Praise for

A Black and White Case

How Affirmative Action Survived Its Greatest Legal Challenge

by Greg Stohr
Bloomberg News Supreme Court Reporter

"Greg Stohr has found the grays in *A Black and White Case.* He has
written a full, fair and scrupulously balanced account of the surprising legal battle that was supposed to end the use of race as a factor
in college admissions, but instead gave affirmative action its biggest
win ever in the Supreme Court."

DAVID SAVAGE
SUPREME COURT REPORTER FOR THE *LOS ANGELES TIMES*

"By setting out in detail the constitutional questions posed by racial
preference, and the individual lives of litigants, advocates, and judges
directly involved in these landmark cases, Greg Stohr's book supplies
a valuable chronicle for the national discussion that necessarily continues. No one who honestly wants to reach common ground can fail to
be benefited by canvassing the ground already traversed with *A Black
and White Case* as their guide."

DOUGLAS W. KMIEC
CHAIR & PROFESSOR OF CONSTITUTIONAL LAW
PEPPERDINE UNIVERSITY

"*A Black and White Case* raised my understanding of last year's Supreme
Court cases on affirmative action to an entirely new level. This makes
the book essential reading for college admissions professionals. The
surprise bonus is that it is truly a page-turner, immensely readable,
engaging in human terms, and well informed. It's a special pleasure to
learn a lot from a book you also enjoy with every passing page."

WILLIAM M. SHAIN
DEAN OF UNDERGRADUATE ADMISSIONS
VANDERBILT UNIVERSITY

"An engrossing, thought-provoking, fast-paced read, *A Black and White Case* thoroughly and even-handedly captures both sides of an epic legal struggle that will affect American race relations for decades to come."

DEBRA DICKERSON
AUTHOR, *THE END OF BLACKNESS* AND *AN AMERICAN STORY*

"A fascinating and compelling account of landmark cases on an issue of enormous importance in American society. Greg Stohr's description of the University of Michigan affirmative action cases is a terrific account of litigation that will affect America's colleges and universities for years to come."

ERWIN CHEMERINSKY
ALSTON & BIRD PROFESSOR OF LAW
DUKE LAW SCHOOL

"Every major decision by the Court is but the culmination of a fascinating drama, one that may have taken years to unfold. It takes a particular gift for a writer to reconstruct such a story and to sustain a lively interest in it even though we know what its last chapter will say. Greg Stohr has given us an impressive retelling of this story, with vivid portraits of the actors and a richly detailed account of the maneuvering, manipulating, and massaging that went into each side's strategy."

LYLE DENNISTON
SUPREME COURT REPORTER SINCE 1958
COVERED THE MICHIGAN CASES FOR THE *BOSTON GLOBE*

A BLACK AND WHITE CASE

A BLACK AND WHITE CASE

How Affirmative Action Survived
Its Greatest Legal Challenge

GREG STOHR

Bloomberg News Supreme Court Reporter

A complete list of titles published by Bloomberg Press
is available at www.bloomberg.com/books

First edition published 2004
1 3 5 7 9 10 8 6 4 2

Library of Congress Cataloging-in-Publication Data

Stohr, Greg
   A black and white case : how affirmative action survived its greatest legal challenge / Greg Stohr. --
1st ed.
      p. cm.
   Includes bibliographical references and index.
   ISBN 1-57660-170-6 (alk. paper)
   1. Grutter, Barbara--Trials, litigation, etc. 2. Bollinger, Lee C., 1946– --Trials, litigation, etc.
3. Discrimination in higher education--Law and legislation--Michigan. 4. Affirmative action programs
--Law and legislation--United States. 5. University of Michigan--Admission. I. Title.

   KF228.G78S76 2004
   342.7308'7--dc22

                                                        2004009630

Book Design by LAURIE LOHNE / DESIGN IT COMMUNICATIONS

To Anne

Contents

Litigation Timeline

1 9 9 5

December 18
   Michigan professor Carl Cohen files his first request under the Michigan Freedom of Information Act seeking documents describing the university's affirmative action policies.

1 9 9 7

February 1
   Lee Bollinger takes office as the twelfth president of the University of Michigan.

October 14
   Unsuccessful undergraduate applicants Jennifer Gratz and Patrick Hamacher file suit, claiming Michigan illegally discriminated against them on the basis of race.

December 3
   Barbara Grutter sues, alleging illegal discrimination by Michigan Law School.

1 9 9 8

July 6
   U.S. District Judge Bernard Friedman rules that student supporters of affirmative action may not intervene in Grutter's law school case.

July 7
   U.S. District Judge Patrick Duggan rejects a student intervention request in Gratz and Hamacher's undergraduate case.

August 6
   Two federal judges in Detroit recommend that the law school case be reassigned from Friedman to Duggan. Friedman refuses to consent to the transfer.

September 17
   Deposition of Jennifer Gratz.

1 9 9 9

February 9

Deposition of Lee Bollinger.

August 8

Former President Gerald R. Ford announces his support for Michigan through an op-ed in the *New York Times*.

August 10

The Sixth U.S. Circuit Court of Appeals reverses Friedman and Duggan and orders that the student supporters of affirmative action be allowed to take part in the cases.

2 0 0 0

July 17

General Motors files a friend-of-the-court brief supporting Michigan.

December 13

Duggan upholds the point system used by the undergraduate admissions office. He declares a previous policy unconstitutional.

2 0 0 1

January 16 through February 16

Friedman holds a trial in the law school case.

February 26

Duggan rejects an alternative defense for Michigan's affirmative action policies offered by student-intervenors.

March 27

Friedman strikes down the Michigan Law School admissions policy.

April 5

The Sixth Circuit stays Friedman's ruling, letting the law school resume its race-conscious admissions program.

October 19

The Sixth Circuit postpones arguments that had been scheduled for October 23 before a three-judge panel and announces that the nine-judge *en banc* court will hear the cases.

December 6

The Sixth Circuit hears arguments in both cases.

2 0 0 2

May 14

The Sixth Circuit, voting five-to-four, upholds the law school admissions policy. The court takes no action in the undergraduate case.

August 9

Barbara Grutter seeks Supreme Court review of her appeal.

October 1

Jennifer Gratz and Patrick Hamacher ask the Supreme Court to review the undergraduate case and bypass the Sixth Circuit, which still hasn't issued a ruling.

December 2

The Supreme Court agrees to hear both cases.

2 0 0 3

January 16

The Bush administration urges the Supreme Court to strike down both Michigan admissions policies.

February 18

The Supreme Court receives more than seventy friend-of-the-court briefs siding with Michigan.

April 1

The Supreme Court hears arguments from lawyers for the university, the Bush administration, and the three rejected white applicants.

June 23

The Supreme Court rules in *Grutter v. Bollinger* and *Gratz v. Bollinger.*

Prologue

THE ENVELOPE was way too thin. Mixed in among the bills and catalogs, the letter to Jennifer Gratz from the University of Michigan admissions office could only mean bad news.

Jennifer had wanted to attend the University of Michigan in Ann Arbor for as long as she could remember. It was the flagship school in her home state, an ideal place to pursue her dream of becoming a forensic doctor. The campus was forty-five minutes from her suburban Detroit house, far enough that she could be on her own and immerse herself in the college atmosphere, yet close enough that she could easily get home to share a quiet weekend with her parents and younger brother. Jennifer pictured herself walking to class across the green grass of the "Diag" in the center of campus, making new friends in one of the ivy-covered dormitories, getting decked out in maize and blue for the football weekends that turn Ann Arbor into a daylong, 100,000-person party. The University of Michigan was the essence of college. It would be a perfect fit for Jennifer Gratz.

Jennifer thought she was a shoo-in. A pretty, outgoing blonde with an engaging smile, she was as impressive on paper as she was in person. She carried a 3.8 grade point average at Southgate Anderson High School, placing her in the top 5 percent of her class. She scored a twenty-five on a thirty-six-point scale on the ACT college admissions test, placing her in the eighty-third percentile—higher than all but 17 percent of the test-takers nationwide. She was a cheerleader, the student-body vice president, and homecoming queen. Jennifer volunteered at a "prom" for senior citizens, organized a blood drive, and served as a math tutor. She even offered a background that might appeal to Michigan's admissions officers. She came from a distinctly working-class neighborhood, growing up in a modest home half a block away from a run-down strip of auto repair shops and liquor stores. She was the daughter of a police sergeant and a hospital lab worker and planned to be the first member of her family to graduate from college. Jennifer knew of students in previous Anderson classes who had enrolled at Ann Arbor with lesser credentials. She felt so sure of her chances that she would have applied only to Michigan for admission into its fall 1995 entering class had her mother not insisted that she add a couple of fallback schools, Wayne State and the University of Michigan at Dearborn.

For two months in the fall of 1994, Jennifer had worked on her application. She brought it with her to school basketball games, poring over the materials in the stands until it was time to start leading cheers. She wrote and rewrote her essay, continually tinkered with the listing of her school activities, and asked friends and family members for advice.

The first inkling of a problem came in January 1995, only a few weeks after she had submitted the application. A thin envelope had arrived then, too, with a letter saying the university wouldn't decide on her application until April. The letter said Jennifer was "well qualified, but less competitive than the students who have been admitted on first review." The letter forced Jennifer to take a step back and re-evaluate her situation, and she hastily decided to submit an application to Notre Dame as well. Still, she remained optimistic about Ann Arbor. She knew of students who had been admitted to Michigan from the waiting list, and she expected to join them.

By spring, she was rushing home every day after cheerleading practice to check the mail. Finally, one afternoon in the last week of April, Jennifer burst into the house, picked up the stack of bills and letters, and pulled out the thin envelope. Her father, Brad, sat across from her in the living room and watched. She scanned the first few sentences until she got to the part that said, "I regret to inform you we are unable to offer you admission." Then she burst into tears.

She felt devastated, angry, and embarrassed all at once. Jennifer thought about all the hard work on her studies, extracurriculars, and application. She had no idea what she would say to the friends who knew how she yearned to attend Michigan.

Jennifer was sure that something had gone horribly wrong. She understood that Michigan used affirmative action in admissions, though she knew nothing of the specifics. Her thoughts flashed to a Hispanic classmate who had been admitted to Michigan with lower grades than hers.

Finally, Jennifer uttered the first words that came to her.

"Dad," she said. "Can we sue them?"[1]

———

GRATZ MAY HAVE had her heart set on Michigan, but she might have encountered the same result anywhere in the country. At the time she applied, virtually every elite U.S. college and professional school was using affirmative action to boost enrollment of minorities—typically, blacks, Latinos, and Native Americans.

The reason for race-based admissions was clear, even if the wisdom was debatable. If highly selective schools such as Michigan, Harvard, and the University of California at Berkeley were to rely solely on the numbers—that is, test scores and grades—enrollment by those three minority groups would plummet. A statistical study by two former university presidents, Princeton's William G. Bowen and Harvard's Derek Bok, had concluded that a race-neutral admissions policy would reduce the share of blacks in the 1989 entering classes at five highly selective colleges from 7.1 percent to between 2.1 and 3.6 percent. Black, Hispanic, and Native American students would be almost entirely shut out from America's single most important ticket to advancement: an education at a premier school. More than a quarter century after the civil rights movement promised racial equality, few if any university administrators were prepared to accept numbers that low.[2]

Considering race in admissions was the most straightforward way to address the imbalance. By giving minorities a few extra points in the evaluation process, admissions officers could turn a class that was 3 percent black and Latino into one that was 8 or 10 percent. By adding targeted recruiting and perhaps race-based scholarships to the mix, many top universities could increase their minority enrollment percentages to levels that approached those in the population at large.

But in a country where black-white tensions had been an entrenched part of the social landscape for more than two centuries, explicit use of race in admissions was guaranteed to spark resentment.

The practice amounted to racial discrimination. Even if the goal was a laudable one, applicants indisputably were being treated differently because of their skin color; preferences favored African Americans and Hispanics, disfavoring whites and, increasingly, Asians. How, many would ask, could that be squared with Martin Luther King Jr.'s vision that his children would "not be judged by the color of their skin but by the content of their character"?

So for three decades—from the mid-1960s to the mid-1990s— universities operated their admissions programs behind closed doors. Publicly, they provided few details about their admissions policies, couching their efforts to enroll minorities in generalities such as "affirmative action" and "diversity" or suggesting they used race only to differentiate among candidates who were otherwise equally qualified. Privately, universities took the steps necessary to find and enroll significant numbers of capable black and Latino students.

Although race-based admissions began in the 1960s, the Supreme Court didn't consider the issue until the 1978 *University of California Regents v. Bakke* case.[3] The high court struck down the particular admissions program it was considering, a University of California at Davis Medical School system that set aside seats for minority applicants, as a violation of the U.S. Constitution's equal protection clause. At the same time, five of the Court's nine justices said that schools could use race in at least some contexts to make admissions decisions. Those five didn't agree on a single rationale. School administrators nonetheless universally read Justice Lewis Powell's opinion, which endorsed affirmative action for the purpose of ensuring a diverse classroom, as the law of the land.

In the mid-1990s, an opposition movement began to gather steam in response to affirmative action. A little-known Washington, D.C., public-interest law firm, the Center for Individual Rights, pressed a lawsuit on behalf of white students who were rejected when they applied to the University of Texas Law School. The suit contended that the school's affirmative action program, which used a separate admissions committee to review minority applicants, violated the equal protection clause by illegally discriminating on the basis of race. In March 1996, the Fifth U.S. Circuit Court of Appeals struck down the Texas Law School program in *Hopwood v. State of Texas*.[4] The panel said not only that the separate admissions committee was unconstitutional but also that race couldn't be a factor in admissions at all. The court reasoned that Powell spoke only for himself in *Bakke* and that his opinion therefore wasn't controlling.

Meanwhile, a separate battle was brewing in California, where state-run universities had been using affirmative action since 1964. Governor Pete Wilson made opposition to racial preferences the central plank in his campaign for the 1996 Republican presidential nomination. At the core of Wilson's efforts was a plan to overhaul the admissions practices at the state's top universities. In 1995, the University of California's Board of Regents voted to halt any race-based admissions at the system's nine campuses. The following year, California voters would go a step further, approving a ballot initiative, known as Proposition 209, that abolished affirmative action in state hiring and contracts as well as in college admissions.

The battleground was about to move to Michigan, as Jennifer Gratz would soon become part of the most important legal fight on racial discrimination in at least a generation.

Part One

A Gathering Storm

(December 1995–October 1997)

Chapter One

A Tale of Two Professors

CARL COHEN HAD the smoking gun. The document he held proved that the University of Michigan used different admissions standards for white and black applicants.

Amid the stacked books and scattered piles of paper in his home study, the longtime Michigan philosophy professor could hardly contain himself. Even on routine days, the wiry, gray-haired Cohen was easily excitable, his arms and hands seemingly in constant motion, his head prone to bobbing when he had a point to make. Today was no routine day. After months of politely but doggedly pressing the university to explain how race factored into its admissions decisions, Cohen finally had irrefutable proof that the university relied on massive racial preferences. The professor's blue eyes darted back and forth across the page as he double- and triple-checked to make sure he was reading the material correctly.

The document, titled "College of Literature, Science, and the Arts/Guidelines for All Terms of 1996," instructed admissions counselors and clerks on the proper handling of applications for the coming fall's entering class. The key page was a grid of ninety boxes that represented various combinations of high school grade point averages and standardized test scores. Each box, known as a "cell," gave coded instructions to admissions office staffers. Applicants in the upper right-hand corner—students with grade point averages near 4.0 and ultra-high SAT or ACT scores—were automatic admits. Those in the

Philosophy professor Carl Cohen was a spirited civil libertarian who sought information about Michigan's admissions policies and wouldn't let up until he had proof that the university considered race as a factor. Cohen was stunned to discover the extent of Michigan's racial preferences.

lower left, the worst performers, were to be rejected. In between were various shades of gray: applications that would get a closer look by an admissions counselor or would be held pending fall semester grades or some other piece of additional information.

What struck Cohen was that the instructions in the cells were different depending on the race of the applicant. According to the grid, a white or Asian American student with a combined SAT score from 1010 to 1080 and a GPA from 3.2 to 3.3 was to be rejected. An "underrepresented minority" with the same numbers got an acceptance letter. Likewise, for applicants who combined low 850–920 SATs with perfect 4.0 GPAs, whites were rejected but minorities were either accepted or deferred. In cell after cell, throughout the middle band of the grid, blacks had a better chance of admissions than whites with identical grades and scores. For Cohen, the document was confirmation of his worst fears.

Cohen was no right-winger. Since joining the Michigan faculty in the 1950s, he had rankled conservatives at least as often as liberals. In the 1950s, Michigan's "Red Squad," an arm of the state police that investigated suspected communists, opened a file on the twenty-four-year-old professor after learning about his enthusiastic classroom presentations of Marxism. Later, Cohen defended the rights of high school boys to wear long hair in class. He was critical of the Vietnam War. And in 1978 Cohen, a Brooklyn-born Jew, defended the rights of Nazis to march through the streets of Skokie, Illinois. Along the way Cohen served as the head of the local chapter of the ACLU and as a steadfast supporter of the NAACP Legal Defense and Educational Fund. At bottom, he was a feisty civil libertarian who relished a good debate and the chance to defend an unpopular cause.

Cohen broke most sharply with his liberal friends on the question of race—or, as he saw it, racial preferences. Cohen was a passionate advocate for blacks and other racial minorities so long as the issue was preventing discrimination against them. Once the question shifted toward giving special advantages to minorities, Cohen disagreed. The aim, as he saw it, was ending discrimination. That goal was the same regardless of the target of the discrimination. Cohen believed that systematic bias against whites was as foreign to the American promise of equal opportunity as discrimination against blacks and Hispanics.

Cohen had been reading, writing, and speaking about questions of race in university admissions as far back as 1973, when as a member of the national board of the ACLU he unsuccessfully urged his colleagues to support a rejected white applicant who was suing the University of Washington Law School. It was not until 1995, though, that Cohen thought to investigate what was happening at Michigan. That was when he read an article in the *Journal of Blacks in Higher Education* detailing the marked disparity in admissions rates for blacks and whites at some of the most selective U.S. colleges. Cohen wondered what was happening at Michigan, one of the most selective public universities in the country. If the university he had called home for forty years was discriminating on the basis of race, Cohen wanted to know about it.

Finding out didn't prove to be easy. Cohen had first sought out colleagues who were involved in the admissions process and asked them what the school's policies were. Each told him the answer was confidential. Frustrated, Cohen decided to invoke the Michigan Freedom of Information Act, known as FOIA. That law, like similar statutes in other states and at the federal level, gives private citizens broad access to government documents. As a state-run institution, the University of Michigan was subject to FOIA. Cohen crafted a series of letters, requesting documents from the law, medical, and undergraduate schools. He asked for information explaining the admissions policies for applicants of different races. He also wanted any data the university had on admissions rates by race.

At first, the FOIA process proved no more fruitful than the informal approach. Cohen was disappointed by the first package of material he received from the university's chief FOIA officer, Lewis Morrissey. The envelope contained only summary information breaking down the applicant pools and entering classes by race; it included little to indicate whether different criteria were being used depending on the race of the applicant. Cohen fired off another letter, six pages long, painstakingly detailing the types of information he was seeking and including sample documents compiled by other universities. He met with Morrissey and his assistant to discuss the new letter point-by-point. At the end, Morrissey said he understood what the professor wanted and asked Cohen for more time. Cohen readily agreed.

Now, on a cold winter evening, Cohen's patience and persistence were starting to pay off. The mail had arrived late in the day, as it always did on the quiet, woodsy street where Cohen lived with his two children, just a ten-minute walk from campus. He saw the envelope from the university right away, plopped himself in front of his desk, and eagerly began digging through the documents Morrissey had sent. When he got to the grid, Cohen caught his breath in disbelief.

The packet also included a document that showed admissions data for the fall 1994 undergraduate entering class. It indicated, not surprisingly in light of the instructions that Cohen now knew admissions clerks had been given, that minorities with various combinations of grades and test scores had been admitted at a much higher rate than white applicants with similar numbers.

Morrissey had also sent a description of the admissions criteria for the university's combined pre-med and medical school program. Again, minority candidates were subject to more lenient admissions standards than their white counterparts. Later, Morrissey would send additional information indicating the use of racial preferences at Michigan Law School as well.

Cohen pored over the documents into the night, occasionally pulling out his calculator to figure out admissions rates for particular types of candidates. By the time he went to bed, Cohen knew what his next step would be. He would put his findings into a report. He would write the university's regents and outgoing president Jim Duderstadt and ask whether they could possibly support such policies. He would spread the word that Michigan was engaging in blatant race discrimination.[1]

———■———

WHILE COHEN DESPAIRED about the state of his university's admissions, an old colleague 800 miles away in New Hampshire contemplated a possible future at Michigan. Lee Bollinger had been Dartmouth College's provost for only two years, but he already had higher aspirations. With Duderstadt planning to step down as Michigan's president, the handsome, charming Bollinger was envisioning himself in the job.

Unlike Cohen, Bollinger already was well-versed in Michigan's affirmative action policies—or at least the ones at Michigan Law School. Bollinger had served as dean of the school from 1987 to 1994 and engineered a comprehensive rewrite of its admissions policies, in part to protect its affirmative action efforts from a legal attack.

As a boy, Bollinger hadn't had much occasion to think about race. The oldest of six children, he was born in Santa Rosa, California, a predominantly white city in the heart of wine country, where his father was in the newspaper business. When Bollinger was young, the family moved to Baker, Oregon, a picturesque town in the Blue Mountains that once served as a supply center for gold miners. His father bought a stake in the local paper, the *Democrat-Herald*, and became its editor and publisher. Like Santa Rosa, Baker had only a handful of minorities.

Newspapering was a family business for the Bollingers. Lee held down a variety of jobs at the paper, from janitor to film developer. He learned to love journalism, admiring the way it could mingle the spirit of public responsibility with a fierce sense of independence, even as he realized that it wasn't his long-term calling. He became the first in his extended family to attend college when he enrolled at the University of Oregon. He dabbled in student government, but soon realized that his heart was in academics, and in 1968 he graduated Phi Beta Kappa. Bollinger went on to attend Columbia Law School in New York, where he began to develop an expertise in the free-speech clause of the U.S. Constitution's First Amendment. He performed so well that he landed a prized position as a clerk for a federal appellate judge and then for Chief Justice Warren Burger on the Supreme Court.

Bollinger decided he wanted to teach law, rather than practice it, and his Supreme Court clerkship made him an attractive candidate to top universities. He settled on Michigan Law School, whose recruitment efforts had included a dinner with fellow First Amendment scholar Carl Cohen.

Bollinger arrived in Ann Arbor having spent his entire life surrounded by other white people—and mostly other white men, at that. Yet he had come to believe that his education would have been a richer experience with a more diverse set of classmates. His wife, fellow Oregon graduate Jean Magnano, was an important influence, offering a distinctly female perspective on certain issues. Lee saw how Jean experienced the sting of gender discrimination and felt pressure to go into traditional female occupations, such as nursing or teaching. Jean also told him of her frustrations with her Catholic Church and its refusal to allow women into its hierarchy. Bollinger's teaching experience reinforced his views on the benefits of diversity. Female students, Bollinger saw, brought a special element to First Amendment debates over pornography. The growing number of African American students had a similar impact in discussions about hate speech.

In 1987, fourteen years after joining the faculty, Bollinger was named dean of Michigan Law School. He soon began familiarizing himself with the nuts and bolts of the admissions process. Bollinger discovered that decisions on applications were almost entirely in the hands of one man, law school admissions director Allan Stillwagon. Bollinger thought the faculty needed to be more involved in the process, working with the admissions office to ensure the best possible mix of students for their classrooms. Bollinger also had concerns about the legality of the law school's admissions policies. He was troubled that, by all appearances, no one had reviewed the system to determine whether it complied with the decade-old *Bakke* decision, or at least with Justice Powell's opinion in *Bakke*. More broadly, Bollinger wanted a comprehensive review of the law school's "special admissions program," which accounted for most of its minority students.

In the fall of 1991, Bollinger decided to appoint a faculty committee to draft a new admissions policy for the law school. The committee would be chaired by Professor Richard Lempert, an expert on law and sociology. Its members would include Ted Shaw, one of two blacks on the faculty and a former lawyer for the NAACP Legal Defense and Educational Fund, as well as Jeffrey Lehman, an up-and-coming professor who specialized in tax and welfare law. The new admissions director, Dennis Shields, also would serve on the committee. (Bollinger had asked Stillwagon to resign after concluding he was too inflexible.)

When the new policy was released the following April, it echoed the language of Powell's opinion in *Bakke,* saying that diversity, particularly with regard to race, was a paramount interest. The policy expressed "a commitment to racial and ethnic diversity with special reference to the inclusion of students from groups which have been historically discriminated against, like African Americans, Hispanics and Native Americans, who without this commitment might not be represented in our student body in meaningful numbers." Those students "are particularly likely to have experiences and perspectives of special importance to our mission." The school would seek a "critical mass" of minority students to ensure "their ability to make unique contributions to the character of the Law School." The policy also drew a line, saying the school would not accept any applicants who couldn't be expected to graduate without any serious problems. Bollinger was pleased, and a few days later the faculty overwhelmingly adopted the policy.

The following year, in the fall of 1993, Bollinger received a visit from Samuel Issacharoff, a lawyer representing the University of Texas Law School in a suit that was challenging its admissions policies. Issacharoff asked Bollinger to testify in the Texas case. Bollinger initially was concerned that his testimony might make Michigan the next target, but after consulting with several colleagues, he agreed to

By the time Lee Bollinger sought the Michigan presidency in 1996, he had established himself as a staunch—and shrewd—defender of affirmative action. While serving as dean of Michigan Law School, Bollinger had reshaped its admissions policies, in part to protect against a legal attack.

take part. Bollinger testified that classroom diversity was an essential part of a top-notch legal education and that schools like Michigan cannot achieve diversity without using race in the admissions process. He also said Michigan needed to have at least 10 percent black enrollment to ensure that those students were in a comfortable learning environment. The testimony, it turned out, largely escaped notice in Ann Arbor, not coming to Carl Cohen's attention until years later.

In 1994, Bollinger took another step up, moving to Hanover, New Hampshire, to become Dartmouth's provost, with responsibility for the institution's entire academic program. The position rounded out Bollinger's résumé, giving him experience beyond the insular world of law and making him a top candidate to return to Ann Arbor as Michigan's next president. In March 1996, the Michigan Board of Regents began its formal search for Duderstadt's successor. Bollinger decided to submit his name.

At age fifty-one, Bollinger looked as much like an actor as an intellectual. With a handsome, chiseled face and a mop of wispy brown hair that grayed as it swept over his ears, he bore a vague resemblance to Robert Redford, but with cuff links. He was an avid runner, having won the unofficial title of "nation's fastest dean" in 1988 when he ran a quarter-mile in 55 seconds in the master's division of the Millrose Games, the premier U.S. indoor track and field meet. (His relay team finished third.) Bollinger coupled his physical attractiveness with the grace of a seasoned politician. He could discuss art or Shakespeare as fluently as the law. He loved to teach and to write and was accomplished at both. If one had created a model for an ideal university president, it might have looked like Lee Bollinger.[2]

———•———

CARL COHEN WAS not one to keep things bottled up. With the grids in hand, he now had confirmation that the university was using race to make admissions decisions, and he needed to spread the word. Cohen's fervor stemmed from his incredulity at what schools throughout the university were doing. Michigan's course catalog said the university was "committed to a policy of non-discrimination and equal opportunity for all persons regardless of race, sex, color, religion, creed, national origin or ancestry ... in employment, educational programs and activities, and admissions." Cohen thought the university was violating that pledge, engaging in hypocrisy as well as race discrimination. He couldn't believe that others at the university, once they learned the facts, could condone what was going on.

His first step was to put the documents he had uncovered into a coherent format. In a ten-page report titled "Racial Discrimination in Admissions at The University of Michigan," Cohen laid out his evidence. He described the grids, extricating a few choice examples of the differing treatments afforded to majority and minority students upon first review of their applications. He also discussed the results of those policies, laying out the rates at which minorities and nonminorities with various combinations of test scores and grades were offered a place in the class. As one example, he pointed out that black and Hispanic applicants with A- grades and combined SAT math and verbal scores between 800 and 890 had a 100 percent admission rate; by contrast, only 12 percent of the nonminorities with identical numbers were accepted.

Michigan Law School, Cohen went on, was doing the same thing. According to other documents he had obtained, whites with 3.00–3.24 GPAs and LSATs from 148 to 163 (out of a possible 180) were accepted 2.2 percent of the time; blacks with those numbers were accepted at a 74.3 percent rate. Every Mexican American applicant with those same grades and an LSAT of 161 or higher was admitted, while only

14.8 percent of whites were. Cohen added that he had indications that Michigan Medical School was also using race in admissions, although he acknowledged he lacked the detailed numerical evidence that he had for the undergraduate and law schools.

Cohen wrote: "The question arises: Do the University officers who make the public declaration of commitment to equal treatment know or believe that in fact our practice does not accord with that profession? If they do, troubling issues of honesty arise. If they do not, if they have been truly unaware of the racial preferences we give in admissions, then changes certainly ought to be made very promptly now."

Then Cohen hit the road. He brought copies of the report with him to Lansing, where he testified before a legislative subcommittee on a pending bill to abolish affirmative action in the state. He distributed more copies at a campus forum at which he accused the school of deception. "We cheat," Cohen told the gathering. "We give racial preferences knowingly while saying that we do not, but we hide that fact with murky references to 'diversity.'" He attached a copy of the report when he wrote his letter to Michigan president Duderstadt and the regents. Duderstadt responded with a polite but terse, five-sentence letter. "It will come as no surprise to you that we disagree on this matter," the president wrote. Undeterred, Cohen published his findings as part of a broad attack on racial preferences in one of his favorite opinion journals, *Commentary*.

By July 1996, Cohen had created enough of a buzz that the *Detroit News* published a 1,500-word feature on his research, complete with a chart that laid out the different success rates of minority and non-minority applicants. In that story, the university acknowledged that it used race in admissions. "We are in compliance with the law as it stands now," Dennis Shields, Michigan Law School's dean of admissions, told the paper. "You can take any set of numbers and focus purely on meritocratic theory and make it appear that the system is discriminatory. But we are not running a two-track system. We do not have a separate review of files, nor do we have a different standard for minority applicants. Professor Cohen is simply incorrect."

Cohen continued to press the university for more information, using the papers he received to help him frame additional inquiries. In some cases, he succeeded; in others, he didn't. One of the early documents referred to the "Affirmative Action Objectives" at the undergraduate school. What, Cohen wanted to know, were those objectives? He was certain there must be some document that gave the answer; a capitalized phrase like Affirmative Action Objectives surely didn't exist only in someone's head. But a series of letters to and from the school's Freedom of Information Act officer failed to produce any such document. Cohen eventually concluded that was one piece of paper he would never see.

———•———

SUPPORT FOR AFFIRMATIVE action was practically a job qualification for a new Michigan president. From the very beginning, several members of the Board of Regents made clear that the next president had to make minority admissions a priority. When Carl Cohen stood up at a regents meeting to decry the use of race in admissions, he found little support. Regent Laurence Deitch said that board support for affirmative action was "almost a given."

Michigan had been admitting black students since the nineteenth century, starting with literary student John Summerfield Davidson and law student Gabriel Franklin Hargo in 1868. But until the mid-1960s, African Americans were admitted only as part of the general applicant pool and with no special consideration. Because the test scores and grades of black applicants tended to be significantly lower than those of whites, the result was that just a handful of minority students—if that—attended the university every year. In 1966, the institution had only 400 black undergraduate students, 1.2 percent of the school's total. And those black students who did enroll found that they might face university-sanctioned discrimination. Through the 1950s, student organizations were allowed to limit their membership based on race, religion, or color. As of 1959, not a single fraternity or sorority had ever accepted a black member. Students in campus housing also could refuse to share a room with a classmate of another race.

The history of difficulties African Americans encountered at UM in some ways reflected their story of second-class status throughout the state. From the moment large numbers of blacks began arriving in Detroit during World War I, they encountered hostility. Blacks who tried to move into all-white neighborhoods were greeted with physical attacks, vandalism, and arson. In 1943, the racial tension boiled over, setting off riots that killed thirty-four people, twenty-five of them black. When the Detroit School Board announced a plan in 1960 that would let black students transfer to formerly all-white schools, white parents boycotted classes. Blacks found they were shut out of entire sections of the labor market. Large sections of the state were virtually all white—and would remain so into the twenty-first century.

In the mid-1960s, with the civil rights movement reaching its height, universities across the country began looking at their minority enrollment numbers. At Michigan, the figures were cause for worry. The dearth of minority students was especially evident at the law school. The 1965 graduation of Harry Edwards, who later returned to teach at Michigan Law School and then became a federal appeals court judge in Washington, left the school without a single black student. The numbers were only slightly better campuswide, with barely 1 percent black enrollment.

Michigan administrators decided they needed to do more to attract African Americans to campus. Their first attempts at affirmative action were somewhat bumbling. In 1964, the undergraduate school instituted the Opportunity Program to seek out black high school students who seemed to have untapped potential. Seventy enrolled at Michigan for the 1964–65 school year and were given both financial and tutorial assistance. Many found they couldn't meet the academic challenges of Michigan; twenty-two were unable to continue beyond their freshman year.

Michigan Law School, which had separate admissions policies and recruitment programs, also struggled. Acting Dean Charles Joiner first tried dispatching the school's admissions director on recruiting missions to historically black colleges. A number of students from those schools enrolled at Michigan Law School, but most proved badly unprepared. The admissions office then broadened its search for qualified black students, and within a few years it was enrolling a significant number of students who were capable of performing the required work. By 1970–71, seventy-seven African American law students were attending Michigan, second only to Harvard in total number.

For an increasingly vocal group of UM activists, the increase was insufficient. Campuswide, black enrollment was less than 4 percent in 1970. Several campus groups agreed to join forces and press for change in a push that became known as the Black Action Movement, or BAM for short. Leaders demanded an increase in minority enrollment by 1973 to 10 percent, a figure that would match the proportion of blacks in the general population of the state. The group called for increased recruiting, financial aid, and support services to help reach that level. BAM leaders also demanded the school begin recruiting Hispanic students, who were all but nonexistent on campus. University president Robben Fleming said the university could commit to 7 percent black enrollment, but he was skeptical of reaching 10 percent without dramatically lowering admissions standards. Not satisfied, BAM leaders called a campuswide strike, nearly shutting down the university. Eight days later, Fleming agreed to a goal of 10 percent, though not a commitment to it, and the strike came to an end.

Much as Fleming predicted, the university failed to meet the 10 percent target. African American enrollment topped 7 percent in 1973 and then began to decline. With university administrators preoccupied by budgetary concerns, by 1983 the figure had slipped below 5 percent.

The problem was slightly different at the law school. Although the percentage of enrolled black students was high—reaching 15 percent one year—their academic achievement was not. In 1985 Dean Terrance Sandalow noticed that not a single black student had graduated in the top 10 percent of the class since Harry Edwards twenty years earlier. And the vast majority graduated in the lower half the class. The problem, Sandalow observed, was that there were too few top-notch black students to go around. The very best African American minds in the country were going to Harvard and Yale, rather than Michigan. Sandalow decided to, in effect, buy some of those students. The school set up a new black-only scholarship, named after famed white alumnus Clarence Darrow. Recipients received full tuition, room, and board, regardless of financial need. Over the next several years, the program served to bring some of the top black students in the country to Michigan.

Racial tensions nonetheless were back in full force at Michigan in 1987. In January, someone distributed a slur-filled flier declaring "open season on porch monkeys." The next month, a student disc jockey encouraged callers to tell racial jokes on the air. A few months

later, a new furor erupted over a group of race-based jokes posted
on an electronic bulletin board. The incidents drew attention from
the *New York Times* and PBS's *Frontline.* Minority students decided
to fight back. Under the banner of "BAM III"—"BAM II" had taken
place in 1975, with minimal impact—students held a series of rallies
and a sit-in at the Fleming Administration Building. President Harold
Shapiro quickly agreed to a six-point plan that included an increased
commitment to attracting and retaining black students and faculty.

That same year, Bollinger took over as dean of the law school, a
post he would hold for the next seven years. Over the course of his
tenure, Bollinger moved to both refine and ingrain the school's affirmative action efforts. Concerned about the legality of the Darrow
scholarship program, he decided it should be open to students of all
races. In 1992, Bollinger oversaw the adoption of the new admissions
policy and its expressed commitment to seeking racial diversity. That
policy also ended the legally questionable practice of using minority
students to help review applications from other minorities.

While Bollinger worked to hone the law school's policies,
Michigan president James Duderstadt, who took office in 1988, was
launching a much broader affirmative action effort across the university. Duderstadt's program, which he called the "Michigan Mandate,"
aimed to increase the number of minority students, faculty members, and administration officials at Michigan. Under the Michigan
Mandate, the university implemented more than a hundred diversity
initiatives, both large and small. One program, known as Target of
Opportunity, instructed academic units to hire any minority teaching
candidate who would add something to the department, even if there
wasn't an open slot that fit the person's specialty. Other efforts focused
on reaching out to minorities in high schools that hadn't traditionally
sent students to Michigan. Duderstadt even tied the compensation
of deans to their success in advancing diversity. By 1995, the end of
Duderstadt's tenure, African American enrollment rose to almost 9
percent, and racial minorities of all types constituted a quarter of the
students on campus.

The ups and downs of minority admissions at Michigan masked a
common thread. For all the issues on the table—the recruiting budget, the support services, the level of commitment by top university
officials—one subject that wasn't in dispute was the use of race-based

admissions in the first place. Students and administration officials alike presumed that race was a desirable—and legal—factor to consider in admissions. Candidates who were black, Latino, or Native American got a boost in the admissions process because of their race. Inevitably, the result was that minority applicants were accepted over whites whose qualifications, under more traditional measures, were superior.[3]

———•———

IN A PUBLIC interview before the Board of Regents, which had narrowed the presidential field down to four candidates by the fall of 1996, Bollinger made it clear that he fit right into the Michigan tradition on affirmative action. He told the regents that he supported the aims of the Michigan Mandate and that higher education had a duty to help students "cross boundaries" and learn "how other people see the world."

His support for affirmative action was just one of the factors in Bollinger's favor. The regents marveled at his indisputable love for the university, intellectual firepower, and vision of a school where faculty members are accessible to students. It didn't hurt that former colleagues met him with hugs and handshakes when he entered the meeting room. Six of the eight regents made Bollinger their first choice, and only one, Deane Baker, voiced any dissent. (Baker, a Republican, said he was troubled both by Bollinger's testimony against Supreme Court nominee Robert Bork and by a "very heavy-handed political campaign to put Lee Bollinger in the office of president of Michigan.")

When the search committee co-chairwomen called Bollinger, to offer him the job as Michigan's twelfth president, he responded, "Oh, my God. What a wonderful day!"

Chapter Two

Getting Lawyered Up

C OHEN MAY NOT have had a big fan club at Michigan, but he had two strong supporters on the East Coast. From their Washington, D.C., office building, Michael Greve and Michael McDonald had been reading the professor's commentaries on racial preferences. Like Cohen, they abhorred the idea that a state-run university would engage in what they considered to be race discrimination. And they had founded a public-interest law firm, known as the Center for Individual Rights, that aimed to stop the practice.

Greve and McDonald made for an unlikely duo as they approached age forty. The German-born Greve was an extrovert who enjoyed both sharp debates with adversaries and golf games with potential supporters. His lingering German accent seemed to add an edge to the witticisms and wisecracks that flowed from his tongue. His naturally optimistic and ambitious demeanor was fueled by his love of the American political system and the possibilities it offered for bright outsiders looking to make an impact.

Greve, the son of a Hamburg tax consultant, was fascinated by public policy long before he knew how he would translate his interest into a professional career. He started out in life with liberal leanings, then grew to distrust the inefficiencies of the West German welfare state and its cradle-to-grave financial protections. As a student at the University of Hamburg, he saw rampant abuses of the stipends the government gave to almost everybody who enrolled; most students,

Greve observed, simply pocketed the money while doing essentially no academic work. Greve studied philosophy and political science under a series of libertarian professors who helped reinforce and refine his suspicion of powerful government.

By the time he received his degree, Greve had concluded he didn't like the German system of political debate any better than he liked the government's policies. The only way to make an impact, as he saw it, was to advance through the bureaucracy of one of the political parties. The type of think tanks and political advocacy groups that flourished in America simply didn't exist in West Germany. Greve was a freethinker, and the idea of becoming a party hack was anathema. A Fulbright Scholarship brought him to the United States by way of Cornell University in 1981, just as Ronald Reagan was taking office as a champion of smaller government. Greve never looked back.

At Cornell he earned his Ph.D., writing his dissertation on the politics of the environmental movement. He joined the Smith Richardson Foundation as a program officer, helping distribute millions of dollars in grants to conservative policy research projects. In 1988, Greve accepted a position as a resident scholar at the Washington Legal Foundation, a legal advocacy group that was becoming one of many private-sector havens for conservatives and libertarians looking to keep the Reagan Revolution alive even after the president left office.

Greve's partner, McDonald, was by contrast a natural pessimist whose frugal tendencies led friends to joke that he would make an excellent accountant. Several inches shorter than Greve and always seeming to need a shave, he had a brooding appearance. He preferred working at his desk with the door closed to attending receptions or conferences. His hobby was Italian literature.

McDonald was the son of working-class parents. His father grew up in the Irish section of a small Pennsylvania mining town, his mother not far away in the Italian enclave. After World War II, the family moved to the Maryland suburbs of Washington, where McDonald's father laid marble and tile. Although neither parent attended college, both stressed education and sent their son to Catholic University. McDonald then attended George Washington University Law School, where he was one of only a handful of conservatives. He honed his arguments debating his liberal classmates and writing for the law school newspaper on such topics as abortion and affirmative action.

After graduating and passing the bar, McDonald, like Greve, joined the Washington Legal Foundation, for a time running an offshoot organization known as the American Legal Foundation, which specialized in media issues. McDonald spent much of his time fighting the Federal Communications Commission's efforts to grant more radio and television licenses to women and racial minorities. McDonald later went back to the parent organization as head of its legal studies division.

Just one office away from each other, Greve and McDonald soon became friends. By the middle of 1988, they discovered they shared the same view of the state of conservative public-interest law. Groups like WLF, they thought, tended to spread themselves too thin, taking on so many issues they had only a limited impact on each one. Greve and McDonald also questioned WLF's reliance on amicus, or "friend-of-the-court," briefs, which outside groups file in existing lawsuits. Amicus briefs had their place, the pair thought, but they were no substitute for original litigation when it came to pressing an agenda.

Both men were hungry for a new challenge. They developed a plan to start their own public-interest law firm to focus on a few niche issues, including civil rights, free speech, and environmental law. The unifying theme would be a goal of limiting government interference with private lives. The Center for Individual Rights, or CIR as it would come to be known, would loosely follow the model used by public-interest groups on the left, such as the NAACP Legal Defense and Educational Fund, by finding representative plaintiffs to file suits. In a variation on the NAACP approach, they would initiate only a handful of suits, targeting them carefully to ensure maximum impact on the law. And in perhaps their most important innovation, they would tap the talents of the many lawyers who were now moving from the Reagan administration into the private sector. Greve and McDonald would persuade outside attorneys to donate their legal services, leaving CIR responsible only for expenses.

Each man had something to contribute to the partnership. Greve would focus on charming potential donors. He had retained his contacts in the world of conservative philanthropy from his days at Smith Richardson, and would tap those to finance the new organization. Greve would also serve as the group's strategic thinker and develop its policy positions. McDonald contributed the law degree, plus a

Convinced that conservative legal groups weren't doing enough to forge changes in the law, Michael McDonald (left) and Michael Greve formed their own public interest law firm, the Center for Individual Rights. They scored several early successes, including a 1996 federal appeals court decision that outlawed university racial preferences in three Southern states.

modest amount of litigation experience. McDonald would scout out opportunities for new lawsuits and supervise the day-to-day progress of the pending litigation.

McDonald quit WLF in September 1988 and set up shop in his apartment in Washington's lively Dupont Circle neighborhood. He put down $10,000 of his own money toward incorporating the organization and securing the necessary tax exemptions. Greve came on board a few months later and quickly brought in $220,000 in seed money. Both men would have to take about a $20,000 pay cut, but they were ready to get to work.

CIR's first case was one that McDonald had wanted to sponsor in his old job. The FCC had awarded a Maryland radio license to Barbara Marmet, a woman with no broadcasting experience, favoring her over Jerome Lamprecht, a man with five years in the business. As part of its efforts to diversify the airwaves, the agency had given Marmet extra credit because she was a woman. Lamprecht wanted to sue. McDonald and Greve agreed to take the case and persuaded Michael Carvin, McDonald's old colleague from law school and a CIR board member, to argue the case. In a two-to-one decision in 1992, a federal appeals court in Washington struck down the FCC policy.

Other successes followed, many of them fighting what Greve and McDonald saw as an increasingly dangerous tide of "political correctness" on college campuses. CIR won its defense of Michael Levin, a philosophy professor at New York's City College who faced disciplinary action for saying that blacks were intellectually inferior to whites. The group succeeded in overturning the punishment imposed by George Mason University on a fraternity that held an "ugly woman contest" with racist and sexist overtones. It won a fight to reinstate University of New Hampshire professor Donald Silva, who had been fired for making references to sex in class, including a description of belly dancing as being "like Jell-O on a plate with a vibrator under the plate." (CIR celebrated by throwing a Jell-O party at the school.) And in 1995, CIR made its first trip to the Supreme Court, winning a five-to-four decision on behalf of a religious student magazine that sought a share of the funding provided by the University of Virginia to other campus organizations.

Courtroom success begat fund-raising success. As Greve was well aware, people like to bet on a winner. Over the next several years, he secured hundreds of thousands of dollars apiece from such foundations as Richard Mellon Scaife's Carthage Fund, the Lynde and Harry Bradley Fund, the Smith Richardson Foundation, and the John M. Olin Foundation. Companies also made donations, including Archer-Daniels-Midland Co., Chevron USA Inc., Pfizer Inc., and Philip Morris Cos.

CIR also received financial assistance from a more controversial source—the Pioneer Fund, a foundation that was gaining notoriety for funding research purporting to show that blacks were genetically inferior. CIR had represented a Pioneer Fund grantee, sociology professor Linda S. Gottfredson, in her fight to stop the University of Delaware from cutting off her funding. Pioneer Fund president Harry Weyher sent Greve a $10,000 check as a thank-you. Greve sought more donations in future years, and Weyher obliged, sending $20,000 in 1993 and $5,000 in both 1995 and 1996. By the mid-1990s, however, the foundation was facing increasing public criticism, and McDonald convinced Greve that the small sums weren't worth the potential trouble. CIR stopped soliciting donations from Weyher.

By 1996, CIR was approaching $1 million a year in contributions. Greve and McDonald had a five-person staff, including three lawyers.

They moved to a larger, fancier office, a glass-doored suite in the heart of downtown Washington, D.C.

As the group won cases, it also gained enemies. Greve's penchant for sarcasm fueled the fire. In a monthly newsletter to supporters, Greve would belittle adversaries, particularly when he thought they were being hypocritical or deceptive. "Like the Japanese soldiers in the caves of Iwo Jima," Greve once wrote, "officials in the basement of the University of Texas Law School refuse to surrender." Greve's barbs occasionally would backfire, as they did when a trial judge rejected a CIR request for attorney's fees, citing a newsletter comment that suggested the CIR lawyers were drinking margaritas while preparing for the case. Opponents began denigrating CIR as childish.

No one could question the impact CIR was having, however, and in March 1996 McDonald and Greve scored their biggest victory yet. The case was the lawsuit against the University of Texas Law School, the one that had occasioned Bollinger's testimony in support of race-based admissions. CIR represented a pair of white students, including lead plaintiff Cheryl Hopwood. To argue the case before the New Orleans–based Fifth U.S. Circuit, the firm secured the services of one of Washington's top appellate lawyers, Ted Olson, the former head of the Office of Legal Counsel in the Reagan Justice Department. Olson won, as the court declared race-based admissions unconstitutional in *Hopwood v. State of Texas*. Judge Jerry E. Smith wrote for the court: "The law school has presented no compelling justification, under the Fourteenth Amendment or Supreme Court precedent, that allows it to continue to elevate some races over others, even for the wholesome purpose of correcting perceived racial imbalance in the student body."

The ruling hit the higher education establishment like a thunderbolt. Although the Fifth Circuit ruling applied only in three Southern states—Texas, Mississippi, and Louisiana—it portended broader application. University administrators across the country took a fresh look at their admissions policies, asking whether those plans might also be vulnerable to legal challenge. Michigan officials paid $10,000 to the Washington law firm Hogan & Hartson to review the school's admissions rules. Admissions directors commiserated at conferences, sharing advice on how to minimize the impact of the *Hopwood* decision.

Greve and McDonald weren't satisfied. True, the *Hopwood* decision had made a splash. But ultimately the vast majority of institutions kept their affirmative action programs intact, save for some tinkering around the edges. Greve thought part of the problem was public relations. Until then, CIR had employed a series of inexperienced people to put together press releases and handle media inquiries. Greve thought the group needed someone more seasoned and more sophisticated.

———•———

THE MAN GREVE had in mind was Terry Pell, a lawyer and philosopher whose style was as serious as Greve's was flip. The two had met through their joint membership in the Telluride Association, a self-governing residential community at Cornell that brought together students studying a range of disciplines to foster intellectual inquiry and leadership skills.

Fair-skinned with neatly parted blonde hair and a preference for starched white shirts, Pell was straight-laced in appearance as well as demeanor. He was cautious with people he didn't know well enough to trust and, unlike Greve, didn't especially enjoy the limelight. But underneath his reserve was an ardor for the principle of race neutrality. Pell was smart and conservative and, crucially for Greve, had some experience in driving a national debate.

Pell was born into an archetypal suburban Rochester, New York, family. His father, a World War II Navy veteran, worked as a physicist at Xerox Corporation, while his mother looked after the three children. As a boy, Terry found his interests lay in the tangible: downhill skiing, woodworking, and photography. He worked as a boat builder and contemplated becoming an architect.

The Pell family paid scant attention to politics and public policy. What opinions Terry's parents expressed tended to be liberal ones. When race riots beset the segregated city of Rochester in the early 1960s, the Pell family posted yard signs of support for the city's black residents. Through high school, Terry considered himself a Democrat, applauding much of the social activism that shaped the 1960s. At the same time, he maintained vague doubts about the role of government. The families he knew took care of themselves; they didn't turn to public agencies to solve their problems.

After graduating from a private high school, Pell enrolled at Haverford College outside Philadelphia, where he developed a love for the more abstract pursuits of philosophy and political theory. His adviser and favorite professor was Paul Desjardins, a charismatic scholar of classical philosophy. Desjardins taught his students the difficult art of reading a classic work—Plato's *Republic* was one of Pell's favorites—from the perspective of the author's era, without the cloud of a twentieth-century political lens. Desjardins emphasized intellectual honesty, candor, and a healthy skepticism about conventional political arrangements—traits Pell would recognize years later when he got to know another philosophy professor, Michigan's Carl Cohen.

Pell decided to attend law school, concluding it would be both a natural extension of his academic interests and a stepping stone to a productive career. He enrolled at Cornell, where he found himself increasingly on the conservative side of debates with his classmates over the wisdom of large government programs as a cure for social ills. When Reagan ran for president in 1980, Pell was an enthusiastic supporter.

Pell practiced law for several years at a large Washington law firm before accepting a position as deputy assistant secretary for civil rights in the U.S. Department of Education under Secretary William Bennett. The experience was an eye-opener for Pell in more ways than one. Bennett used his office as a bully pulpit to advocate a core curriculum that focused on traditional Western thought and included character as a key component. Bennett traveled the country, giving speeches and teaching sample lessons, and the department produced a steady stream of documents describing ways to reinvigorate education. The school boards and teachers' unions that Bennett fought were powerful—he derided them as the "education blob"—but the secretary managed to put his ideas about education in the forefront of the debate, a remarkable accomplishment given the relatively low profile of the department he headed.

Pell also gained first-hand experience on issues of race and education. He and his staff reviewed a series of court orders around the country that were designed to desegregate school districts. The question in each case was whether the district had achieved "unitary status"—that is, whether desegregation had taken hold, permitting the court to end its oversight. Pell concluded that about a third of the districts had achieved unitary status. Another third might with additional steps. The last third seemed hopelessly segregated, with no end in sight.

When Bennett moved to the drug czar's office under President George H. W. Bush, Pell moved with him, serving as general counsel and chief of staff. Later Pell earned his Ph.D. in philosophy at Notre Dame, completing his dissertation from the office space he rented from CIR and his old friend Michael Greve.

Greve's suggestion that Pell come to work at CIR proved well-timed. Pell had been contemplating becoming a professor and even received one job offer, but he had concluded that a university salary couldn't support his growing family, which now included two boys and a third child on the way. A position with CIR wouldn't pay much more, but Pell thought it would be a good fit. Over lunch at a restaurant a few blocks from the office, the two men sealed the deal. Pell would come aboard as a PR man. He would both deal with reporters and work to place his own articles in academic journals and newspaper op-ed pages.

Shortly after joining CIR, Pell wrote a *Wall Street Journal* piece that blasted a Clinton administration official for suggesting ways to limit *Hopwood*'s impact. "Not since George Wallace blocked the schoolhouse door has an elected official so openly and willfully encouraged state officials to defy a federal court," Pell wrote.

The *Hopwood* success left Greve and McDonald—and now Pell—eager for more university affirmative action battles, dreaming of someday persuading the Supreme Court to strike down racial preferences across the country. In March 1997, CIR filed a new lawsuit on behalf of a white woman rejected from the University of Washington Law School. The trio was also keeping a close eye on the unfolding controversy in Michigan.[1]

———■———

PRAISING DIVERSITY IN higher education was one thing. Defending it was quite another, as Lee Bollinger quickly discovered upon taking office in February 1997.

Three weeks into Bollinger's term, Carl Cohen made clear that the new president was in for a fight on affirmative action. Cohen penned a blistering commentary in Michigan's in-house weekly magazine, the

University Record. "University of Michigan records obtained using the Freedom of Information Act reveal that what is going on beneath euphemisms and obfuscation is, in a word, shocking."

Bollinger figured a lawsuit was coming, and he wanted to be prepared. One of his first orders of business was to take stock of the university's admissions policies. He was familiar with the law school policy, of course, but did not know the workings of the other university admissions systems.

He didn't like what he saw at the undergraduate level. The grids not only made for bad public relations, they also failed to capture what Bollinger thought the university should be trying to accomplish. Bollinger didn't want a mechanistic approach that automatically admitted applicants—white or black—based solely on grades and test scores. University officials told Bollinger that the grids were a useful tool to cope with the 14,000 applications received every year at the College of Literature, Science, and the Arts, Michigan's largest academic unit. (Of the 14,000, roughly 10,000 would be admitted to produce an entering class of 3,500–4,000 students.) Bollinger said he wanted a more individualistic approach that focused on the particular contributions each candidate could make to the class.

Bollinger made other changes, too. When he took office, he inherited Jim Duderstadt's wide-ranging Michigan Mandate. Bollinger approved of the aim—that is, diversifying the campus and making it more hospitable to minority students, faculty, and staff—but not the implementation. Bollinger quietly ratcheted down some of the programs and ended others. And, concerned that the phrase "Michigan Mandate" suggested that the school was doing something unique in higher education, Bollinger instructed his staff to stop invoking the expression.

Finally, Bollinger wanted to have his own administrative team in place. He quickly sought and received the resignation of the university's general counsel, Elsa Kircher Cole, and launched a national search for a new one. To fill the leadership void in the meantime, he tapped a pair of university attorneys, Elizabeth Barry and Daniel Sharphorn, as interim co–general counsels. Sharphorn, who had been an assistant under Cole, would manage the day-to-day operations of the office. Barry, previously the director of academic human resources, was tasked with advising the new president and Board of

Regents on various legal matters, including the growing affirmative action controversy.

Bollinger also filled a vacancy in the office of the provost, the university's chief academic officer. His choice was Nancy Cantor, dean of Michigan's Rackham School of Graduate Studies and former vice provost. Cantor, a psychologist, strongly believed that racial diversity had real, measurable benefits in the classroom, and she felt it had special, historical importance at Michigan. Diversity was in the lifeblood of Michigan, and it was clearly a principle worth fighting for, Cantor thought. Her appointment itself was an example of diversity, as she became the school's first female provost.

Beyond the specifics of Michigan's policies and staff, Bollinger had a more fundamental problem. Race-based admissions might well have the support of the Board of Regents, but they weren't always so popular outside Ann Arbor. The 1996 *Hopwood* decision by the Fifth Circuit, coupled with the passage that same year of Proposition 209 in California, had created a sense of inevitability about race-based admissions policies. To Bollinger, it was as if a tidal wave were headed straight toward affirmative action, threatening to wash it away.

Bollinger first tried to shore up his support among his fellow universities. He had seen from his involvement in the Texas case that many institutions were skittish about associating themselves with a school that was being sued. Although Bollinger wasn't the only law school dean who testified for Texas, he knew that a number of others had refused, preferring to keep their distance.

At the annual spring meeting of the Association of American Universities in Washington, Bollinger turned his charm and powers of persuasion on his colleagues, imploring them to stand together on the question of race-conscious admissions. The AAU, made up of sixty-two of the nation's largest research institutions, seldom issued public proclamations. But with the attack on race-conscious admissions policies gathering momentum, a majority of the presidents concluded that an exception was warranted. After a lengthy debate, the presidents decided to issue a statement that not only praised the value of classroom diversity but said outright that universities needed to consider race as an admissions factor to achieve their educational goals. For good measure, the group ran the statement as an advertisement in the *New York Times*.[2]

———◼———

MICHAEL GREVE WAS used to getting phone calls from people he didn't know. After CIR's success in *Hopwood*, he and Michael McDonald had received a slew of inquiries from people who wanted the firm to file lawsuits on their behalf. Greve had learned that the best approach was to promise nothing and ask callers to send information about their situation. CIR couldn't afford to sue every school that used race in admissions. The group had to choose its battles.

The call from Deborah Whyman and David Jaye was nonetheless intriguing. The two were Michigan state representatives, both Republican and both fiercely opposed to racial preferences. On speakerphone, they told Greve that they had learned about Carl Cohen's research and wanted to do something with it. Whyman pitched their idea: she and Jaye would find people who were rejected because of their race, and CIR would file suit.

Greve gave Whyman and Jaye his now-standard line, saying that CIR would consider representing the people they came up with, but that he couldn't promise anything. Privately, Greve harbored concerns about Jaye. Over the course of his nine-year career, Jaye had repeatedly drawn charges of race-baiting, frequently from members of his own party. Most recently, he was criticized for an election flyer that referred to his opponent as a "friend of Jesse Jackson." On the phone, Jaye struck Greve as a loose cannon.

On May 1, 1997, Whyman, Jaye, and two other legislators issued a press release attacking Michigan's "discriminatory racial preference policies," referring specifically to the undergraduate and law schools. Students were told to contact the lawmakers if they had been denied admission or scholarships because of the university's racial preferences. The release included an ambiguous comment from Greve, who noted that CIR had received a "large number of requests for assistance" and that the group "can handle only so many cases."

Stories appeared in both the *Detroit Free Press* and the *Detroit News,* and Whyman further publicized the campaign on radio talk shows. Over the next several weeks, Whyman's office fielded dozens of calls from parents and students distraught over rejection letters from the University of Michigan. An aide carefully took down the information and told the callers to send a copy of their application along with their grades and test scores. Whyman's office then forwarded the information to CIR.

Greve followed the news coverage with interest. He had concluded that Jaye was more trouble than he was worth and needed to be jettisoned from the team. At the same time, the tremendous response to the press release seemed to confirm Greve's intuition that Michigan was ripe for a lawsuit.[3]

—•—

IN AN IDEAL world, CIR would have found a lawyer in Michigan to lead the potential litigation against the university. The case or cases probably would need to be filed there for jurisdictional reasons, and it would be logistically helpful not to be waging the fight on completely foreign turf. But McDonald, whose job it was to find an attorney, had learned over the years that big-firm lawyers—and he already knew he would need the resources of a substantial firm—rarely were looking to sue one of the most powerful institutions in their home state. Besides, McDonald had a lawyer from Minnesota in mind, one he'd been trying to bring over to the conservative cause for almost two decades.

Kirk Kolbo had sported a "Ted Kennedy for President" button when McDonald met him at George Washington Law School. Born and reared in overwhelmingly white South Dakota, the baby-faced, dimple-cheeked Kolbo was a product of a staunchly Democratic family. His father was a state legislator and an ally of future U.S. Senate Democratic Leader Tom Daschle. His mother was a legal secretary, and, as a boy, Kirk would visit her at her law firm and help her reorganize books. He took an interest in politics himself and at Augustana College in Sioux Falls, he became president of his campus chapter of the Young Democrats.

Despite their ideological differences, McDonald and Kolbo became close friends in law school. They were part of a group that would go out on weekend nights and debate the latest Supreme Court cases. After graduating with high honors, Kolbo returned to the Midwest and accepted a job as a litigator at Faegre & Benson, a large Minneapolis law firm. He dabbled in Democratic Party politics in his new city but discovered he had little in common with the more liberal brand of Democrats he met there. As time went on, Kolbo realized he was becoming more conservative and increasingly in agreement with his old friend McDonald, with whom he kept in touch. Kolbo admired his friend's decision to take a risk and form CIR.

By the end of 1994, Kolbo was ready to take on a case for CIR. The client was a male professor at a northern Minnesota community college who was being accused of making sexually harassing remarks to female faculty members. When the college placed a letter of reprimand in his file, CIR and Kolbo sued on behalf of the professor. Within a few months, the school agreed to rescind the letter.

In 1995, Kolbo moved to a smaller firm, seventy-lawyer Maslon Edelman Borman & Brand, in the same downtown Minneapolis skyscraper. Maslon, founded in the 1950s by Jewish lawyers who had faced anti-Semitism, had a history of combating discrimination. Most notably, Maslon lawyers had led the legal fight to desegregate the public schools in Minneapolis in the 1970s.

Soon McDonald had another Minnesota case to offer his old friend. This one involved race-based tuition assistance at the University of Minnesota. Kolbo wanted to take the case, but Maslon's management committee concluded that suing the state's flagship university raised conflict-of-interest issues. The school had previously been a client and probably would be again in the future. Kolbo was frustrated, but he had to turn McDonald down. "If you get another case, give me a call," Kolbo said.

A few months later, McDonald telephoned Kolbo and told him about the Michigan situation. Kolbo ran it past his partners, and this time the firm cleared him to take the case. Kolbo was pleased. The case was a chance to liven up an otherwise staid corporate litigation practice. Kolbo's client list included insurance companies, construction firms, and manufacturers. He spent his days poring through building codes and interviewing witnesses about policy limits. Cases presenting fundamental questions of constitutional rights were few and far between.

Kolbo's docket reflected his style: workmanlike and solid, not prone to attract attention. Tall and hefty with graying hair, he was partial to the dark suits that were practically a uniform among corporate litigators. He was unquestionably a good lawyer—the attorney information service Martindale-Hubbell gave him its highest rating—but, at age forty, not one who had yet won the awards that some of his partners collected every year from local legal publications and attorney organizations.

Kolbo didn't have McDonald's passion or knowledge about the issue of racial preferences. But his instincts now told him that his old friend was on the correct side of the debate. Racial discrimination was wrong, regardless of the color of the victim, Kolbo felt. As a courtroom lawyer accustomed to advocating for a client, Kolbo was more than comfortable taking on the CIR cause.[4]

———•———

THE PUBLICITY SURROUNDING Representative Whyman's efforts erased any lingering doubts Bollinger might have had about the inevitability of a lawsuit. He decided it was time to put together his legal team. When Texas Law School had been sued, it chose to rely on donated, or "pro bono," legal work from professors and a local law firm, along with the services of the state's attorney general. It was an unusual arrangement for a wealthy university, but it had saved the school more than $1 million.

Bollinger wanted a more formal relationship with the legal team, one in which he could be sure the university could control the litigation and call on its attorneys to do whatever work was necessary. It would be expensive, and he anticipated the price tag might cost him support on the Board of Regents. But Michigan had a self-funded insurance plan, which Bollinger expected would cover much, if not all, of the legal defense costs. And Bollinger was convinced that cutting corners on the school's legal defense would prove counterproductive.

Bollinger turned to Wilmer Cutler Pickering, an elite Washington firm whose revenue and profits typically ranked among the top five in the city each year. The firm had been co-founded in 1962 by John Pickering, who had earned his undergraduate and law degrees from Michigan and gone on to become one of the university's most influential alumni. The eighty-one-year-old Pickering was past the point of taking the lead role on such a momentous case, but he told Bollinger he had a partner, John Payton, who seemed a good fit.

Payton was a rare combination—a black partner at a top Washington firm. Fifty years old, he had a salt-and-pepper beard, hazel eyes, and a receding hairline that emphasized his broad fore-

©2003 JAY MALLIN

For Minneapolis corporate litigator Kirk Kolbo, fundamental constitutional questions were few and far between—until the Michigan cases came along. His representation of Barbara Grutter and Jennifer Gratz marked a new high in his career. The one-time liberal's opposition to racial preferences would grow more fervent as the case progressed.

©THE REGENTS OF THE UNIVERSITY OF MICHIGAN.
BY MARCIA L. LEDFORD

Michigan's lead attorney, Washington litigator John Payton, brought a no-nonsense style and decades of experience in civil rights. He set out to prove that diversity had educational value. Payton thought that proposition indisputable, but experience had taught him not to count on the Supreme Court to make even what seemed an obvious assumption.

head. His booming voice and blunt speaking style made him seem taller than his barely average height. Some people thought he bore a vague resemblance to television journalist Ed Bradley.

Throughout his adult life, Payton had never strayed far from the cause of minority rights. He was a Los Angles native who attended nearby Pomona College in the middle of the turbulent 1960s. He discovered he was one of only three African American students there and soon became one of the leaders of the campus protest movement, pressuring the school to enroll more black and Hispanic students and create an environment where they could thrive. When the school retained a law firm to negotiate with the protestors, the students hired their own attorney, giving Payton his first glimpse at the contributions a lawyer could make to the cause of civil rights. The school eventually responded to the student complaints, setting up special minority admissions offices and study centers. The school even offered Payton a job in the admissions office recruiting black candidates and vetting their applications. Seeing the admissions process up close reinforced Payton's belief that affirmative action was morally right. Admissions, he discovered, wasn't a matter of simply picking the applicants with the highest grades or test scores. It was also putting together a class where students would get along and learn from each other. That meant sometimes admitting students with relatively low numbers if they seemed likely to make nonacademic contributions to the class.

Payton enrolled at Harvard Law School in the fall of 1974. When he arrived, Boston was exploding with violence over school integration. For the first time, white and black students were being bused across the city as part of a court-ordered desegregation plan. Many whites reacted by throwing rocks, beating up students, and even firebombing a bus full of children, all of whom managed to escape with their lives. Payton and other Harvard law students took down statements from some of the firebombing victims in an effort to help a local judge figure out how to quell the violence.

Payton took advantage of Harvard's new clinical course offerings, working as a public defender during his third year. He discovered he was a natural courtroom lawyer, able to think quickly on his feet and sway judges, jurors, and witnesses. He considered working at a public-interest organization but couldn't resist the trappings of a large firm. He learned that Wilmer Cutler Pickering was representing the NAACP in a case that threatened to bankrupt the group. White Mississippi merchants, claiming an NAACP boycott was an antitrust violation, had won a multimillion-dollar award. When Wilmer offered Payton a job, he accepted on the condition that he could work on the NAACP appeal. The firm agreed, and he joined a team led by Lloyd Cutler that in 1982 won unanimous reversal of the verdict at the U.S. Supreme Court in *NAACP v. Claiborne Hardware*.[5]

At Wilmer, Payton split his time between the firm's staple commercial litigation practice and civil rights. In the late 1980s, the city of Richmond, Virginia, asked Payton to argue a Supreme Court appeal seeking to revive a set-aside program that directed city construction work to minority-owned businesses. Payton readily agreed to take on the case, but soon discovered he faced a daunting obstacle. The city's lawyers at the lower court level, for whatever reason, had made no effort to show why minorities received only a tiny fraction of the city's construction dollars. Payton was sure that decades of racism played a significant role, but he couldn't make that argument at the Supreme Court unless he could point to evidence that had been introduced at the trial court. In a six-to-three ruling known as *City of Richmond v. J. A. Croson Co.*, the Supreme Court, pointing to the very dearth of proof that had troubled Payton, ruled against the city. Justice Sandra Day O'Connor's majority opinion said that "the city points to no evidence that qualified minority contractors have been passed over for city contracts or subcontracts, either as a group or in any individual case." She added: "Blacks may be disproportionately attracted to industries other than construction." Shortly after the decision, Payton first encountered Lee Bollinger, who co-wrote a *Harvard Law Review* article criticizing the *Croson* ruling.

In 1991 Payton, like so many of his Wilmer colleagues had done over the years, left the firm for a government job, serving as the top lawyer for the District of Columbia. He stayed at that post until 1994, when he traveled to South Africa in advance of its first presidential election in the post-apartheid era. Payton's wife served on the commission that ran the balloting while he served on an international observer team. He returned to Wilmer and its high-priced offices in the summer of 1994.

The Michigan fight was a chance for the fifty-year-old Payton to do what he hadn't been able to do in *Croson*—build a defense for affirmative action from the ground up. He recognized that a lawsuit against the university had the potential to reach the Supreme Court. If that happened, Payton was determined to have the type of evidentiary record that was missing in *Croson*. He wouldn't simply assume that classroom diversity was of great value; he would prove it by finding experts who could explain its importance in detail. Nor would he simply point to Justice Powell's opinion in *Bakke* for support; he would demonstrate that Powell was right.[6]

BOLLINGER HAD COME to the conclusion that a top-flight law firm should be only part of his response to a lawsuit. Long conversations with his new provost, Nancy Cantor, and his wife, Jean, had helped convince him that the university needed to wage its fight to defend affirmative action on multiple fronts.

Bollinger decided that he, Cantor, and other top university officials should launch a public education campaign. They would vie to win the hearts and minds of people both in Ann Arbor and around the country. On campus, university officials would host a series of symposia and bring in speakers to explain why diversity and affirmative action were so crucial to the school's mission. They would write position papers and articles for publication, explaining in detail why the school was willing to go to court to defend its position. They would set up a website to make legal documents widely available. They would happily agree to media interviews and set up meetings with key newspaper editorial boards. Michigan would take its case to business leaders and politicians, as well as others in higher education, to put together the broadest possible coalition in support of affirmative action.

Bollinger, in short, wanted to do exactly what Terry Pell at CIR sought to do—start a national debate on the use of race in college admissions. A subject that other university presidents had been reluctant to discuss was soon to be front-page news.

Chapter 3 Three

Gratz, Grutter, and Hamacher

J ENNIFER GRATZ MOVED ON as best she could. After Notre Dame rejected her, she settled on the University of Michigan at Dearborn. Every
day she climbed into her black Mustang and drove twenty minutes
from her parents' house to the suburban campus, located in a town best
known for being the headquarters of Ford Motor Co. She abandoned
thoughts of becoming a doctor, deciding instead to major in math.

She didn't tell anyone outside her family—not even her boyfriend—
the real reason she enrolled at Dearborn. Instead, she told her friends
that she wanted to stay closer to home. They were incredulous, but
Gratz couldn't bear to confess that Michigan had rejected her. The
closest she came was in a composition class her sophomore year at
Dearborn, when she wrote a paper called "Legalized Discrimination
in Educational Institutions." In it, she described a white woman with
credentials identical to hers who was rejected from the University of
Michigan. She contrasted the student with a Hispanic applicant who
had lower grades, yet was admitted.

Late in her sophomore year, Gratz filled out a Michigan transfer
application. She visited the Ann Arbor campus, talked to an admissions officer, and learned that the university wouldn't accept all her
Dearborn credits. She looked at a few apartments, then drove home
to Southgate to talk with her parents. They discussed the activities Jennifer might have to give up to make a transfer feasible. She
had just been offered a position as a cheerleading coach at her old

high school, and she was working at a Michigan cheerleading camp. Together, the family concluded that transferring didn't make sense. Gratz never submitted the application.

She left for cheerleading camp that summer and tried to put Ann Arbor out of her mind. When she returned, her father offhandedly told her about an article he had seen in the *Detroit News* while she was away. Some legislators are trying to put together an admissions lawsuit against UM, he said. She asked if he had saved the article. He hadn't, so Jennifer called the newspaper and tracked down the reporter, who suggested she call State Representative Deborah Whyman's office in Lansing for more information.

As Gratz placed the call, she thought to herself that she would be willing to contribute however she could to a lawsuit against the university. "I'll probably be stuffing envelopes," she thought to herself.[1]

———•———

ALL TOLD, some 200 rejected applicants contacted Deborah Whyman and the other Michigan lawmakers. It was instantly clear that many of them wouldn't be acceptable plaintiffs. Some had applied years earlier, so the applicable statute of limitations had expired. Others lacked the grades or test scores to make them qualified candidates for admission. Still others never sent Whyman copies of their applications or changed their minds after initially expressing interest.

By September 1977, the CIR team had whittled the list down to about a half dozen people. Michael McDonald in Washington and Kirk Kolbo in Minneapolis made plans to travel to Michigan and meet their potential clients in person.

Their first stop was Carl Cohen's office. Cohen was sitting on the steps outside the building when the two lawyers arrived. He whisked the visitors into his office and offered them a beer. For two hours, Cohen was a whirlwind, pulling sheaves of documents from his files, pointing out example after example of unfairness in the Michigan admissions system.

McDonald and Kolbo then set up shop at a hotel near the Detroit airport. They had arranged for a small conference room, which they discovered was outfitted with squeaky chairs and a blackboard. In coats and ties, the two old friends waited for their first appointment to arrive.

The two men knew what they were looking for. They wanted to find plaintiffs, of course, but only the right type of plaintiffs. McDonald and Kolbo needed people who would get involved for the proper reasons. Money or personal gain couldn't be the goal, although a modest damage award was a possibility. (McDonald once had a client who insisted on holding out for millions of dollars.) The plaintiffs had to be people who were involved in the case simply because they believed that what the university was doing was wrong. Equally important, McDonald and Kolbo wanted people who demonstrated a commitment, who wouldn't back down in the face of inevitable public criticism and the prospect of years of fighting. Over the next several days, they met three people who seemed to meet those criteria.

Jennifer Gratz arrived with her mother, fresh from a pep rally at her old high school. Almost as soon as the two women entered the room, Kolbo and McDonald both realized they had a strong candidate. Jennifer was well organized and had brought all her application materials with her. She told the two men that she felt strongly that a wrong had been committed. She said she understood that nothing could be done for her—by the time the case was resolved, she likely would have her degree from Dearborn—but she wanted to help change the school's admissions policies.

McDonald and Kolbo explained the personal price she might have to pay. Her involvement might not sit well with future employers, they told her. "I'm not worried," she replied. She said that, if an employer couldn't understand why she was doing this, she didn't want to work for them. The group shook hands and promised to stay in touch. In the car on the way home, Jennifer told her mother that she wanted to be a plaintiff.

———•———

THE NEXT DAY, McDonald and Kolbo met a very different type of candidate, Barbara Grutter, an unsuccessful law school applicant. Grutter was a mother of two who ran her own health-care consulting firm from her home in the Detroit suburb of Plymouth. Grutter had applied to Michigan Law School the previous year as a forty-three-year-old interested in health-care law. Her credentials included a 3.8 undergraduate GPA from Michigan State, and her LSAT score of 161 ranked in the eighty-sixth percentile. Like Jennifer Gratz at the

Two women came to symbolize
the national campaign against
university racial preferences. Rejected
undergraduate applicant Jennifer Gratz
(right) was a police officer's daughter
who graduated in the top 5 percent of
her suburban Detroit high school class.
Barbara Grutter, a forty-three-year-old
mother of two with her own consulting
business, sought to study in the imposing
gothic halls of Michigan Law School.

JAY MALLIN/BLOOMBERG NEWS

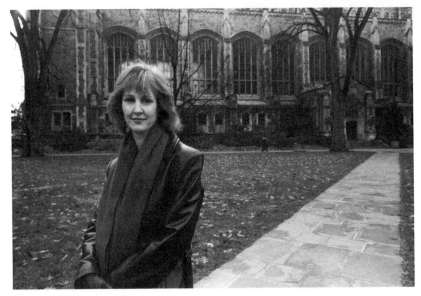

MICHELLE ANDONIAN

undergraduate school, Grutter initially was placed on the waiting list
and ultimately was rejected.

The slender, brown-haired Grutter came to the hotel by herself.
She had more questions than Gratz did. How long would it take?
What would it mean for her family? Since she hadn't enrolled in any
other law school, was there a chance the lawsuit might earn her a

place at Michigan? Beneath her many questions, both Kolbo and McDonald detected a firm commitment. Like Gratz, she was convinced she had been wronged. If she decided to get involved, she wouldn't back down.

Kolbo and McDonald's final appointment was in East Lansing, the home of Michigan State University. There they met Patrick Hamacher, an unsuccessful undergraduate applicant for the class of 1997. Hamacher had scored a 28 on the ACT, in the eighty-ninth percentile, and earned a 3.4 high school GPA. He also was a varsity football and baseball player, took part in the school choir and Quiz Bowl team, and worked several part-time jobs. He was just starting his freshman year at Michigan State, having enrolled there after being wait-listed at Michigan. Although Hamacher held out some hope of being able to transfer to Ann Arbor, Kolbo and McDonald told him that wasn't likely, at least not as a result of the lawsuit. Hamacher said he was interested in suing the university anyway.

As Kolbo and McDonald boarded their respective airplanes home, they had reason for optimism. Three possible plaintiffs had indicated strong interest. All three could make the case that they were more qualified than many of the minority students who were admitted with the help of affirmative action. Together, the group could provide the basis for suits challenging both the undergraduate and law school admissions policies. (The medical school would be spared, in large part because CIR lacked a plaintiff.)

Importantly for McDonald, two of the three were women. He didn't want to give opponents the chance to characterize the case as a bunch of "angry white men."[2]

———•———

WHILE KOLBO AND McDONALD prepared for litigation, the university quietly moved the target, eliminating the increasingly controversial grids. By the fall of 1997, a new undergraduate admissions system was ready, just in time for the flood of applications for the following year's entering class.

The new system scored each applicant on a 150-point scale, with the admissions cutoff falling somewhere between ninety and one hundred each year. Students could earn as many as 110 points for academic factors, including eighty for a 4.0 grade-point average in their high school academic courses. A 3.0 was worth sixty points, and a 2.0, forty. Applicants could get up to ten points for attending an exceptionally strong high school, eight points for taking a challenging curriculum, and twelve points for performing well on their standardized tests. (The admissions office reasoned that test scores were so highly correlated with grades that they added relatively little to the process.) Ten points were awarded for being a Michigan resident, five for personal achievement or leadership, four for alumni connections, and one for an outstanding essay.

Race would be factored in through a category called "miscellaneous," which gave twenty points to underrepresented minorities, socioeconomically disadvantaged students, scholarship athletes, and other applicants at the discretion of the provost. Applicants could receive the twenty points only once. In other words, a poor, black scholarship athlete got twenty miscellaneous points, not sixty.

On a surface level, the point system alleviated one problem with the grids—the implication that the university had two different sets of standards for judging minority and nonminority candidates. The new system ensured that the university no longer would have one column or sheet for blacks, Hispanics, and Native Americans and another column for whites and Asians.

But the point system didn't change the fundamental fact that race made a difference in some admissions decisions. Indeed, the new system underscored just how significant a factor race was. It was worth the equivalent of one grade point. A black "B" student stood on the same footing as a white "A" student.

———■———

THE COALITION TO DEFEND Affirmative Action by Any Means Necessary lived up to its name. The group had waged war in support of affirmative action in California for the past two years. Student members occupied admissions offices, walked out of classes, shut down regents' meetings, and occasionally got arrested. They didn't think twice about branding an opponent or a contrary idea as "racist." They embraced the description "militant."

The group's leader, Shanta Driver, was a Detroit-based socialist and union activist who hadn't been a student herself since 1975, when she graduated cum laude from Harvard. Driver was the daughter of two professors, one an African American, the other an immigrant from India. She was convinced that mainstream civil rights advocates weren't putting up an adequate fight for affirmative action.

Driver started BAMN, as the group was known, across the country at the University of California at Berkeley during what she considered to be a time of crisis. (Driver's group wasn't formally affiliated with BAM movements at Michigan in the 1970s and 1980s, despite the similarities in acronyms.) The university's regents had just voted to end race-based admissions, and opponents were pursuing a state ballot initiative that would even further undermine affirmative action. Mainstream liberals responded with what Driver saw as defeatism. The Reverend Jesse Jackson's Rainbow/PUSH Coalition decided to focus its efforts not on the ballot initiative but on electing more Democrats to office in 1996. President Bill Clinton conceded that many affirmative action programs were flawed, issuing a call to "mend it, don't end it." Even those groups who were working against the ballot initiative, the one that would come to be known as Prop 209, seemed to do little more than register blacks and Latinos to vote.

For Driver and her allies, affirmative action was something to be embraced, not apologized for or hidden behind a euphemism like "diversity." She saw affirmative action as a natural extension of the Supreme Court's 1954 *Brown v. Board of Education* school desegregation decision. Far from giving minorities some kind of special advantage, affirmative action merely offset the deep-seated racism (and sexism) that permeated American society, Driver thought. For BAMN, the issue was equality, not diversity.

Driver believed that the only way to defeat the attack on affirmative action was with a massive, nationwide civil rights movement that would revive memories of the 1950s and 1960s. As she saw it, progress would come not from isolated court cases or legislation, but from a social struggle that would force change. Driver envisioned inspired blacks and Latinos demanding the equality and justice they were being denied at virtually every level of the American power structure. She saw minorities coming out to vote against Prop 209 and fight racist police brutality. And, Driver thought, once millions of people took to the streets, politicians and judges would have to listen.

But Prop 209 had passed, and now the battleground seemed to be moving into Driver's backyard of Michigan. Driver had already fought one civil rights battle in Ann Arbor, helping organize protests at UM over the 1994 firing of three black Dental School workers accused of falsifying their time cards. The workers, represented by local civil rights attorney George Washington of Scheff and Washington, eventually were reinstated and given jobs in different departments.

As the school year began in 1997, Driver and two UM students decided to open a new chapter of BAMN at Michigan. More than fifty students took part in BAMN's first rally on the Diag in the center of campus. Carrying a banner with the new group's name, the demonstrators chanted slogans and exhorted their fellow students to join the cause. Some did, spontaneously jumping into the demonstration. Others watched with curiosity, and one told the student newspaper, the *Michigan Daily,* he worried what the group meant by the phrase "by any means necessary." The protestors marched to the building that housed the *Daily* and demanded a retraction of an editorial cartoon that had depicted a squirrel protesting a lack of rights.[3]

——■——

GREVE'S EFFORT TO KEEP the flamboyant legislator David Jaye on the sidelines was only partially successful. Jaye scheduled a public hearing on the university's admissions policies in his hometown of Shelby Township in the northern suburbs of Detroit, with Carl Cohen as the featured speaker.

By the time Cohen arrived at Shelby Township Hall in the early evening, two dozen BAMN members, many of them nonstudents, were out front, shouting slogans and carrying signs. Jaye invited them in. Once at the podium, he told the 150-person crowd that he planned to push for a Michigan equivalent to California's Prop 209. The protestors stood up and began shouting at Jaye. "Change your nametag to George Wallace!" one said. Jaye snapped back at them: "Do you behave like this in the classroom? Do your parents know how you're behaving?" The chanting protestors moved in front of the podium, blocking Cohen and the other would-be speakers. Someone called the police, whose headquarters were in the same building. The officers tried to persuade the protestors to leave and, when that didn't work, attempted to drag the demonstrators out. Then the police turned to pepper spray. The fumes sent some people into coughing fits and caused others to vomit. Protestors, participants, and audience members alike cleared the building. Police arrested four people and charged them with disorderly conduct.

Jaye reconvened the hearing later in the evening, holding it in the lobby because the pepper spray still lingered in the meeting room. Cohen, his adrenaline flowing, launched a blistering attack on the university's policies. Others stood up in defense of affirmative action. Another legislator vowed to introduce a bill that would bar disruptive protests. The remaining BAMN members stayed outside, blocked by police from re-entering the meeting hall. The protestors resumed their chanting: "We won't take resegregation! We demand an education!"

The battle over affirmative action at Michigan had begun. And, as Cohen told a reporter, race relations at the university were as bad as they had ever been.[4]

Part Two

Trial Court

(October 1997–April 2001)

Chapter Four

Equal Protection

W E'VE BEEN WAITING for this," said the clerk behind the counter at the Detroit federal courthouse. A local lawyer working with CIR handed over the complaint and watched it get stamped with the date, October 14, 1997.[1]

The document covered only Gratz and Hamacher, the CIR team having decided to file a separate lawsuit later over Grutter's application to Michigan Law School. The complaint boiled down Gratz's and Hamacher's grievances to four and one-half pages. It described how both students were wait-listed and rejected from the College of Literature, Science, and the Arts (known as LS&A or LSA) before enrolling in other universities. The lawsuit sought class action status on behalf of rejected LS&A applicants dating back to the 1995–96 school year. Jennifer Gratz and Patrick Hamacher would be the representatives of all rejected applicants who were disfavored because of their race—primarily whites but also Asian Americans. The complaint sought an injunction that would force the admissions office to stop considering race. It requested damages to compensate the applicants for the "humiliation, emotional distress, and pain and suffering" they endured upon learning they were rejected and again upon learning that they had been discriminated against because of their race. The plaintiffs sought additional compensation for the reduced earnings they could expect as a result of attending a less prestigious university. The suit also requested unspecified punitive damages against the uni-

versity and demanded that Michigan pay the white students' legal fees
and court costs. Finally, it asked that Patrick Hamacher be offered a
place at Michigan as a transfer student from Michigan State.

The complaint accused Michigan of violating three federal statutes. Two of those, known to lawyers as sections 1981 and 1983,
are Reconstruction-era laws authorizing some suits over civil rights
violations. The third, Title VI of the 1964 Civil Rights Act, bars race
discrimination by recipients of federal funds. For the purposes of the
lawsuit, all three statutes pointed to a central principle: the students
claimed the university had violated the Constitution's equal protection clause.

Perhaps no single phrase in the Constitution has as much importance in the day-to-day life of the average American as the one that ends
Section 1 of the Fourteenth Amendment: "Nor shall any state ... deny
to any person within its jurisdiction the equal protection of the laws."
The words resonate with one of the basic tenets of American society,
harkening back to the Declaration of Independence and its promise that
"all men are created equal." Approved by Congress in 1866 in the wake
of the Civil War and ratified by the necessary twenty-seven of thirty-six
states over the next two years, the Fourteenth Amendment, by its terms,
pledged to give newly freed slaves the same legal rights and privileges
as whites.

But for black Americans, the promise of equality continued to ring
hollow for the better part of the next century. Blacks held second-class
status under the law. In 1883, the Supreme Court struck down a new
civil rights law that sought to open hotels, restaurants, railroads, theaters, and other businesses to black patrons.[2] Justice Joseph Bradley
said the equal protection clause reached only public actions, such as
laws or decisions by state administrators, not the "private rights" that
are at stake when a business opens its doors to customers.

In 1896, the Supreme Court upheld a Louisiana law that required
railroads to seat black and white passengers in separate cars. That
case, *Plessy v. Ferguson,* enshrined the notion of "separate but equal"
into the law.[3] By an eight-to-one majority, the court ruled that neither
the Thirteenth Amendment, which bans slavery, nor the Fourteenth
barred the Louisiana law. Justice Henry B. Brown said the Fourteenth
Amendment "could not have been intended to abolish distinctions
based upon color, or to enforce social, as distinguished from political,

equality, or a commingling of the two races upon terms unsatisfactory to either." The lone dissenter, Justice John Marshall Harlan, made an impassioned argument that, in the eyes of the law, "there is in this country no superior, dominant, ruling class of citizens." Our Constitution, he said, "is color-blind."

The *Plessy* decision institutionalized state-sanctioned segregation in Southern and border states until the 1960s. "Jim Crow" laws, named after a racist nineteenth-century minstrel song, forced blacks to use separate water fountains, restrooms, parks, beaches, and hospitals. More often than not, the facilities for blacks were grossly inferior—older than and not as well maintained as those for whites. Restaurants that served blacks did so in separate sections. Buses had whites-only seats in the front; "Negroes" and "colored" had to sit in back. Theaters relegated blacks to the balconies. And, of tremendous long-term significance, schools in twenty-one states were racially segregated. Black children often had to trudge miles to attend decrepit schools with leaky roofs, inadequate supplies, and poorly trained teachers. Enforcing the regime of white superiority was the constant threat of violence against anyone who dared to challenge the system. Thousands of people, both blacks and whites, were lynched or killed in race riots.

In 1944, the Supreme Court gave racial minorities a theoretical boost, though not one that produced any immediate tangible benefits. In *Korematsu v. United States*, the Court for the first time said it would give especially tough equal protection scrutiny to state-sponsored racial classifications.[4] "All legal restrictions which curtail the civil rights of a single group are immediately suspect," the Court wrote. The ruling revived the notion that race discrimination by an arm of the state was generally forbidden. At the same time, the *Korematsu* decision itself upheld the forced detention of Japanese Americans during World War II, saying the practice was justified by a pressing government need.

For African Americans, Jim Crow remained the law of the land in almost half the country. In Topeka, Kansas, a young black girl named Linda Brown traveled a mile every day to all-black Monroe School, usually walking part of the way along the railroad tracks before catching a bus. One September morning in 1950, seven-year-old Linda's father took her for a walk to Sumner School, an all-white school in their neighborhood, and he tried to enroll her. The principal refused. Soon Oliver Brown was in touch with the local chapter of the National Association for the Advancement of Colored People, and the landmark lawsuit bearing his name was under way. The lead attorney would be future Justice Thurgood Marshall, the founder of the NAACP Legal Defense and Educational Fund.

Brown v. Board of Education was actually five cases that the Supreme Court decided together in 1954. Overturning *Plessy*, the court said segregated public schools were "inherently unequal." For black children, a separate school "generates a feeling of inferiority as to their status in the community that may affect their hearts and minds in a way unlikely ever to be undone," Chief Justice Earl Warren wrote. To back up that conclusion, Warren took the novel step of citing seven sociological and psychological studies of the effects of racial segregation.

Though only thirteen paragraphs long, the decision spoke volumes, in large part because of the unanimity that Warren had struggled behind the scenes to ensure. The ruling signaled that a fundamental change in American society was coming. "In its 164 years the court had erected many a landmark of U.S. history," *Time* magazine declared a week after the ruling. "None of them, except the Dred Scott Case (reversed by the Civil War) was more important than the school segregation issue. None of them directly and intimately affected so many American families."

Directly and intimately, perhaps, but, as it turned out, not immediately. The change would take time. The following year, in a ruling known as *Brown II*, the court said school districts need not desegregate right away.[5] They could instead move with "all deliberate speed," an oxymoronic standard that confounded judges and school officials while giving a legal opening to segregationists already predisposed toward defying the *Brown* decision.

Southern leaders reacted with defiance, mounting a campaign that came to be known as "massive resistance." More than a hundred members of Congress from Southern states signed a declaration condemning the *Brown* decision. States passed new laws intended to circumvent the Supreme Court ruling. Arkansas Governor Orval Faubus sent units of the state's national guard to prevent nine black children from entering Little Rock Central High School. Only after

President Dwight Eisenhower sent federal troops and the Supreme Court issued two more rulings did Faubus relent. Little Rock high schools opened their doors to both black and white students in the fall of 1959.

For opponents of segregation, the *Brown* ruling and others that followed represented the dawn of new possibilities. On December 1, 1955, no longer willing to tolerate second-class status, a black woman named Rosa Parks refused to give up her seat to a white man on a Montgomery, Alabama, bus and sparked a citywide boycott. Protestors staged nonviolent "sit-ins" at whites-only lunch counters. Others boarded buses for interracial "freedom rides" through the South. In 1963, a quarter of a million people marched in Washington, D.C., and listened as Martin Luther King Jr. delivered his famous "I Have a Dream" speech. Congress enacted the 1964 Civil Rights Act, which barred race discrimination by private businesses and employers.

Segregationists reacted to these developments with violence. When John Lewis and Hosea Williams led a group of marchers into Selma, Alabama, to demand voting rights and to protest a recent shooting death, heavily armed state troopers attacked them with clubs, whips, and tear gas. Television cameras brought the bloodshed into the living rooms of a horrified nation. Five months later, Congress passed the Voting Rights Act, which wiped out the poll taxes, literacy tests, and other bureaucratic obstacles that had denied black Americans their right to vote.

The Supreme Court put itself squarely on the side of integration. The justices quickly upheld the 1964 Civil Rights Act. In 1967, the Court struck down a Virginia law that punished people who married outside their race.[6] And a series of unanimous decisions called on school districts to move more quickly to integrate. By 1968, the justices had seen enough foot-dragging. "This deliberate perpetuation of the unconstitutional dual system can only have compounded the harm of such a system," Justice William Brennan wrote in a Virginia case. "Moreover, a plan that at this late date fails to provide meaningful assurance of prompt and effective disestablishment of a dual system is also intolerable.... The burden on a school board today is to come forward with a plan that promises realistically to work and promises realistically to work now."[7]

———◼———

AFFIRMATIVE ACTION WAS a child of the civil rights movement. The phrase itself was coined by President John F. Kennedy in a 1961 executive order. The generally accepted aim of affirmative action, at least as originally conceived, was to ensure that blacks no longer would face discrimination. Affirmative action would involve temporary steps to ensure the playing field was leveled. In the words of President Lyndon B. Johnson: "You do not take a person who, for years, has been hobbled by chains and liberate him, bring him up to the starting line of a race and then say, 'you are free to compete with all the others,' and still justly believe that you have been completely fair."

Johnson in 1965 signed an order that required government contractors to "take affirmative action" to hire and keep minority employees. But shedding the centuries-old vestiges of slavery and state-sponsored discrimination didn't prove easy. In Philadelphia, for example, the unions that dominated the construction industry were only 1.6 percent minority by 1969, a small fraction of the percentage in the city as a whole. The situation there prompted President Richard Nixon to issue his "Philadelphia Order," which for the first time required federal construction contractors to meet specific goals and timetables for increasing minority employment.

The private sector followed suit. Companies set up their own hiring and promotion goals, both for minority workers and for women, steps that helped insulate businesses from lawsuits claiming discrimination against those groups. And universities, including Michigan, worked to recruit and admit more blacks and Hispanics. By the 1970s, college affirmative action programs were commonplace, and the percentages of enrolled African Americans rose steadily.

The sudden ubiquity of affirmative action programs created a host of new legal issues. For starters, only a blurry line separated efforts to wipe out bias against minorities from programs that discriminated *in favor* of them. Goals and timetables could be seen as a tool to help ensure that subtle discrimination against minorities didn't take place, but the specifics got messy. Which races and ethnic groups should benefit? Could a construction company hire a black carpenter over a more qualified white candidate, reasoning that past discrimination had prevented the African American worker from gaining more job experience? Was it acceptable for a university to admit a black applicant with relatively low grades and test scores on the grounds that discrimination had forced her into inferior grade and high schools? Even if an affirmative action program really was "reverse discrimination," might it nonetheless be justified in the name of compensating for centuries of societywide injustices suffered by minorities?

By the mid-1970s, the Supreme Court was ready to explore this new area in the context of university admissions. The first dispute to reach the court was a washout. The 1974 case, *DeFunis v. Odegaard,* involved a white applicant who had been rejected by the University of Washington Law School.[8] A five-justice majority concluded the case was moot—that is, it no longer presented a live legal controversy. A trial judge had ordered Marco DeFunis admitted to Washington, and by the time the case reached the Supreme Court, he was finishing up his third year of law school. Since DeFunis had secured all that he was seeking in his lawsuit, the majority concluded there was nothing left to decide.

In 1977, the Supreme Court agreed to consider the case that would prove to be the central legal precedent in the Michigan fight. The question was whether the medical school at the University of California at Davis should have admitted Allan Bakke, a white engineer the school rejected twice. Much like Jennifer Gratz and Patrick Hamacher would do three decades later, Bakke said the school was using a double standard. The lawsuit said Bakke would have been admitted had he been allowed to compete for the sixteen seats the university had set aside in each 100-student class for minority applicants. The numbers gave him some support. Bakke's undergraduate grade point average was 3.46, 3.44 in science courses. By contrast, students admitted under the so-called special admissions program in 1973 had an average GPA of 2.88, 2.62 in science courses. Special admittees in 1974 had even lower scores: 2.62 and 2.44 for science. And Bakke's MCAT scores put him in the ninety-sixth, ninety-fourth, ninety-seventh, and seventy-second percentiles in the test's four categories. Special admittees in 1973 averaged the forty-sixth, twenty-fourth, thirty-fifth, and thirty-third percentiles; in 1974 they averaged the thirty-fourth, thirtieth, thirty-seventh, and eighteenth percentiles.

The case, known as *University of California Regents v. Bakke,* splintered the Court. Four justices—John Paul Stevens, Potter Stewart, William Rehnquist, and Chief Justice Warren Burger—sided with Bakke. They said that, under Title VI of the 1964 Civil Rights Act, the University of California and other schools receiving federal funding couldn't use race as an admissions factor. The group said the statute was so "crystal clear" that it didn't need to take the more momentous step of deciding whether the equal protection clause imposed similar restrictions on *state*-sponsored affirmative action programs.

Four other justices—William Brennan, Thurgood Marshall, Harry Blackmun, and Byron White—said the university's affirmative action policy was justified. Writing the main opinion for the group, Brennan dismissed the notion that the Constitution mandated absolute color-blindness. That, he said, "must be seen as aspiration rather than as description of reality." Brennan went on: "[We] cannot ... let color blindness become myopia which masks the reality that many 'created equal' have been treated within our lifetimes as inferior both by the law and by their fellow citizens."

After concluding that Title VI imposed no restrictions on affirmative action that weren't already mandated by the Constitution, Brennan described how he would determine whether racial preferences favoring blacks go too far. The test, he said, shouldn't be the "strict scrutiny" standard used by the court to judge discrimination against minorities. Under that demanding test, government discrimination was permissible only if it served a "compelling purpose" and was "narrowly tailored"—that is, if a policy used race only so much as was necessary to serve the compelling purpose. Brennan said the test for affirmative action should be less onerous. Invoking a standard that would come to be known as "intermediate scrutiny," Brennan said programs needed only to serve "important governmental objectives" and be "substantially related to achievement of those objectives."

Brennan had no trouble finding that important government objective. Davis was seeking to remedy the lingering effect of past discrimination in a society where many states once punished those who sought to educate blacks. It didn't matter that there was no evidence of discrimination by Davis itself. "Davis clearly could conclude that the serious and persistent underrepresentation of minorities in medicine ... is the result of handicaps under which minority applicants labor as a consequence of a background of deliberate, purposeful discrimination against minorities in education and in society generally, as well as in the medical profession."

Brennan argued that affirmative action wouldn't stigmatize beneficiaries as inferior. The black students attending Davis were "fully qualified to study medicine." Finally, he dismissed contentions that the Davis program was especially egregious because the school set aside a number of seats for minority applicants, rather than simply using race as one of many factors to be considered with each application. "For purposes of constitutional adjudication, there is no difference between the two approaches.... [A]ny given preference that results in the exclusion of a white candidate is no more or less constitutionally acceptable than a program such as that at Davis."

Each of the justices who signed Brennan's opinion added some of his own words. The most poignant came from Thurgood Marshall, the nation's first African American justice. Marshall described a sorry 350-year history that began with blacks being dragged to America in chains and continued through the dismantling of the Jim Crow system of segregation. He wrote: "[I]t must be remembered that, during most of the past 200 years, the Constitution as interpreted by this Court did not prohibit the most ingenious and pervasive forms of discrimination against the Negro. Now, when a State acts to remedy the effects of that legacy of discrimination, I cannot believe that this same Constitution stands as a barrier."

———■———

THE DECIDING VOTE in *Bakke* belonged to Justice Lewis Powell. He issued an opinion that would be analyzed and re-analyzed countless times in future years.

Writing only for himself, Powell said he read Title VI to impose the identical standards as the equal protection clause. He then said racial classifications should be subject to the same level of review—strict scrutiny—whether they were designed to help minorities or hurt them. While the Fourteenth Amendment may have been drafted for the benefit of freed slaves, it lay dormant until the twentieth century, by which time "the United States had become a

Nation of minorities," Powell wrote. "It is far too late to argue that the guarantee of equal protection to all persons permits the recognition of special wards entitled to a degree of protection greater than that accorded others." Judges, he said, shouldn't get into the sticky business of determining which racial groups are entitled to special protection. "The kind of variable sociological and political analysis necessary to produce such rankings simply does not lie within the judicial competence—even if they otherwise were politically feasible and socially desirable."

So, did any of the University of California medical school's stated purposes for its special admissions program constitute the required compelling purpose under the strict scrutiny test? The school had four rationales: increasing the number of minority doctors and medical students, countering the effects of societal discrimination, training doctors who will serve poor areas, and attaining a diverse student body. Powell quickly dismissed the first three arguments. He gave remarkably short shrift to the first, dismissing it with just three sentences of explanation. "Preferring members of any one group for no reason other than race or ethnic origin is discrimination for its own sake," he wrote. "This the Constitution forbids."

Powell also disagreed with Brennan on the question of societal discrimination. That was "an amorphous concept of injury that may be ageless in its reach into the past," Powell said. Courts and government agencies can use race to redress specified instances of discrimination, but "[w]ithout such findings of constitutional or statutory violations, it cannot be said that the government has any greater interest in helping one individual than in refraining from harming another."

It was diversity—or, more precisely, "the educational benefits that flow from an ethnically diverse student body"—that struck a chord with Powell. Again writing only for himself, he said that universities have a right, stemming from the First Amendment's free speech guarantee, to decide how best to select their student bodies. "Academic freedom, though not a specifically enumerated constitutional right, long has been viewed as a special concern of the First Amendment," Powell wrote. "The freedom of a university to make its own judgments as to education includes the selection of its student body."

Invoking a 1957 opinion by Justice Felix Frankfurter, Powell pointed to "four essential freedoms" for academia: who may teach, what may be taught, how it shall be taught, and who may be admitted to study. Frankfurter had said those freedoms lead to a climate of "speculation, experiment, and creativity." Powell took his predecessor's reasoning a step further, saying that atmosphere was promoted by a diverse student body. Quoting from another Supreme Court ruling, Powell wrote: "[I]t is not too much to say that the 'nation's future depends upon leaders trained through wide exposure' to the ideas and mores of students as diverse as this Nation of many peoples."

Nonetheless, Powell said, the Davis program went too far, failing the "narrow tailoring" part of the inquiry. He faulted the medical school for focusing solely on ethnic diversity. "The diversity that furthers a compelling state interest encompasses a far broader array of qualifications and characteristics of which racial or ethnic origin is but a single though important element," he said.

And Davis was wrong to set aside a specified number of slots for minorities, Powell said. He contrasted the Davis program with the one in place at Harvard College. Quoting from the Ivy League school's admission policy, Powell said:

> When the Committee on Admissions reviews the large middle group of applicants who are "admissible" and deemed capable of doing good work in their courses, the race of an applicant may tip the balance in his favor just as geographic origin or a life spent on a farm may tip the balance in other candidates' cases. A farm boy from Idaho can bring something to Harvard College that a Bostonian cannot offer. Similarly, a black student can usually bring something that a white person cannot offer.

Unlike Davis, Harvard didn't explicitly set a minimum number of black students for each class. "In such an admissions program, race or ethnic background may be deemed a 'plus' in a particular applicant's file, yet it does not insulate the individual from comparison with all other candidates for the available seats," Powell said. Critically, the Harvard program "treats each applicant as an individual in the admissions process." Powell acknowledged that the line between a "plus" system and the Davis program was a thin one. The difference was that Davis showed a "facial intent to discriminate."

———•———

THE *BAKKE* CASE was unquestionably a blockbuster, but what exactly it meant was far from clear. Five justices—Powell, plus the Stevens four—had agreed that universities can't set aside a certain number of seats for members of particular races. (That group also ruled that the medical school must admit Allan Bakke.) A different group of five—Powell, along with the Brennan four—had said that admissions offices may consider race for some purposes. The problem was that the latter fivesome had used two different rationales. Powell had said limited consideration of race was acceptable for purposes of diversity; Brennan had conspicuously failed to adopt that reasoning.

The immediate reaction to the decision was in large part one of confusion. The president of the American Association of Medical Colleges issued a statement expressing disappointment, then revised it a few hours later to say he was pleased. Others scratched their heads at the questions left unanswered. "This isn't a landmark decision," former Nixon administration Solicitor General Robert Bork told the *Washington Post*. "It doesn't tell us how much race counts. We're told that we can count race somewhat but not too much. That's going to be difficult to apply." Both sides in the fight claimed at least a partial victory.

Over time, university administrators and their attorneys concluded that the differences in the Powell and Brennan rationales were, for practical purposes, irrelevant. What mattered, the thinking went, was that five justices had made clear they thought a plan modeled after Harvard's would be constitutional. Put another way, because Powell would place more restrictions on affirmative action than the other four, his opinion controlled. So long as a plan met Powell's diversity test, it was constitutional, at least in the minds of university officials.

A few schools revamped their admissions systems. The UC-Davis medical school shifted to a point system that rated all applicants on a single scale and gave extra points to minorities. Some schools abolished special committees that had been set up to screen minority candidates; others opened their minority-admissions systems to disadvantaged white students. But few if any universities stopped using race altogether in admissions. University affirmative action was here to stay, at least until the next Supreme Court case.

THE COURT FOLLOWED up its *Bakke* decision with additional endorsements of affirmative action in each of the next two years. The first decision, *United Steelworkers v. Weber,* allowed private employers to voluntarily set up affirmative action programs that favored blacks over whites.[9] The second, *Fullilove v. Klutznick,* upheld a federal set-aside program that guaranteed that minority-controlled contractors would get 10 percent of the funds under a U.S. public works program.[10]

Those cases would prove to be the high-water mark for affirmative action at the Supreme Court. Ronald Reagan's election in 1980 installed an administration interested in rolling back racial preferences. To Reagan, preferences were simply a new form of racial discrimination, as vile and unconstitutional as bias directed against minorities. His Supreme Court appointments—Sandra Day O'Connor, Anthony Kennedy, and Antonin Scalia as associate justices and William Rehnquist for elevation to chief justice—reflected that philosophy, at least to some degree. All tended to be skeptical of, if not opposed to, racial preferences. Kennedy's appointment in 1988 proved especially significant because he replaced Powell, the Court's swing vote in *Bakke.*

With the Reagan appointees in place, the Court dealt a significant blow to affirmative action in 1989 in *Croson,* the case argued by John Payton. The justices struck down a Richmond, Virginia, program that required contractors on city construction projects to subcontract at least 30 percent of each contract to minority-owned businesses. Justice O'Connor's opinion said that local and state governments can't use affirmative action to remedy societywide discrimination. The Court also ruled for the first time that strict scrutiny was the appropriate test for those local and state rules. And O'Connor said government agencies have a duty to investigate whether they can accomplish their goals through race-neutral means.

The following year, the Court took what proved to be a temporary step in the other direction with *Metro Broadcasting v. Federal Communications Commission.*[11] A five-to-four majority led by Justice Brennan upheld FCC rules that gave preferential treatment to racial minorities to increase their ownership of broadcast licenses. Reasoning that the Fourteenth Amendment gives Congress special power to enact affirmative action programs, the majority said the federal government need meet only the less demanding "intermediate scrutiny" test articulated by Brennan in *Bakke*. That is, federal preference programs must serve "important governmental objectives" and be "substantially related to achievement of those objectives." The objective at stake, Brennan said, was the same one Powell cited in *Bakke*. "The diversity of views and information on the airwaves serves important First Amendment values," Brennan wrote.

That victory for affirmative action was short-lived. The 1991 appointment of Clarence Thomas to fill Thurgood Marshall's seat replaced the Court's most passionate advocate of affirmative action with its most ardent opponent. (President George H. W. Bush a year earlier had named David Souter to fill the seat of the retiring William Brennan. That appointment had little impact on affirmative action because Brennan was a supporter and Souter, much to the dismay of conservatives, proved to be as well.) In Thomas's first racial preference case, his vote was the difference as the Court overruled *Metro Broadcasting*. The case, *Adarand Constructors Inc. v. Pena*, concerned financial incentives given under a federal road-construction program to contractors that used minority subcontractors.[12] Writing for the five-to-four Court, Justice O'Connor said the federal government must meet the same strict scrutiny test that applies to local and state agencies.

———■———

IF THE TREND of the Supreme Court's decisions on racial preference gave the Michigan plaintiffs and their lawyers reason for optimism, so did the first round of news reports. Terry Pell, CIR's point person on publicity, at first wasn't sure the national media would be interested in the case. He called the *New York Times* anyway and offered an exclusive for the morning the suit was to be filed. Somewhat to Pell's surprise, the paper accepted. Pell arranged for the reporter to interview Gratz and provided some of the most damning evidence Cohen had uncovered. The result was a 900-word story and an accompanying graphic that used the data from Cohen's grids to show how minorities were far more likely to gain admission than majority applicants with identical grades and test scores. The story ensured the lawsuit would be in the headlines for two days running.

It also meant that the other media outlets had to treat the suit the way the *Times* did—as big news.

For Gratz, October 14, 1997, marked the day her life changed forever. For the month before, she had managed to keep her role in the lawsuit secret, even from her closest friends. Even when Pell asked her to fly to Washington to give media interviews on the day of the lawsuit, Jennifer told only her family the real reason for the trip. Her friends learned the truth—and why she didn't attend Michigan—when they woke up Wednesday morning to discover her photo on the front page of the local newspaper.

Pell quickly saw that Gratz was a natural at handling press interviews, using many of the same qualities that had helped her succeed as a cheerleader. Gratz was articulate, poised, and attractive—and she had a compelling story to tell. In the weeks and months after the suit was filed, Pell shepherded her through dozens of interviews. She appeared on *Today* and the *McNeil/Lehrer Newshour.* She granted interviews to *Time* and *Newsweek* and posed for photographs for the *Washington Post* and *Glamour* magazine. Although Patrick Hamacher spoke to the media as well, Gratz quickly became the star, the poster child for principled opposition to racial preferences.

Pell was surprised by the intensity of the media spotlight and, in retrospect, concluded CIR had been woefully unprepared for it. The firm had filed the suit in a bit of a rush, scrambling to meet an arbitrary deadline Greve had set. Kirk Kolbo, in fact, had been out of the country for the week leading up to the filing, leaving the drafting of the complaint largely up to CIR attorney Michael Rosman. The rushed filing meant the team had neglected a few details. In particular, CIR had done next to nothing to check out Gratz's background and ensure that she really was what she seemed. As time went by, Pell was relieved to conclude that CIR's three plaintiffs indeed were good citizens and solid candidates for admission to Michigan. "We are," Pell told his colleagues, "extremely lucky to have the clients we do."

——■——

FOR SHANTA DRIVER and BAMN, the Gratz and Hamacher lawsuit meant it was time to mobilize. The case, as Driver saw it, underscored the seriousness of the attack on affirmative action. She hoped it would spur students who previously had been content to sit out the battle. On the day the complaint was filed, a handful of protestors gathered outside the student union building with a banner calling for a defense of affirmative action. On October 27, demonstrators in California, Texas, and Michigan took part in a coordinated "National Day of Action." The biggest of those demonstrations took place in Sacramento, the state capital, where Jesse Jackson spoke to a crowd of more than 2,000 people. In Ann Arbor, seventy students braved bitterly cold winds on the campus Diag to hear Driver and other speakers. "The fight for affirmative action is the fight for equality, the fight for dignity, the fight for the future of America," Driver said. "We need to remind America about its racist past." It wasn't exactly the massive civil rights movement Driver had in mind, but it was a start.

———■———

BOLLINGER TOOK THE NEWS of the suit in stride. He and other university officials vowed publicly to mount an aggressive defense. He told the Board of Regents that the university would hold a series of symposiums on campus to discuss affirmative action and the lawsuit. And he predicted it would be a long fight that might reach the Supreme Court. "This will be a difficult time," Bollinger told the regents. "It will test the character of the institution."

Bollinger also told the board of his intention to be personally involved in planning the school's litigation strategy. It already was clear that the courtroom defense would have to center on Justice Powell's opinion in *Bakke* and his diversity justification. The diversity explanation, of course, was far from foolproof. In the *Hopwood* case in Texas, the Fifth Circuit concluded that Powell spoke only for himself, not for a binding majority of the Court. But diversity was really all Bollinger had, short of taking the position that Michigan needed to remedy its own past discrimination against minorities. Powell had ruled out every other possible justification. Goals such as removing the effects of societal discrimination and increasing the number of college-educated minorities were legally irrelevant.

Privately, Bollinger thought Powell was wrong to take those issues off the table. As Bollinger saw it, the legacy of societal discrimination was an important part of the justification for affirmative action. Discrimination had helped create a racially segregated country where blacks and Hispanics were still attending inferior schools from kindergarten through high school. Affirmative action at the college level could help rectify that imbalance, ensuring that minorities could make it into the ranks of professionals and civic leaders. Diversity was important in a college environment, but Bollinger thought the real value of affirmative action lay in its ability to help integrate America.

Speaking before the Michigan faculty two weeks after the suit was filed, Bollinger pointed to a Supreme Court decision that Powell had mentioned only in passing—*Brown v. Board of Education.* "To my mind," Bollinger said, "the question is this: Do the ideals of *Brown v. Board of Education,* with their profound commitment to integration and to the fundamental role of education in realizing that national goal, still have vitality and meaning at the end of the century, or will they slip into obscurity, a noble but largely failed effort of the romantic twentieth century?" He told the faculty that he didn't see diversity as the central issue: "I prefer to think and speak in terms of integration and of segregation and of education's role in helping us arrive at the former state. What we learn from integration—and it is absolutely a matter of learning—is as much or more about similarity as it is about difference."

Bakke might be the controlling legal precedent, but in Bollinger's mind, *Brown* needed to be the starting point for the public debate. Opponents of affirmative action had captured and carried off the language of civil rights. They had turned the issue from a fight over school integration and the rights of minority students into a battle over the rights of Jennifer Gratz. Bollinger wasn't sure that diversity or the legacy of *Bakke* offered a powerful enough counterargument. But, more than four decades after *Brown* was decided, it still had a hold on the American consciousness like perhaps no other Supreme Court case.[13]

———•———

NOT EVERYONE WAS impressed with the university's staunch defense of its admissions policies. In his October 1997 newsletter to supporters, Greve was in rare form.

"The 'Michigan Mandate,' is a thing of beauty," Greve wrote. "It's a plan, a strategy, a manifesto. It's diversity-speak, Newt Gingrich on acid, and TQM [Total Quality Management] gobbledygook. Enacted

and periodically updated by Kaiser Duderstadt, the Mandate committed U of M to do anything and everything nice for minorities."

Greve apparently prepared his comments before he saw Bollinger's
comments in the wake of the lawsuit. That didn't stop him from sav-
ing one of his choicest barbs for Bollinger in a critique of a recent
speech by the new Michigan president.

"In the national craze to disconnect airbags," Greve wrote, "who
forgot to deflate Lee Bollinger?"

Chapter **5** *Five*

Arguments
Michigan Wouldn't Make

U NDER THE RANDOM assignment process of the federal court in Detroit, Gratz and Hamacher's lawsuit against the undergraduate program at Michigan landed on the desk of U.S. District Judge Patrick Duggan. The assignment, at first blush, seemed to favor the Center for Individual Rights. Duggan was a former Republican activist nominated to the bench by Ronald Reagan. If he shared the philosophy of the man who appointed him, the university was in trouble.

Duggan, an Irish Catholic, grew up in a middle-class, all-white neighborhood in East Detroit. His father was an emigrant from Ireland who began as a factory worker and eventually started his own real estate company. Duggan's mother, a Detroit native, focused her attentions on raising Patrick and his three older sisters. Dinner-table conversation often centered around Notre Dame football, a passion of Patrick's father.

Duggan majored in economics at Xavier University in Cincinnati, then attended law school at the University of Detroit. He joined a small, general-practice law firm in Detroit, handling mostly plaintiff-side civil work along with an occasional criminal case. In the late 1960s, Duggan began to develop an interest in politics and found that his sympathies lay with the fiscal conservatism he saw from Republican candidates. He joined the Republican Party in his hometown, the Detroit suburb of Livonia, and worked on the gubernatorial campaign of moderate Republican William Milliken.

His family helped balance out the politics of the household. His wife, Joan Duggan, served as chief administrator for Livonia Mayor Ed McNamara, who later became one of the state's most powerful politicians as the Democratic Wayne County executive. Joan Duggan herself ran for Livonia mayor in 1987, losing in a nonpartisan runoff. Years later, their son Mike would serve as McNamara's deputy in the county executive's office.

Duggan's political connections paid off in 1977, when then-Governor Milliken appointed him to fill a vacant seat on the Wayne County Circuit Court. Duggan threw himself into the heavy workload at the court, a popular venue for lawsuits because of its reputation for large jury awards. In the mid-1980s, three seats opened up on the federal district court in Detroit. Duggan applied but was passed over. Then a fourth slot opened up, and he got the nod.

On the federal bench, Duggan developed a reputation as a moderate. In a long-running race discrimination case involving hiring practices by a Detroit suburb, Duggan split the difference, awarding damages to one unsuccessful black applicant while rejecting other claims. Overall, local lawyers gave Duggan mixed reviews, praising his legal skills and efficiently run courtroom but criticizing his tendency to snap at attorneys. "He's a little overbearing," according to one lawyer's anonymous evaluation in the *Almanac of the Federal Judiciary*. "He has a high-pitched voice, and he just screams at people."

———•———

Bollinger and Payton were prepared to defend the school's admissions policies on the merits, but the Michigan team wasn't averse to the possibility of winning on a technicality.

On December 3, seven weeks after the lawsuit was filed, the university filed its formal answer. Buried among the legalese of the six-page document was a passing mention that Gratz and Hamacher lacked "standing"—that is, that they had no legal right to sue because they weren't injured by the university's actions. Michigan said that both applicants had been offered a position on LS&A's waiting list and that neither had accepted the invitation. Some students had been admitted off the waiting lists. Michigan was suggesting that Gratz and Hamacher should blame themselves, not the university, for their failure to gain admission.

The lawyers at CIR scoffed at the suggestion. The letter to Gratz had made clear that the waiting list was a long shot. It said: "We expect to take very few students from the Extended Waiting List, and recommend students make alternative plans to attend another institution." No one could receive that letter and feel any reason for optimism, the CIR team thought. And if it weren't for the university's policy, Jennifer and Patrick might never have received the wait-list letters in the first place.

In any event, the university stopped short of putting its arguments about standing into a formal motion. So for now that issue wasn't in front of Judge Duggan.

———•———

THE SAME DAY the university filed its answer in the undergraduate case, CIR opened a new front, filing its suit against the law school on behalf of Barbara Grutter. The complaint was virtually identical to the undergraduate suit, save a few technical changes. As with Hamacher, the suit sought Grutter's admittance to the law school.

This time the university community reacted almost as if getting sued was becoming commonplace. Students didn't rally. Television camera trucks didn't descend on campus. Instead, 250 students filed into Hutchins Hall, the sixty-four-year-old Gothic building that housed most of the Law School's classrooms, and listened calmly as Provost Nancy Cantor and Dean Jeff Lehman discussed the case and the stakes.

———•———

THE JUDGE FOR the second lawsuit was well aware of the stakes. For Bernard Friedman, a federal judge in the same Detroit courthouse as Duggan, the complaint represented a once-in-a-lifetime case, and he was thrilled to learn he had received the assignment. In almost a decade on the federal bench, he had never before presided over a case of such magnitude.

Friedman, a Detroit native born in 1943, came from a family of doctors. His father was a general practitioner who served mostly blacks and started his own hospital when existing local facilities wouldn't accept his patients. To his father's dismay, Bernie Friedman wasn't especially interested in medicine or anything else that required much studying. His interests lay in work and community activities, not in books. Concluding that a bachelor's degree from a four-year institution would do him little good, Friedman attended a Detroit junior college instead.

Friedman applied to Detroit College of Law almost on a whim, in part because it protected him from the draft. Friedman hadn't yet earned an undergraduate degree nor taken the LSAT, but the school had a policy of accepting a broad range of students and then weeding them out. Friedman had to promise the dean he would take the LSAT at some point. Law school was a perfect fit, and for the first time in his life, Friedman plunged into his studies. He did so well the dean decided the LSAT wasn't necessary after all.

After graduating from law school in 1968, Friedman began working at the Wayne County prosecutor's office, where one of his mentors was Jim Brickley, a Republican who later ran for lieutenant governor. Although Friedman came from a family of Democrats, he helped raise money for Brickley and before long was an active Republican himself. Friedman later left the prosecutor's office, teaming with two other men from the office to found one of the first racially integrated law firms in the state.

In the early 1980s, Governor Milliken appointed Friedman as a state court judge. The new job gave Friedman countless opportunities to do what he loved: get involved in his suburban Detroit community. He set up an open-door policy so police officers, lawyers, and citizens could wander in whenever they needed his help. Occasionally he would even move his entire court into the local high school, holding traffic adjudications and other proceedings there so that students could learn about their legal system.

Friedman's political connections helped him get something he had long sought in 1988, when Reagan nominated him for a seat on the federal district court. Friedman found the issues he encountered on the federal bench to be intellectually stimulating, but he missed the fast pace of the state court and the more intimate environment that let him follow up on his cases there.

Friedman, with his penetrating green eyes and frequently furrowed brow, conveyed the impression of a thoughtful judge who wanted to hear what lawyers and litigants had to say to him. His pleasant demeanor made his a popular courtroom among local lawyers. "He couldn't be more civil," one lawyer told the *Almanac of the Federal Judiciary*. "He's almost too nice for his own good."[1]

—•—

AFTER THE SECOND CASE against the University of Michigan was filed, Payton decided he needed another high-powered Wilmer Cutler Pickering attorney. He turned to Jane Sherburne, a hard-nosed litigator recently returned to the firm's plush downtown Washington offices from scandal-management duty in the Clinton White House. Payton asked Sherburne to assume responsibility for the day-to-day work in the undergraduate case. Payton would focus on the law school case and the broad defense strategy for both suits. He also would handle all the courtroom appearances.

Ann Arbor soon became a second home to the two Washington-based lawyers. They spent hours talking over the case with Nancy Cantor in the provost's office and discovered she had a wealth of ideas for buttressing the university's case. Cantor was convinced that racial diversity had measurable benefits—academic, as well as social—and she told the lawyers that much of the supporting research had already been done.

Cantor urged Payton to get in touch with the chairman of Michigan's psychology department, Patricia Gurin, who had been studying students' experience with diversity on the campus since 1990. Gurin was analyzing a study that tracked the diversity-related experiences of 2,500 students who entered the school in 1990. Gurin also was studying the impact of an academic program at Michigan designed to foster interracial dialogue through academic courses.

Cantor also suggested Payton talk to William Bowen, the former president of Princeton University. Bowen and former Harvard President Derek Bok had just completed work on their book *The Shape of the River*, a detailed statistical study of the long-term consequences of race-based college admissions. And Cantor gave the attorneys the name of Claude Steele, a Stanford psychology professor who had studied the effect of race on standardized test performance.

Before long, Payton had close to a dozen names of historians, statisticians, social scientists, educators, economists, and other experts. He began to see the outlines of a case that would actually prove the value of diversity—how it enriched a university, produced more thoughtful citizens, and helped overcome the racial segregation that still permeated American society.

Piece by piece, Payton was putting together the type of aggressive legal defense Bollinger had envisioned. But at a cost as high as $350 an hour, the tab was growing quickly. University Regent Andrea Fischer Newman, an attorney, was concerned. She was a supporter of affirmative action and Bollinger's decision to fight, but for months she had grumbled privately about the costs. In March she went public, telling the *Detroit News* she was troubled that the university had paid $425,000 in legal fees in 1997 alone. She told the paper: "I think it's absurd if the case isn't even going to trial till sometime later in the year."[2]

———•———

WHEN THE NEW admissions system became public in February, both sides tried to downplay its significance. "The grids were not eliminated because of the lawsuit," UM Associate Vice President Lisa Baker told the *Detroit Free Press*. "They were eliminated to simplify the process."

CIR attorney and publicist Terry Pell told the press that "if race continues to be a major factor in determining admissions, the new system suffers from the same problems as the old."

———•———

AMID THE WORN CARPETING and civil rights memorabilia of the NAACP Legal Defense and Educational Fund in New York, Ted Shaw was taking both a professional and a personal interest in the Michigan cases. Shaw, a freckle-faced black man with a gentle speaking style and a love of good conversation, had made university affirmative action a top priority since becoming the LDF's associate director-counsel in 1993. As a refugee from a South Bronx housing project, the forty-three-year-old Shaw knew first-hand how crucial affirmative action was for young African Americans seeking to improve their lot. Shaw also was intimately familiar with the policy at issue in the Michigan Law School case; he had helped draft it when he was a law professor there.

Ted's mother died when he was three, and his father drifted in and out of his childhood. That left a stepmother to raise five children in the increasingly violent and segregated Castle Hill housing project.

Education was Ted's salvation. He attended a Catholic grade school where the nuns had high expectations of their pupils. Ted, a voracious reader and eager learner, didn't disappoint them. Equally importantly, he learned how to cope in a white-dominated world. Ted and his siblings, the lone black children in the school, more than once felt the sting of a racial slur. But Ted also learned that not all of his white classmates were alike; some were racist, but most weren't.

The civil rights struggle was in his blood. One grandmother would take him to Abyssinian Baptist Church in Harlem to hear the charismatic Congressman Adam Clayton Powell Jr. preach. His other grandmother tried to take him to the 1963 March on Washington and, when Ted's stepmother refused to let him go for fear that violence might erupt, brought him back a treasure trove of handbills and buttons.

In high school Ted joined a church-sponsored leadership organization for black youths. The priest who ran the program saw Ted's potential, encouraged him to attend college, and helped him get accepted to Wesleyan University, an elite liberal arts school in central Connecticut. Shaw graduated from Wesleyan with honors in 1976 and moved on to Columbia Law School, where Lee Bollinger had graduated five years earlier. Shaw hated the cutthroat competition he found at Columbia, but in three years he graduated with a coveted position as a trial attorney in the Justice Department's Civil Rights Division.

It was a dream job at first, putting Shaw on the front lines of the fight against school and housing discrimination. But with Ronald Reagan's election, things began to change. The new assistant attorney general, William Bradford Reynolds, opposed affirmative action and ordered the line attorneys to take a less aggressive approach toward discrimination against racial minorities. When the administration in 1982 threw its support behind Bob Jones University, which advocated race discrimination and was fighting to preserve a tax exemption, Shaw decided he'd had enough. As he was composing his resignation letter, he got a call from Jack Greenberg, then the head of the LDF. When Greenberg offered a job, Shaw didn't hesitate to accept.

For the next eight years, Shaw had his second dream job. He directed the LDF's education docket and litigated school desegregation and capital punishment cases around the country. It took Lee Bollinger, the University of Michigan, and the Michigan Mandate to lure Shaw away. In 1990 Michigan Law School had only one black professor—John Payton's cousin Sallyanne—and the school wanted to increase that number. Bollinger, then the dean, was impressed by Shaw's track record and extended him an offer.

Michigan gave Shaw time to read, write, and think. It also gave him a chance to get to know the congenial Bollinger. The two occasionally would debate the extent to which the free-speech clause guarantees the right of individuals to engage in private discrimination. Bollinger held firm to his First Amendment principles, but Shaw was impressed by the dean's thoughtfulness.

Shaw also told Bollinger he had concerns about the legality of the school's admissions practices. Before long, Bollinger was asking Shaw to serve on the faculty committee to rewrite the policy. Shaw agreed and made it his mission to ensure the new system was *Bakke*-compliant. He told his colleagues that flexibility had to be a central component. Test scores should be de-emphasized, and individualized consideration of each application stressed. Shaw also advocated eliminating the practice of having minority students help review minority applications; that smacked of the two-track review system that Justice Powell had condemned in *Bakke*. When that change was announced, drawing grumbles from some of the school's African American students, Shaw took it upon himself to meet with the students.

Shaw endorsed the idea of a "critical mass" of minorities as the goal of the school's affirmative action program. He himself had experienced isolation as a rare black professor at Michigan. For students, it was even more important that they not feel like tokens, Shaw felt. But he fought a colleague's suggestion that the plan mention a numerical range for minority enrollment. That, Shaw believed, would make the policy too easy a target in the likely event of a legal challenge. The concept of a critical mass was already susceptible of being misconstrued as quota, he thought; numbers would only exacerbate the problem.

Shaw had retained his ties to the LDF, and in 1993 he returned to the organization as its number-two staff lawyer. (Although Shaw technically took a leave of absence from Michigan, Bollinger suspected it would prove permanent. "You won't be coming back," the dean predicted.) Higher education was at the top of Shaw's agenda for his new job. The LDF unsuccessfully defended a blacks-only University of Maryland scholarship program that was being challenged by a Hispanic student. Shaw's team then tried and failed to intervene on behalf of minority students in the *Hopwood* case and in a similar fight at the University of Georgia. And now there was Michigan.

———•———

SHAW STUDIED Jennifer Gratz's complaint from his desk at the LDF's headquarters in New York's resurgent Tribeca neighborhood. His small corner office was invariably a mess, the clutter equal parts litigation paperwork and civil rights souvenirs. Pictures of Malcolm X and Frederick Douglass adorned the walls, along with a sketch of Shaw arguing before the Supreme Court in 1995 and a sign reading, "We serve colored. Carry out only." With its institutional metal doors and narrow hallways, the LDF offices were anything but glamorous, but they were rich with history.

Shaw knew the LDF needed to play a role in the Michigan cases. He expected the university would staunchly defend affirmative action as necessary to foster campus diversity. Bollinger's early statements, coupled with Payton's hiring, had confirmed that intuition. But Shaw also expected the university would pull its punches on another potential argument—that the policies were justified as a remedy for the school's own history of discrimination against minorities. Making such an argument would not only be embarrassing for the university; it also might open the school to lawsuits by black and Latino students who faced discrimination. If Shaw could intervene in the cases on behalf of some of the beneficiaries of affirmative action, he could make the arguments that the university wouldn't.

Shaw quickly assembled a coalition that included the Mexican American Legal Defense and Educational Fund, known as MALDEF, and the American Civil Liberties Union. (The ACLU, much to Carl Cohen's displeasure, had long since decided that affirmative action was warranted to offset the persistent racial inequalities in American society, despite arguments that state-sponsored preferences were anathema to the notion of civil libertarianism.) Shaw had worked with MALDEF and the ACLU in the past and was happy to team up with them in Michigan. He knew they all shared the same basic approach toward civil rights litigation.

One other group presented a stickier situation. Detroit civil rights lawyers Milton Henry and Godfrey Dillard were considering getting involved in the Michigan cases as well. A decade earlier, Henry and Dillard had successfully sued the University of Detroit Law School, and the case had given the two men great confidence in their ability to litigate issues of racial discrimination in higher education. Shaw thought their self-assuredness misplaced: the local lawyers had something to contribute, but he had the experience in dealing with university affirmative action. Dillard and Henry flew to New York for a meeting with Shaw and his LDF colleagues. Tensions were high at first, but eventually the group agreed to work together, with Shaw taking the lead in formulating and presenting the arguments.

The first task was to win the right to take part, no small hurdle. Federal courts are resistant when outsiders try to jump into a pending dispute. Additional parties can bog a lawsuit down, adding new layers of complexity, not to mention more briefs. Shaw wanted to gain "intervenor" status, invoking a rule that lets people with a legal interest in a matter ask a federal court to consider their rights as part of the case. Winning the right to intervene would mean Shaw's team could demand documents from the other litigants, conduct sworn interviews of university officials and other people, call witnesses at a trial, and appeal any adverse decision. Shaw had tried and failed to intervene in the Texas and Georgia cases. But the law in the Sixth Circuit was especially favorable to would-be intervenors, so he was optimistic.

The lawyers faced an array of tactical questions. Most fundamentally, whom would they represent? As a general matter, the aim was to argue for the beneficiaries of affirmative action. But not all beneficiaries were the same. Minority high school students who planned to apply to Michigan clearly would be affected by any change in the undergraduate admissions policy. The impact would be less direct for current black and Hispanic students at Michigan, who at least were already admitted. And what about white students? Shaw thought they learned from the diversity that affirmative action brought, but that connection was even more tenuous.

The lawyers also needed to decide what their case would say. In particular, should they attack the use of standardized tests? Many civil rights organizations, including the LDF, thought the test was racially biased. But, as Shaw himself had once told his colleagues at Michigan Law School, he thought the tests at least were valuable measures for people with especially high or low scores.

For Shaw, the primary goal was to ensure the group could intervene. That meant a narrow intervention motion that would give a judge as few excuses as possible to reject it. Shaw and his colleagues decided that, in the undergraduate case, they should represent only black and Latino high school students, plus a nonprofit organization composed of prospective Michigan students and their families. No white students would be part of the group. And the case wouldn't include an attack on standardized tests. Shaw feared a judge might see that issue as being too far afield from the questions raised in the lawsuit.

Shaw's Michigan-based colleagues recruited seventeen Michigan high school students, predominantly black but including one Mexican American. All had solid academic records, and all said they intended to apply to Michigan. On February 5, 1998, Shaw filed his motion on behalf of those students in the undergraduate dispute.

In the other case, Barbara Grutter's suit against Michigan Law School, there was a wrinkle. Because Shaw had helped draft the law school's admissions policy, he was a potential witness in that case, and he couldn't ethically serve as an attorney in it as well. The team of lawyers would have to create a wall so that Shaw was not involved with the work for that case. It would be extremely awkward, and he wasn't sure exactly how they would manage it.

As it turned out, they didn't need to. Another lawyer was about to beat Shaw and his coalition to the punch.

———■———

MIRANDA MASSIE would have been the first to concede she wasn't a top-flight litigator. Only a year out of law school, Massie had a fraction of the experience of Payton, Kolbo, or Shaw. Nor did she look the part of the seasoned attorney. The occasional streak of gray in her wavy, brown hair couldn't disguise the fact that her sharp-featured face was only thirty years old. Massie also lacked the resources of a big firm—or the LDF, for that matter. She was one of three attorneys— all white—in the spartan offices of Detroit's Scheff and Washington, which specialized in representing victims of sexual harassment, police brutality, and racial discrimination.

Massie would have had it no other way. Unlike so many of her classmates from New York University Law School, she had no desire to work at a large firm, regardless of the salaries, perks, or prestige. Even after she passed the bar exam a few months into her job at Scheff and Washington, Massie considered herself an activist as much as a lawyer.

Massie was raised in New York State in what she considered to be a privileged family. Miranda's parents weren't especially interested in politics, but she grew up reveling in stories of her grandmother's civil rights exploits. Molly Todd helped organize coffee shop sit-ins in Nashville, brought a chapter of Planned Parenthood to Tennessee, and served as a plaintiff in a lawsuit that led to an important Supreme Court voting-rights decision. By the time Massie graduated from Cornell University, she was deeply involved in activism herself, particularly union organizing and support. She enrolled at Yale to pursue her master's degree in history and American studies. While there, she fought to unionize teaching assistants, protested against the Gulf War, and joined in abortion-rights marches.

At Yale, Massie flirted with the idea of becoming a professor, but she decided that academia was too much theory and not enough activism for her tastes. She wanted to play a role building a new progressive movement, and law school seemed a perfect fit. While attending NYU, Massie's younger brother, Luke, told her about his work as an activist in Detroit. Luke described a case involving three black dental school workers who had been fired by the University of Michigan over time-card discrepancies, a small law firm called Scheff and Washington that had represented them, and an ambitious activist named Shanta Driver. Massie spent half a summer as an intern at Scheff and Washington, then readily accepted an offer of full-time employment upon graduation. One of her early assignments sent her to California, where she helped represent one of two BAMN members who had been charged with assaulting police officers at a debate involving David Duke.

Massie saw the two Michigan lawsuits as both a threat and an opportunity. Like Driver, Massie thought the litigation could be a launching pad for a civil rights movement that would transcend whatever the outcome might be in court. Win or lose, the cases could energize young people to demand the racial equality that was miss-

Ted Shaw and Miranda Massie brought very different styles to their bids to intervene in the cases on behalf of affirmative action beneficiaries. Shaw, an NAACP lawyer who had helped draft the Michigan Law School admissions policy, focused his efforts on the courtroom. Massie, a fledgling attorney at a tiny Detroit law firm, saw the cases as a springboard for demonstrations and petition drives.

ing even at schools that used affirmative action. The cases were also an opportunity for Massie to make a name for herself and make an impact. She badly wanted to play a central role, and she persuaded George Washington, one of the firm's partners, to let her take the lead for the firm.

The question was how to get involved. Massie knew she didn't have the answer, but Driver had an idea: what about intervening in the case on behalf of students who benefit from affirmative action? Massie hadn't even studied intervention in her law school civil procedure class, but the more she looked into it, the more she loved the idea. Intervention would let the group present evidence to show that affirmative action was necessary for equality and integration. And it would put human faces on their side of the case, showing the real-life benefits of race-conscious admissions.

Together, Massie and Driver set out to find people to represent. Unlike Shaw, they wanted a wide range of students, white as well as black, high school as well as undergraduate. They sought students from California and Texas to ensure a connection to the other flash points for affirmative action around the country. Most importantly, Massie and Driver sought students who would be leaders in the movement and would speak out publicly for affirmative action. Some students they approached were more eager than others. Many said they were worried that involvement would paint them as radicals or affect their career prospects. Nonetheless, by February, the two women had three dozen students willing to sign on to an intervention motion.

Massie wasn't surprised when she got word that Shaw had filed in the undergraduate case. She looked over his intervention motion and, even though it was designed to bolster Michigan's defense, decided it was lacking. The motion didn't use the phrase "affirmative action," suggesting to Massie that Shaw's group was ashamed of it. The motion also said nothing about bias in standardized testing, which Massie thought had to be a central component in any student-intervenor case. And Massie knew the LDF wouldn't be using the case as a springboard for a new civil rights movement. Massie and her colleagues concluded their involvement was as necessary as ever. The only thing that had changed was that the LDF, by filing its motion to intervene, had put the undergraduate case off limits. Since no judge was going to allow two groups of student-intervenors in the same case, Massie and BAMN would have to focus their efforts on the law school dispute.

—■—

IN NEW YORK, Shaw was still trying to figure out how the LDF could take part in the law school case without his involvement. He got word that another Detroit group was considering its own intervention motion. Shaw asked Godfrey Dillard if he could find out who it was. Dillard reported back that the firm of Scheff and Washington was leading the effort. A lawyer on Shaw's team placed a call to George Washington to discuss the case. Washington passed the message on to Massie just as she was putting the finishing touches on her motion.

Massie decided not to return the call. The way she saw it, there was nothing to talk about. Less than a week later, she filed her motion in the law school case.[3]

———◆———

WARD CONNERLY was used to getting a hostile reception. He had been experiencing a lot of them since 1995, when he started his campaign to wipe out racial preferences.

In 1995, Connerly, a Sacramento businessman and University of California regent, sponsored a motion to bar race-based admissions at the system's nine campuses. With the backing of Governor Pete Wilson, the motion passed. Connerly then took the reins of the drive to get what became known as Proposition 209 on the California ballot, leading to the abolition of affirmative action in state hiring and contracts as well. In 1997, Connerly turned his sights to the rest of the nation, forming the American Civil Rights Institute with an eye on ballot initiatives in other states.

Connerly seemed to inspire a particularly virulent strain of hostility. His mixed-race heritage—he was a quarter black, the rest white and Native American—drew charges that he was a "sellout" and an "Uncle Tom." Connerly's blunt, combative style only deepened his opponents' antagonism toward him.

With Michigan quickly becoming the central battleground over affirmative action, Connerly decided to visit the state and scheduled a speech in Ann Arbor on March 18. BAMN leaders wanted to make sure he felt especially unwelcome. For days leading up to the speech, student activists distributed flyers depicting Connerly as a marionette. Connerly, the leaflet said, "is heading the racists' campaign against every policy and law designed to offset the impact of racist and sexist inequality and discrimination."

Connerly's first stop was Lansing, where he testified in support of a proposed Michigan constitutional amendment that would have banned racial preferences in employment, education, and public contracting. The predominantly black audience greeted him with jeers and catcalls. "How do you sleep at night?" one spectator shouted.

When he arrived at the Michigan League in Ann Arbor, it was overflowing with protesters. Some 600 people packed the ballroom, while another 100 outside chanted, "Let us in!"

Inside, Connerly told the crowd about the hardships he endured growing up in Mississippi. He described how he came to the conclusion that preferences did more harm than good to racial minorities. He wasn't against all forms of affirmative action, Connerly said, but he opposed preferences that treated people differently because of their race.

The questions from the audience were uniformly hostile. "You are glib about the results in California, but you had no idea what you were getting into coming to Michigan," said law student and BAMN member Jodi Masley. "Well, bring it on," Connerly shot back. He added: "We'll see what happens at the polls." Undergraduate Boyd White III told Connerly to "go to the Detroit Board of Education and tell those children that you're taking away their hope." Connerly responded: "I would go to the Board of Education and say you have the opportunity to be the best you can be." As the session deteriorated, Connerly threatened to walk out if the crowd didn't quiet down and let him answer a question. A handful of people held signs supporting Connerly, but not one made it to the microphone to ask a question.

Connerly left wondering why he had bothered coming. The crowd, he thought, was little better than a pack of animals. Universities were supposed to be a forum for enlightened debate, but his presentation had ended up as nothing more than a shouting match.[4]

———■———

A FEW WEEKS after the intervention motions were filed, Shaw, Massie, and their respective colleagues met in Godfrey Dillard's Detroit office to try to coordinate their efforts. Although the two teams were involved in separate cases—Shaw and his coalition for minority high school students in the undergraduate suit, Massie for her broader group of clients in the law school fight—they still might be able to work together on evidence, witnesses, and litigation strategy.

The session was tense. Shaw made no secret of his annoyance that Massie hadn't returned his colleague's phone call before she filed her motion. Massie explained her interest in creating a new civil rights movement. Shaw was skeptical, and he told her so. He questioned whether Massie's group would have the money to mount a serious defense of affirmative action in court. And Shaw made no secret that he believed Massie was badly lacking in experience, no matter how bright or energetic she might be. He thought the far-flung nature of her intervention motion might be just the first of a series of errors.

BAMN's militancy and confrontational style concerned Shaw, too. He had no qualms about demonstrations, and he was well aware of the vital role they had played during the civil rights struggles in the 1960s. But Shaw saw himself first and foremost as a lawyer, not as an activist or a political figure. The LDF had a long history in litigation, and presumably a long future. Part of Shaw's job was to preserve the organization's credibility in the courtroom. He didn't think he could do that if he was simultaneously organizing rallies on the courthouse steps, and he certainly couldn't if judges perceived that he was using their courtrooms for political ends.

Shaw also thought Massie was far too quick to label people who disagreed with her as "racist." It was a word Shaw rarely used, even though, unlike Massie, he was black. Shaw believed that type of name-calling only antagonized people.

A few weeks after the meeting, BAMN members helped lead a counterprotest as three dozen Ku Klux Klan members held a rally in Ann Arbor. Some of the demonstrators threw rocks, shouted obscenities, scuffled with volunteer peacekeepers, and used a bottle to beat a man sporting a "White Pride" tattoo. Some tried to break the equipment newspaper photographers were using to record the event. Police eventually used tear gas to clear the melee and arrested twenty-one people, including Massie's brother Luke and Shanta Driver.

———■———

SHAW WASN'T SURPRISED to learn that CIR was opposing his intervention request. In papers submitted to Judge Duggan, Kolbo wrote that the minority high school students Shaw and his team represented lacked a "protectable legal interest" in the case. Kolbo acknowledged that the minority students might be able to show that they would benefit from the university's racial preferences. But Kolbo said the standard for intervention was a strict one. The students, Kolbo argued, needed to be able to show they had a legal entitlement to an affirmative action policy. "They claimed none and have none," he wrote. Letting Shaw's group in would unnecessarily complicate the case, Kolbo added.

The university's position was similarly predictable: like the University of Texas in the *Hopwood* fight, Michigan would take no position on Shaw's intervention request. In a four-sentence response, Payton wrote that the minority students had a "substantial interest" in the subject matter of the lawsuit. At the same time, he said, the university planned to mount a "vigorous defense." The neutral stance let the university avoid an awkward situation. Support for the request could have been read as a tacit admission that the university's defense was inadequate. Opposition would have pitted the school against the very students it was professing to help and potentially set off a wave of campus protests.

By the time Massie's wide-ranging intervention request reached Payton's desk for a response, he felt the need for a qualifier to the university's neutrality. After repeating the language he used in responding to Shaw's motion, Payton added that intervention "could significantly complicate" the case.

———————

MASSIE WAS VISITING a client at the Ann Arbor jail when she got the word: Judge Friedman had rejected intervention in the law school case. His opinion was short, suggesting the issue wasn't an especially close one for the judge. Friedman said the students hadn't shown that the university would fail to sufficiently defend their interests. A judge, he added, must have strong evidence before concluding that a governmental entity won't adequately defend itself. "The proposed intervenors have made no showing of inadequacy of representation, to say nothing of the much stronger showing required in this case," Friedman wrote.

Friedman added that Massie's group was raising issues that went well beyond those in the complaint. Her intervention papers suggested she wanted to argue for consideration of gender in admissions, as well as race, and challenge the usefulness of the LSAT. Much as Shaw had predicted, the judge bristled at such an expansive agenda. "The inclusion of these issues would substantially broaden the scope of, and delay the adjudication of, this case," Friedman wrote.

Massie's thoughts turned to the Sixth U.S. Circuit Court of Appeals in Cincinnati, which handled appeals from the federal district courts in Michigan. She thought that Friedman had ignored the cases from that court and that she had a good chance to win reversal on appeal. But even if the Sixth Circuit let her into the case, Massie read Friedman's decision as a bad sign. If he wasn't willing to let the intervenors in the case, how likely could he be to agree with their arguments on the substance?

She vented some of her frustration in the press. "I am absolutely certain the university will inadequately represent the interests of the students," she told the *Michigan Daily*. The university "is notorious in this region for its wretched record" on both racism and sexism.

—■—

DUGGAN AND FRIEDMAN weren't trying to coordinate their cases, so it was by coincidence that Duggan was ready with his decision on Shaw's proposed group of student-intervenors the following day. Duggan's reasoning differed from Friedman's, but the result was the same. Shaw's efforts to keep his intervention motion focused didn't matter. The intervening students were out of the undergraduate case as well.

The minority students "do not have any legally enforceable right to have the existing admissions policy continued," Duggan wrote, mirroring Kolbo's brief. The judge suggested he was skeptical that Shaw's arguments, even if allowed into the case, would amount to much. "The proposed intervenors have failed to establish in any detail any alleged deficiencies in the defendants' intended defense of its admissions policy," Duggan wrote.

Shaw was convinced Duggan had it wrong. The university simply wasn't going to introduce evidence of its own discriminatory history, the lawyer thought. Only the intervening students could make that case. Like Massie, Shaw began preparing his appeal of the intervention ruling to the Sixth Circuit.

———■———

BACK AT CIR, Greve had his pen out again. In a 2,000-word article for the *Weekly Standard,* a conservative publication, he accused universities of using race-based admissions solely to enhance their own public image. "Elite universities want an egalitarian veneer of minority students," he wrote.

Top universities, Greve went on, were being dishonest. He said they claimed that race was only a small factor in admissions despite "incontrovertible evidence" that it was a major consideration. He went so far as to compare universities to Texaco Inc., where company executives had been caught on tape disparaging black workers.

"Were we to demand of university presidents the honesty and candor on diversity policies that we demand of, say, the management of Texaco," Greve wrote, "they'd all be in jail."

Chapter Six

A Clash in Chambers

FRIEDMAN'S LAW CLERK reached the judge on his wireless phone as he and his wife drove up Interstate 75 toward Charlevoix, a resort town on Lake Michigan where they were planning to spend a long weekend relaxing at a friend's house.

"Do you know that Judge Feikens and Judge Cook are holding a hearing about reassigning your case?" the clerk said. "I just saw Mr. Payton arriving."

Friedman couldn't believe what he was hearing. He had known that Michigan had a pending request for reassignment of the law school case, but he was stunned that two other judges were now hearing arguments on the matter.

The issue dated back to the filing of the law school complaint, when Kolbo noted that it was a potential "companion case" to the undergraduate lawsuit. Under the court's local rules, if Friedman and Duggan were to agree that the suits involved "substantially similar" evidence and parties, Friedman would designate the cases as companions and, because his was the second case, transfer his suit to Duggan. Friedman and the lawyers had discussed the issue at the first scheduling conference back in February. The judge later asked one of his clerks to research the question. Friedman and his clerk decided that the two cases were separate matters and shouldn't be formally linked, and Friedman had told the lawyers of his conclusion at the second scheduling conference, in April. He also talked to Duggan about the matter. Duggan said that he hadn't looked into the issue but that his views were irrelevant since the consent of both judges was needed. "If you don't think they're companion cases, then I don't think they're companion cases," Friedman later recalled Duggan as saying. Friedman had thought the matter was settled.

Three months later, however, Friedman had received what he considered to be an unusual visit from Judge John Feikens, a Nixon appointee to the Detroit court and a Michigan Law School graduate who hired all his law clerks from UM and decorated his office in maize and blue. Feikens told Friedman he had taken a look at the affirmative action cases. "Bernie, I think they're companion cases," Feikens said. Friedman told Feikens he had looked into the matter and disagreed.

A week later, on July 14, John Payton's partner Jane Sherburne had filed what, to Friedman, seemed a bizarre motion. The first half of the motion was addressed to the court's chief judge, Anna Diggs Taylor, asking her to reassign Friedman's case to Duggan. Sherburne invoked another provision in the court's local rules, one that authorized the chief judge to reassign a case in the interest of "docket efficiency" if both the old and new judges consented. The second part of the motion asked Friedman, as an alternative step, to declare the suits companion cases—the very issue Friedman thought he had resolved in April. Further confusing matters, Sherburne seemed to have filed the motion formally only with Taylor; Friedman understood the copy he received to have been a courtesy copy.

From the university's standpoint, its motion carried some risk. Seven months into the law school litigation, Michigan's lawyers were telling Friedman they didn't want him deciding the case. If for whatever reason the move failed, Michigan's lawyers had to wonder whether Friedman might be resentful. Furthermore, Friedman had already indicated he didn't believe the cases were companions. In a bid to soften the impact of the request, the university had sent advance word of its plan to Kolbo and asked whether CIR would go along.

Terry Pell could only speculate as to what Michigan's motivation was. CIR hadn't had the resources to do significant research on Duggan and Friedman, and, in any event, neither judge had much of a track record on the equal protection clause or on race issues. Still, the CIR team figured that Michigan must have a reason for trying so hard to combine the cases. Maybe, Pell thought, the university had come up with some research indicating either that Duggan was likely to favor race-based admissions or that Friedman was inclined to oppose them.

The CIR team had developed a mild preference for keeping the suits in separate courtrooms. The team was confident and figured a second judge only improved its chances. As Pell saw it, a judge would be less likely to duck the central issues knowing that another man down the hall would be looking over his shoulder. Kolbo told the university lawyers that the plaintiffs wouldn't go along with the effort to shift the law school case to Duggan.

There was another twist. Chief Judge Taylor's husband was a University of Michigan regent and therefore a defendant. It was clear that Taylor couldn't take part in the dispute, and Sherburne noted as much in the cover letter to Taylor that accompanied her motion. "We anticipate that you will likely direct this matter to another judge for consideration," she wrote.

After Taylor received the motion, she paid a visit to Friedman. As he had with Feikens, Friedman told Taylor that he wouldn't consent to a reassignment. Then Taylor did a curious thing. As expected, she disqualified herself, but she also took an additional step, transferring the entire motion—including the part addressed to Friedman—to two former chief judges of the court, Feikens and Julian Abele Cook Jr.

Taylor's order was problematic in several respects. First of all, she had transferred a request that, in part, was addressed to Friedman. In addition, under the rules of judicial ethics, her decision to disqualify herself should have ended her participation in the matter, not left her free to choose her successor. And a federal statute said that any motion the chief judge was unable to handle should have gone to the district judge who was next on the court's seniority list.

Friedman was getting annoyed. He wasn't worried that the case would actually be taken away from him. He was sure that could only happen with his consent. But he was angry that Taylor, and now Feikens and Cook, were trying to intervene despite what Friedman saw as their clear lack of authority. Friedman fired off a two-page memo to Taylor. Keeping his tone measured, he said he had "some concerns" about the appointment of Feikens and Cook. A two-judge panel, Friedman said, appeared to be unprecedented. More pointedly, he said that a disqualified judge "probably should not select his or her own successors no matter how prominent or thoughtful or fair-minded the judge is." Most fundamentally, he said, "there really is no issue to decide" because the case couldn't be reassigned without his consent, something he had no intention of giving.

Friedman ended his memo by offering to meet with Taylor. Then he waited. When four days went by with no response, he set out for his long weekend in Charlevoix.

From the road, Friedman told his law clerk that he wanted to dictate a new memo to Feikens and Cook, with copies going to all the judges on the court. This time, Friedman didn't try to mask his irritation. "It is obvious that the two of you, as well as Anna, are determined to direct this case as you see fit, and there is absolutely no precedent for what is taking place. This is the grossest form of judge shopping, and I intend to deal with it in the appropriate form when I return." Friedman asked his law clerk to sit in on the hearing before Cook and Feikens. She told him she wouldn't miss it.

In Friedman's mind, the whole episode seemed like an effort to engineer an outcome favorable to the university. Friedman was far from making a decision on the merits of the lawsuit, and he had no reason to think Duggan was any closer. But as he saw it, nothing else could explain such an egregious breach of court procedure. His suspicions were only heightened when one of his clerks learned that Feikens served on the Michigan Law School's Committee of Visitors, which studied and evaluated the school's operations.

—■—

FEIKENS BEGAN THE hearing by announcing that the question before the panel was whether the two lawsuits were "companion cases"—the issue that had been directed to Friedman—making no mention of the "docket efficiency" rule that had formed the basis of the university's request to Taylor.

Payton argued the issue for the university. He contended that putting the two cases before a single judge would prevent the possibility of inconsistent rulings. "And I think there's just no prejudice in having both cases assigned to a single judge," he said.

Kolbo contended that the lawsuits were distinct cases, involving separate facts and parties, and that they would move along more efficiently if they stayed with separate judges. Kolbo also argued that the companion case question should go first to Friedman. "He's set a scheduling order, he's given us a trial date, and we think that it really ought to be something for his consideration," Kolbo argued.

———•———

FRIEDMAN HOPED he would hear from Feikens or Cook upon his return to Detroit, but the two judges never responded. Instead, a week later, they released a five-page opinion saying they viewed the two suits as "companion cases." The plaintiffs "have made substantially similar claims," and the cases "involve nearly identical parties, with all the defendants being associated with the University of Michigan," Feikens and Cook wrote. The two judges made no mention of the requirement that Friedman consent to any reassignment.

The opinion clearly lacked legal force. It didn't come with the type of corresponding order that typically accompanies judicial opinions. Feikens and Cook were simply offering their advice. Friedman nonetheless was hurt and angry. In his mind, two judges he had respected were acting as renegades, publicly questioning his role in the case. And the multiple, flagrant violations of the court's operating procedures undermined the institution's legitimacy, he thought. If judges couldn't follow the rules, how could it expect litigants to?

For days, Friedman stewed. At first, he hoped that the other judges on the court would intervene. In time, however, he realized that there wasn't much the other judges could do. It wasn't their case any more than it was Feikens's or Cook's. Over lunch one day, one of Friedman's clerks suggested the judge issue his own order wiping the Feikens-Cook opinion from the record. The move wouldn't have any legal significance, but it would at least give Friedman an opportunity to put his views on the record.

Friedman liked the idea and decided to write a full-scale opinion of his own. His first draft was a blistering opinion that questioned the ethics and motives of his colleagues and accused Feikens of a conflict of interest because of his relationship with Michigan Law School. His clerks persuaded him to tone down some of the language. Even with the revisions, Friedman's opinion dripped with contempt. Feikens and Cook, he wrote, "have no authority to take any action or issue any rulings in this case, and their 'opinion' is a nullity." He added: "The docketing of this 'opinion' in a case properly assigned to a judge by blind draw, is an affront to the dignity and the independence of the court and an unlawful intrusion upon and interference and meddling with this court's business." As for Chief Judge Taylor, she had ignored one of the most basic conflict-of-interest principles, Friedman said. She "violated her legal and ethical duty by selecting the judicial officers who were to act in her stead." Her action "tarnishes this court's appearance of fairness and appears to place the court's imprimatur upon a judge-shopping practice which we, collectively as a bench, in the past always have denounced."

The "companion case" issue, Friedman said, should have stayed with him. And he said he saw no reason to combine the two matters. The parties in the two cases, he said, were actually quite different. Not only were there different plaintiffs, but only Bollinger was specifically named as a defendant in both suits. (Friedman neglected to mention that the Board of Regents was a named defendant in each case.) Friedman also wrote that the evidence in each case was proving to be markedly different. An affidavit by Kolbo underscored the point. Kolbo said he had received 5,000 pages of documents from the university in the two cases so far. Of those, not one document had been offered by the university as having relevance in both cases. And when Kolbo had asked the university lawyers to list the people with responsibility for the admissions policies, he received twenty names in the undergraduate case and twenty-two in the law school case, with no overlap between the groups. "The reason for the lack of any overlap," Friedman wrote, "is apparently due to the simple fact that the law school and the undergraduate college operate as independent units within the University of Michigan, and it appears their admissions policies have little, if anything, to do with one another."

Friedman was proud of the opinion, but he wasn't fully satisfied. For a time, he considered filing an ethics complaint with the U.S. Court of Appeals for the Sixth Circuit. Friedman even went so far as to hire a lawyer, a specialist on judicial ethics, before deciding he would drop the matter.[1]

WARD CONNERLY REMAINED intrigued by Michigan, his April visit to Ann Arbor notwithstanding. Buoyed by his success in wiping out racial preferences in California, Connerly had moved on to Washington state, where he had succeeded in placing a similar proposal on the November 1998 ballot there. Michigan seemed fertile ground for a third ballot initiative, possibly in 2000. Carl Cohen's research and CIR's lawsuit had exposed the way in which the University of Michigan used race in admissions. Connerly was convinced the Michigan public wouldn't stand for that kind of double standard.

The Michigan Republican Party apparently thought so, too, at least at first. The party had invited Connerly to speak at its upcoming convention, and he had accepted. Then Connerly's office got a call from an aide to Michigan's Republican Governor John Engler, asking for more information about Connerly and his work on California's Proposition 209, which banned racial preferences by arms of that state. Engler quietly opposed preferences and thought the University of Michigan was violating the Constitution. But conventional wisdom held that ballot initiatives aimed at killing affirmative action would galvanize minority voters and hurt Republican candidates. Although Prop 209 passed in California, the same voters gave Democrats major gains in the state legislature. With Engler's close ally, Texas Governor George W. Bush, seeking the presidency in 2000, the Michigan governor had no interest in making affirmative action a front-page political issue.

A week after the inquiry from Engler's office, Connerly received another letter from the Michigan Republican Party, rescinding the invitation. Convinced that Engler and the party would actively oppose a ballot proposal, Connerly decided that Michigan wasn't the place to launch his next fight. At least for the time being, Connerly thought, he would wait to see how the litigation progressed.[2]

———■———

MICHIGAN WAS STILL without a permanent general counsel. As Bollinger looked to fill that vacancy, his list of criteria wasn't a long one. First and foremost, he wanted someone smart. Universities as large as Michigan tended to have complex legal problems—the affirmative action cases were only one example—and Bollinger thought he needed a first-rate legal mind.

Marvin Krislov certainly met that standard. A Yale Law School graduate and Rhodes scholar, he impressed Bollinger from the first time
they met with his ability to think through legal issues. Bollinger also
sensed that Krislov, a high-energy thirty-nine-year-old with a long face
and rapidly receding hairline, had the values and the type of collegial
personality that would serve the university well. True, Krislov lacked
any experience as a higher education lawyer, and the search committee
for the new general counsel ranked him well down on its list of candidates. But Bollinger didn't mind making unconventional appointments,
and he didn't have to take the search committee's advice.

Born in 1960, Krislov practically grew up on the University of
Kentucky campus in Lexington, where his father was a professor of
labor economics. Marvin's mother was a social worker and an active
Democrat who battled illiteracy, child abuse, and other community
problems. At school board meetings she would urge steps to integrate
the public schools. "We can't brush these problems under the carpet,"
Krislov remembered her saying. The family received hate calls and at
least one death threat.

In college at Yale, Krislov became politically active, working to get
out the vote for Democratic candidates in the 1980 election. He ran
for office himself, winning election as an alderman in New Haven,
before putting politics to the side to study at Oxford on a Rhodes
scholarship. Krislov then returned to Yale to enroll in law school,
where his favorite professors included civil rights leaders Burke
Marshall and Drew Days.

Krislov joined the Justice Department as a career-track attorney in
the Civil Rights Division. For four years, he prosecuted cases involving police brutality, cross burnings, and other hate crimes. In 1993,
a friend from Yale helped Krislov land a plum position at the White
House counsel's office. He started off handling relatively mundane
matters such as Freedom of Information Act requests but soon was
heading up the nomination process for nonjudicial positions. Like
almost everyone in the White House counsel's office, he also found
himself enmeshed in the myriad congressional and independent
counsel investigations of the Clinton administration. After three
years, Krislov moved to the Labor Department and the slightly less
hectic position of deputy solicitor. Soon after, he became acting solicitor, the department's top legal officer.

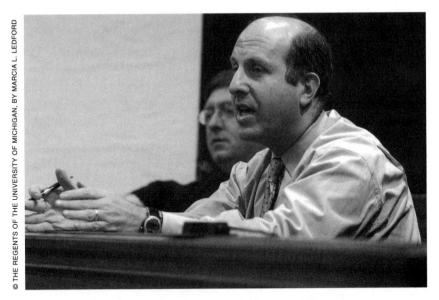

A year into the legal fight, Lee Bollinger tapped Clinton administration lawyer Marvin Krislov to be Michigan's new general counsel. Krislov would quickly become the point person in the university's effort to build support for its case among outside groups.

By the beginning of 1998, Krislov was focused on his next career step. He wasn't keen on a law firm position. His strengths, as he saw them, didn't lie in the brief writing or courtroom presentation that would be the staples of a litigator's work. Krislov saw himself as a problem solver, one who worked best in house, where he could get to know his clients well and figure out how best to serve them. A university general counsel position seemed attractive, but Krislov knew those positions were hard to land.

Krislov thought his initial interview with Bollinger, in Washington, had gone well. But Krislov still had one more significant hurdle, a meeting in Ann Arbor with the full search committee, consisting of about a dozen administrators and faculty members. Midway through the interview, Krislov's beeper sounded. He glanced at the incoming number and realized the caller was his boss, Labor Secretary Alexis Herman, who knew only that Krislov was taking the day off and had no idea he was in the middle of a job interview. Krislov was morti-fied, but he had no choice: he had to call her. He excused himself and ducked into the hall. He returned and had barely finished his profuse apologies when his phone rang a second time, again with a call from Herman. Krislov went back to the hallway.

As he flew back to Washington, Krislov worried about how the committee would react to the incident. Would the members see him as a man who acted with grace under pressure or someone who had spent too much time inside the Beltway to realize when he was being rude?

In the end, it didn't matter. The one person whose opinion really mattered had long since decided he was impressed by Krislov. A cou-ple of phone calls from the secretary of labor weren't going to change Lee Bollinger's mind about his new general counsel.[3]

— ■ —

CARL COHEN WAS in the middle of another campus controversy, only he didn't start this one.

Michigan's Residential College, which Cohen had helped design thirty years earlier, decided to name a new reading room after him. The college put up a plaque and announced it would hold a dedica-tion ceremony on November 20, 1998. But in the weeks before the scheduled event, a group of students mounted a campaign to reverse the decision, denouncing Cohen for his stance on affirmative action. Officials working under Bollinger then announced that, because of pro-cedural irregularities, they would take Cohen's name off the room. The university said the reading room space was actually controlled by the UM housing office, which required an opportunity for student input.

Bollinger backed the decision, at first. "This was not a mere techni-cal oversight," he said in a statement. But as pressure mounted on cam-pus, Bollinger soon concluded he had made a mistake. A month later, he and Provost Nancy Cantor issued a second statement acknowledging that "a significant segment" of the university thought the institution was retaliating against Cohen. "We probably should have foreseen this unruly state of affairs, but the fact is we did not," they wrote. "We have no desire to put the university in a position where misunderstandings and uncertainties about our basic values are circulating." The room, they said, would be named for Carl Cohen after all.

—•—

ALTHOUGH SHAW AND MASSIE had both appealed the intervention decisions, the cases were moving ahead at the trial court level. The other lawyers immersed themselves in "discovery," a litigation tool that lets attorneys ask the other side for relevant documents and demand the opportunity to question potential witnesses.

For Kolbo, representing the three rejected white applicants, the papers Cohen had received from his FOIA request were a good start. But the attorney knew he needed more details to put together a full case. Kolbo already suspected the university was using a massive double standard, and the new documents he received in discovery in the undergraduate case seemed to him to be a confirmation. One item that caught his attention was a 1995 memo written by Admissions Director Ted Spencer. The memo said that minority admissions guidelines were "set to admit all students who qualify"—that is, all applicants deemed capable of doing the required work and eventually graduating. By contrast, Spencer wrote that nonminority students had to compete with one another for the limited number of seats in the class. It seemed to Kolbo that Spencer was conceding that his office used different rules for candidates of different races.

In the law school case, discovery gave Kolbo his first look at the 1992 admissions policy that had guided the review of Barbara Grutter's application. He thought the law school's goal of a "critical mass" was indistinguishable from a quota, and he found some support in the other materials he received. Pre-1992 documents were replete with references to a goal of 10–12 percent minority enrollment. Because the 1992 policy described its mission as being "as much to ratify what has been done and to reaffirm our goals as it is to announce new policies," Kolbo reasoned that the goal must still be in effect. He thought draft versions of the 1992 policy reinforced that conclusion, particularly the suggestion from one committee member that the document mention a numerical target range of 11 to 17 percent.

One place where Kolbo failed was in his effort to find a law school faculty member willing to help the legal case. Kolbo had hoped a law professor might be willing to play a role akin to Carl Cohen's at the undergraduate college, but even the conservative professors at the law school weren't interested in waging a public fight against race-based admissions. Kolbo couldn't even find a faculty member who had opposed the admissions policy back in 1992.

With two cases to put together, Kolbo was beginning to realize he needed more help. He now had dozens of people to formally interview, both university officials who had information about the policies and the team of expert witnesses Payton was assembling. The university had produced thousands of pages of documents that needed to be analyzed and organized. Plus, Kolbo had to prepare for the Wilmer Cutler Pickering lawyers to interview his own witnesses.

Kolbo had already tapped the services of one of the firm's most highly regarded lawyers, appellate and complex litigation specialist David Herr. As chairman of the Maslon Edelman Borman & Brand's Governance Committee, Herr had helped secure the firm's approval for Kolbo to take on the case. Now Kolbo sought help from another of his partners, Larry Purdy, a Vietnam veteran and hard-nosed litigator. Purdy had considered himself a supporter of affirmative action until he learned how Michigan's programs actually worked. He enthusiastically jumped in.

The men divided up the work. Kolbo would be the lead lawyer in both cases, but Herr and Purdy would handle various tasks and provide advice and support. One of the first orders of business was Jennifer Gratz's deposition. Kolbo decided he would handle that one himself.[4]

———

DEPOSITIONS ARE a bit like rehearsal for trial. Lawyers ask questions of sworn witnesses, who are obligated to answer as best they can. Depositions let the lawyers know what a witness would say if called to testify at trial. Because witnesses usually are aligned with one party or the other, depositions tend to be one-sided affairs. In Gratz's case, her lawyers already knew what her testimony would be. It was only Payton's team that needed to question her under oath.

The most significant difference between a deposition and trial testimony is that the former takes place without a judge present. The lawyers for the most part must referee their own disputes. If a lawyer objects to a line of questioning, the other attorney usually has the right to continue on. An objection, however, can still serve a purpose.

It creates a record so that the lawyer later can ask a judge to strike the disputed testimony. Perhaps more importantly, a good lawyer can use objections to influence the direction of the deposition. Objections can both wear down the other side and subtly guide the witness away from revealing important information.

Kolbo arranged for Jennifer Gratz's deposition to take place ten minutes from her house at the office of a local attorney. Payton's partner Jane Sherburne arrived with two colleagues to handle the questioning for the university. Gratz was nervous, knowing that her mother had returned home upset after testifying the day before. But Jennifer wasn't completely out of her element, having testified as a witness before. When she was nineteen, the Southgate Police Department hired her to try to buy alcohol from local stores. After several stores sold to her, she described her experiences in court.

Sherburne wasted little time. A few minutes into the session, she asked Gratz about her grades at Dearborn. Gratz had done well in her first year, earning a 3.7 in her first semester and 3.0 in the second. But in the fall of her sophomore year, she slipped to a 2.6 with three C-plusses. "They were rough classes," Gratz testified. The next semester, she rebounded with a 3.7, but in the fall of her junior year, she fell to 2.5, with a C and a D. "Looks like fall's not your time of year," Sherburne cracked. The following semester, Gratz had withdrawn from a modern algebra course. She explained that she felt she needed to lighten her academic load after a friend committed suicide.

Kolbo sat quietly as Sherburne marched through her questions, giving him few openings for lodging objections that might disrupt her flow. Sherburne turned to Gratz's application to UM, revealing flaws that no doubt hurt her admissions chances. The lawyer pointed to the booklet that had come with Gratz's blank application. The brochure noted that 63 percent of the enrolled freshmen in the fall of 1993 had an ACT score of twenty-seven or higher. Gratz acknowledged that her top score was a twenty-five.

Another section in the brochure encouraged high school seniors to apply as early as possible in the fall. Jennifer's application had arrived in Ann Arbor in January. "Did you have any understanding that there might be an advantage to applying earlier rather than later?" Sherburne asked. "No," Gratz answered.

Sherburne later pressed Gratz about the university's offer to include her on the extended waiting list. Several weeks earlier, Kolbo indicated in writing that Gratz had completed the wait-list application and that she thought she mailed it. Kolbo also produced a copy of the completed application from the Gratz family files. But the university's admissions office didn't have the original form on file, suggesting it was never sent. Sherburne now confronted Gratz with the discrepancy.

Gratz said she didn't remember filling out the form or mailing it. It wasn't a high priority for her. She assumed it would have been futile. She said she read the letter from the admissions office to mean that "there was no hope, and I needed to figure out what I was going to do for the next four years of my life."

"Are you aware," Sherburne said, "that all students who returned this form were admitted that year?"

Sherburne was being a bit imprecise. It was only the Michigan residents on the extended waiting list who were universally admitted. But since Gratz lived in-state, Sherburne's larger point was valid: Jennifer could have attended UM after all.

No, Gratz said, she hadn't realized that.

—■—

IN DECEMBER 1998, Duggan ruled that the undergraduate case could proceed as a class action. The ruling ensured that Kolbo could seek relief that went beyond Gratz and Hamacher; he could request an injunction barring Michigan from considering the race of any future applicant. The decision also opened up the possibility that, if Kolbo won his case, thousands of rejected white and Asian applicants could seek damages or demand that their applications be reconsidered under race-neutral criteria.

Payton had sought to defeat Kolbo's class action motion with a variation of the standing argument he had raised in his initial answer to the complaint. Payton argued that Kolbo lacked a suitable representative of the class because neither Gratz nor Hamacher would benefit from any future change in the university's undergraduate admissions policies. Gratz was too far along in her studies at Dearborn to consider transferring, and Hamacher had neither filed a transfer application nor achieved high enough grades at Michigan State to make himself a viable candidate, Payton argued.

Duggan rejected those arguments, saying Hamacher could be the class representative because he had vowed to file a transfer application as soon as Michigan changed its admissions policies. A month later, Friedman issued a similar decision in the law school case, saying it, too, could go forward as a class action.

——•——

KOLBO AND BOLLINGER shook hands for the first time and sat down at the plain oak table in the conference room of the university's local law firm, Butzel Long. Kolbo wasn't surprised to see that Bollinger had come for his deposition with two lawyers, Jane Sherburne and Michigan's new general counsel, Marvin Krislov. Morning sun came through the window that stretched the length of the room, giving the group a bird's-eye look at a seafood restaurant and children's-clothing store on Ann Arbor's Main Street.

Kolbo had modest goals for Bollinger's deposition. He assumed the president wouldn't know all the ins and outs of the various admissions policies at Michigan, but Kolbo wanted to make clear that Bollinger had at least a general understanding of the way the university used race in admissions. And in the law school case, Kolbo thought Bollinger might have some specific knowledge since he had ordered the 1992 rewrite of the admissions policy.

Bollinger wasn't going to make it easy for Kolbo. From the beginning of the session, Bollinger's answers evinced a strategy of providing few details and not straying far from the comments he had already made publicly in defense of affirmative action. Bollinger professed only the most general knowledge of the pre-1992 workings of the admissions program at the law school. He politely said he hadn't been aware at the time that the school had an avowed goal of 10–12 percent minority representation in each class. When Kolbo asked whether Bollinger had known anything about how precisely race was used, his witness repeatedly avoided the question.

"I don't know what to say more than I've said," Bollinger stated. "You're asking the question how it was used, and I've said that I knew that it was a factor that was taken into account in the admissions process for purposes of trying to achieve a diverse student body."

Kolbo: "To me, that's kind of a broad statement to say it was a factor. I'm trying to find out if you had some knowledge about how it was used, how it was taken into account as a factor in the admissions process."

Bollinger: "Well, again, I'm not sure that I understand what you're driving at. My best answer is that it was taken into account in the same way that geographical diversity was taken into account or life experiences were taken into account or grade point average was taken into account. The admissions process is subtle, complex, and nuanced. You can't just isolate one factor and say, 'How was it taken into account?'"

A few minutes later, Kolbo tried to get Bollinger to agree to the straightforward proposition that minority students admitted to Michigan Law School often have lower grades and test scores than nonminorities. Inquiring specifically about the period before the 1992 policy went into effect, Kolbo asked whether "in order to achieve that diversity or critical mass of minority students, there was a willingness to and a policy to accept minorities with generally lower LSAT and grade point averages than other students."

Bollinger ducked that question, too. The school had a threshold requirement that all students needed to be qualified, he said. "Within the entire range of applications, we would make that a threshold, and above that, it was important to us to take into account a host of factors in deciding who ultimately to admit and who to reject—whom to reject."

"Well, I don't think that answered my question," Kolbo replied. He asked it again.

"Objection," Sherburne chimed in, "asked and answered."

"I don't think it was," Kolbo said.

"Well, his answer is his answer, Kirk. It may not be the answer you want, but his answer is his answer."

"It was a yes-no question, and I got a long statement defending diversity."

"No, it's not a yes-no question."

"Can you answer the question?" Kolbo asked Bollinger.

"I think I have given the best answer I can," Bollinger replied.

The next few hours went much the same way. Kolbo tried to pin Bollinger down on his specific concerns about the pre-1992 policy. Bollinger refused to go beyond generalities, saying he wanted to be "absolutely sure that our policy was consistent with the Constitution."

And when one of Bollinger's answers suggested he was worried about the law school's practice of having minority students review minority applications, he quickly backtracked, rephrasing his answer in more general terms.

Kolbo then tried to elicit whether Bollinger was concerned specifically about the name "special admissions program." Bollinger refused to give a direct answer, simply reiterating that his interest was in ensuring that the policy was consistent with *Bakke*. When Kolbo tried again, Sherburne objected that he had already asked the question and received an answer. Kolbo kept plugging away, asking the question again and again in slightly different form.

"Objection," Sherburne said on Kolbo's eleventh and final try. "You've asked the question eight times now."

"I've not yet gotten a responsive answer to that question. I think the record will reflect that."

"Well, the record will reflect the answer that you've gotten and that you've gotten the same answer to the question now at least eight times. I think you might be better off just moving on, Kirk."

Kolbo gave up. "Well, I think you're probably right," he said.

As the morning progressed, Kolbo's frustration began to show. At one point he snapped at Sherburne, "If we were in a courtroom, you wouldn't sit here and interrogate me about my questions."

Sherburne jumped in again when Kolbo asked whether the "critical mass" goal was part of the pre-1992 policy.

"Kirk, can I just—maybe I can help here," she said.

"I doubt it," he retorted.

"Well, let me try. Are you asking whether the policy that's articulated in the 1992 document with respect to critical mass is different than the way critical mass was perceived by President Bollinger before that period?"

"No, I didn't ask that."

"Okay. Then I don't know what you're asking either."

"And the witness hasn't told me that, but I appreciate your telling me you're not understanding the question," Kolbo replied sarcastically.

———•———

AFTER LUNCH, KOLBO managed to extract a few nuggets. Bollinger acknowledged that a law school class with only 3 percent minorities wouldn't have a critical mass. (Bollinger wouldn't commit, however, when asked about 7 percent.) The witness said the law school had an in-state resident goal of 35–40 percent of each class. Bollinger said a state law school had a duty to ensure a significant number of slots were filled by residents. "And that was true even if some have qualifications lower than those of some applicants from outside Michigan," he added, when prodded.

When Kolbo asked whether that same principle applied to minority applicants, Bollinger became evasive again, saying he didn't understand Kolbo's questions. It was several minutes before Bollinger gave Kolbo some of what the attorney was looking for. Bollinger acknowledged that admitted minorities had lower test scores and grades on average than their majority counterparts. Bollinger then agreed that the gap helped explain why minorities would represent only a small fraction of the class in the absence of affirmative action.

As the afternoon wore on, Kolbo collected another valuable piece of information. He asked Bollinger whether the undergraduate college has a policy of protecting spaces in each entering class for minority candidates who applied late in the application cycle. Bollinger gave a lengthy reply that explained some of the techniques the admissions office used to handle its rolling admissions policy. Kolbo repeated the question, and Sherburne objected that Bollinger had already answered.

"No," Kolbo said. "He answered why some of this stuff is done. I want to know if, in fact, it's done that way. Is that true or not?"

"To the best of my understanding, to the best of my knowledge, it is," Bollinger answered.

At 7:42 p.m., almost eleven hours after the deposition started, Kolbo said he was finished and began packing up his briefcase.[5]

Chapter Seven

Accepted on the Spot

Unlike Jennifer Gratz, Agnes Aleobua didn't have to wait for a letter to learn whether she could attend the University of Michigan. She was accepted on the spot for the fall 1999 class after an interview with a university admissions officer at her downtown Detroit high school, Cass Technical. The fast-track acceptance was part of a program by the university to attract and admit qualified black students. Agnes didn't think twice about accepting the fruits of affirmative action. In her view, it was well deserved.

Aleobua, a heavyset African American woman with a warm smile, knew all about segregation. Her childhood home sat almost precisely on Detroit's racial border, across the street from an all-black housing project and a block from the predominantly Polish American Catholic Church her family attended. In kindergarten and first grade, she was one of just two blacks in her class. She got an early lesson in racial discrimination in first grade after she passed a note to a white boy she liked. He wrote back saying he wasn't interested in her because she was black. Starting in second grade, her parents sent her to a predominantly black school for gifted and talented children.

From there, she went to Cass Technical High School, which passed for the crown jewel of the Detroit public school system. Cass had educated generations of the city's best and brightest, including singer Diana Ross, car designer John DeLorean, and Detroit Mayor

113

Kwame Kilpatrick. It was a magnet school, meaning that it selected its students on the basis of grades and an entrance exam, then required admitted students to choose a curriculum such as vocational music, business administration, or robotics design. Yet its institutional strengths stood in contrast to its dilapidated physical condition and inadequate resources. The school, an eight-story building rumored to have once been a pickle factory, was literally falling apart. Holes went all the way through the walls. Pieces of stairs were missing. The bathrooms lacked stall doors. Snow came in through windows that wouldn't shut properly. Yellow water flowed from the rust-encrusted drinking fountains. Worst of all, the school didn't have enough books to go around. Students were forced to share.

In Agnes's junior year, her physics class got a visit from Miranda Massie and another woman making a pitch for a group called the Coalition to Defend Affirmative Action by Any Means Necessary. They explained they were looking for students to help fight a lawsuit that was challenging the admissions policy of Michigan Law School. The group was organizing demonstrations and petition campaigns and wanted to get more high school students involved. The presentation hit home with Agnes, and she wrote her name on the sign-up sheet for interested students.

She pleaded with her parents to let her take part. Agnes's father, a Nigerian immigrant with a master's degree in architecture, was concerned about what the lawsuit would mean for his daughter and family. Paul Aleobua had a list of questions when Massie visited the family's home to discuss the case. He wanted to know what Massie, a white woman, hoped to gain from the fight. "I never feel more in touch with our common humanity than when I'm fighting racism," Massie responded. Finally, Paul Aleobua turned to his daughter. "Don't you have any questions?" he asked. No, she said. She knew she wanted in. He consented.

In February 1998, Agnes went to a rally in support of affirmative action on Michigan's Diag. Someone asked her to say a few words. Agnes had done a little public speaking before, but this was different and she wasn't prepared. Fighting off her nerves, she approached the microphone and said, "I go to Cass." The crowd cheered. "I'm competent and I deserve the opportunity to go to college," she concluded. It wasn't much, but the audience loved it.

AP/WIDE WORLD PHOTOS

Detroit native Agnes Aleobua was a proud beneficiary of Michigan's race-conscious admissions policies. As an undergraduate, she would become one of the leaders of a militant group, the Coalition to Defend Affirmative Action by Any Means Necessary.

By the time she applied to college in the fall of 1998, Agnes knew she wanted to attend Michigan and be a part of that movement. She felt good about her chances. She was in the top fifth of her class, ultimately graduating eighty-second in her class of 620. Her application was chock full of extracurricular activities and leadership roles in student organizations. Her best ACT score was a twenty-six, one point higher than Jennifer Gratz had scored. Agnes Aleobua was confident she was Michigan material, and she knew what she wanted to do when she got there.[1]

IN THE SPRING of 1999, a year and a half after the lawsuits were filed, Kolbo and Payton filed their summary judgment motions with Friedman and Duggan. Summary judgment is a tool in federal court that lets the judge avoid having to hold a full-scale trial. Litigants typically file for summary judgment after the discovery period has ended. They tell the court, in effect, "We've combed through all the evidence, and any factual differences the two sides have are immaterial." Put another way, trials are designed to resolve issues about the credibility of witnesses and the veracity of what they say. If the answers to those questions don't matter—that is, if one side should win the case as a matter of law even if everything the other side says is true on the facts—the judge should award summary judgment.

By now, it was clear to both teams of lawyers in the Michigan cases that they had little disagreement about the facts surrounding the admissions processes, and the attorneys said as much in their court papers. The university acknowledged it used race as a factor in admissions. Black, Hispanic, and Native American applicants got a boost in the admissions process because of their race, meaning that in many cases minorities were admitted rather than whites and Asian Americans with higher grades and test scores. Michigan also acknowledged that in practice its policies meant the admission of every minority student who appeared qualified to perform well enough at the school to graduate.

The papers revealed that the admissions process at the undergraduate level during the 1990s was both complex and variable from year to year. All applications to the College of Literature, Science, and the Arts went to the Office of Undergraduate Admissions. Applications began arriving every year in the summer (seeking admission for the fall of the following year) and continued through January. Clerks processed the applications, recalculating the high school grade point average to exclude nonacademic courses, adjusting for the strength of the school and curriculum, and putting the grades on a 4.0 scale. A small number of applicants with especially high grades and test scores were automatically sent offers of admission, even without a review of their file by one of the twenty admissions counselors. In theory, applicants with especially low scores and grades could be sent rejection letters, but in practice the clerks rarely did so because they were uncomfortable making decisions without counselor input.

The vast majority of the files then went to the counselor assigned to the applicant's geographic area. The counselor made a "first review" decision on each application, consulting written guidelines that were designed to ensure consistency across the office. In 1995 and 1997, the years Gratz and Hamacher applied, counselors consulted the grids that Carl Cohen had uncovered. In 1995, counselors used four such grids: one for minority students who either lived in Michigan or were "legacies" (relatives of an alum); one for in-state or legacy majority applicants; one for other minorities; and one for other majorities. Which grid was used could make all the difference for an applicant. Gratz's record put her in a box that called for a postponement of a decision; had she been an in-state underrepresented minority with identical numbers, the box would have called for an admission letter. Indeed, in Gratz's application year, all forty-six minority candidates in that box were admitted, while only 121 of 378 majority applicants were.

Postponement of decisions for white applicants was a technique the admissions office used to ensure it obtained sufficient numbers of minority students. Minorities tended to apply relatively late in the application cycle (as did athletes, foreign students, and ROTC candidates). Because Michigan admitted applicants on a rolling basis, the school needed to ensure that seats were available to offer to late-applying qualified minority students. The school's solution was to "protect" a number of seats—that is, to leave them unfilled until the end of the application cycle in the hope that qualified minorities would apply to fill them. If not, the university could fill the spots with white students from the waiting list.

At the same time, the school had a general policy of not putting minority candidates on the waiting list. Michigan found that an early offer of acceptance tended to increase the chance that a minority student would decide to enroll at UM, rather than another college. And if a counselor was in doubt about the qualifications of a minority applicant, the preferred practice was to wait for additional information, such as fall grades, rather than send out a wait-list letter. Minorities, the guidelines said, "will be admitted as soon as high probability of success can be predicted." Or, in the words of Admissions Director Ted Spencer in his 1995 memo, "minority guidelines are set to admit all students who qualify."

The process had changed slightly by the time Hamacher applied in 1997. Instead of four grids, the admissions office used two—one for in-state applicants and legacies, the other for out-of-state, non-legacy students. Each grid had a line of instructions for majorities and another line for minorities. The new system also tweaked the way race was taken into account. The office used minority status (as well as legacy status and socioeconomic disadvantage) to increase the adjusted GPA, meaning that race entered into the process at two points, rather than one. The practical effect of the changes was insignificant because the university continued to admit any minority student who appeared qualified to pass the university's courses.

The 1998 change, the one Bollinger ordered when he became president, was more dramatic in appearance, replacing the grids with the simpler 150-point "selection index." No longer would the admissions office judge applicants using different sheets of paper for different races. Underneath, the point system was less of a change than it appeared. Counselors still admitted virtually all qualified minority candidates. Both Payton and Kolbo told Duggan in court papers that the changes were solely in the mechanics, not in the substance of the policy.

Michigan officials added an additional layer to the process for the 1999 entering class. The university established a panel, known as the Admissions Review Committee, for what Payton called "the more difficult and complex admissions decisions." Counselors were authorized to flag applications that showed particular qualities important to the university, such as minority status or unique life experiences, yet scored below the selection index cutoff (usually between 90 and 100). In most cases, only students with scores of eighty or higher (seventy-five or higher for out-of-state applicants) were eligible for consideration by the new committee, but counselors could even flag applications with lower scores in certain circumstances. The committee then would meet to discuss the flagged applications, disregarding the point system and making an individualized judgment on each.

—■—

THE ADMISSIONS PROCEDURES at the law school were less rigid. With a fraction of the number of applications—3,400 in 1997, out of which 1,163 got offers of admission—the law school admissions office could devote individual attention to each file in a way the undergraduate office couldn't. It took three or four people at the law school to review all the files, compared with the group of twenty at the undergraduate level. A single person, the law school admissions director, made the majority of the decisions, alleviating the need for a scoring system to ensure schoolwide consistency.

Numbers were of primary importance at Michigan Law School. The admissions policy Ted Shaw helped draft described an "index score" that would be a composite of an applicant's undergraduate grades and LSAT scores. "Bluntly, the higher one's index score, the greater should be one's chances of being admitted," the policy said. "The lower the score, the greater the risk the candidate poses. And when scores are extremely low, it is extremely difficult for us reliably to pick out those who would be successful at Michigan and in the practice of law. So we expect the vast majority of those students we admit to have high index scores." The policy said that admissions decisions could be plotted on a grid, with LSAT scores along one axis and GPA on the other. Most admitted applicants, the policy said, should come from the upper right-hand corner of the grid.

Still, individual attention meant the admissions office occasionally could offer admissions to someone not quite in the upper right-hand corner. The policy described two types of applicants who might qualify for admissions despite being "relatively far" from the corner. The first type was the applicant whose record suggested that an index score wouldn't be a good predictor of law school performance. As an example, the policy described a student who had earned high grades in college despite a low SAT score. That student then achieved a mediocre score on his LSATs, yet still was admitted to Michigan Law School. The faculty committee concluded the student's strong undergraduate record would be a better predictor than his LSAT score.

The second reason for admitting a student who didn't land in the upper right-hand corner was diversity and its power to "enrich everyone's education and thus make a law school class stronger than the sum of its parts." The policy laid out some examples: the Bangladeshi immigrant, the single mother from Argentina, the winner of an Olympic gold medal. And, of course, there were groups that had historically suffered from discrimination, specifically, blacks, Hispanics, and Native Americans. "These students are particularly likely to have experiences and perspectives of special importance to our mission."

As to what the admissions criteria would be for racial minorities, the committee was vague. The policy laid out a general minimum requirement: "No applicant should be admitted unless we expect that applicant to do well enough to graduate with no serious academic problems." The policy also pointed to a goal—a "critical mass" of minority students—but didn't define what that meant nor specifically put it in percentage terms. But it also endorsed the previous affirmative action policies, which had featured a goal of 10–12 percent underrepresented minorities and a "special admissions program" to help reach that target.

—■—

WHERE KOLBO AND Payton differed was on the law and how it applied to the Michigan admissions policies.

For Payton, the case was little more than an application of *Bakke*. Adopting the prevailing understanding of *Bakke* from academic circles, Payton argued that Justice Powell's opinion represented the controlling reasoning in the case. That meant diversity was a compelling interest that could justify the use of race as one factor in admissions. Powell, Payton went on, did put some limitations on the use of race. First, universities couldn't establish quotas by setting aside seats that only minority candidates could fill. Put another way, minority applicants couldn't be insulated from competition from majority students. Two-track systems were unconstitutional. Second, Powell suggested (as did the Court in later cases) that beneficiaries of affirmative action needed to be qualified. But beyond that, Payton argued, universities had power to use race as they saw fit.

In Payton's view, the law school case was an especially easy fit into Powell's framework. Admissions officers looked at an applicant's entire file and considered race simply as one factor among many. There was no quota, and even the 10–12 percent target for minorities had been jettisoned, thanks to the insistence of Shaw and other members of the drafting committee that the policy not even allude to a numerical goal. Minorities were considered in competition with all the other applicants, not under the old special admissions program. Finally, the policy itself made clear that only qualified applicants would be admitted.

The undergraduate case required a bit more explanation. There wasn't any quota in the sense of a set percentage below which minority enrollment wouldn't fall. But Carl Cohen's grids and, to a lesser extent the point system, did at least suggest that minorities and majorities were systematically being treated differently. And the grids, with their separate instructions for handling applicants of different races, could convey the impression of a two-track system.

To Payton, those were cosmetics. As at the law school, the undergraduate admissions policy simply used race as one factor among many to achieve a diverse class. The grids showed how race could make a difference in some cases, but they were only one part of the admissions process. Some factors, such as race and legacy status, were considered through the different grids. Other factors, such as high school curriculum, mattered when calculating adjusted grade point average. And the point system was just a simpler method of making the calculations. Payton wrote: "Whether by use of the grids or the selection index, the university has considered race on an individual basis—for some minority students, it is decisive, but for others it is not."

Kolbo thought Payton's interpretation would reduce the *Bakke* decision to a case that invalidated only admissions programs that were identical to the one in use at UC-Davis. As Kolbo saw it, Powell had something much more significant in mind. The justice had insisted that each student be treated as an individual. Neither the law school nor the undergraduate college were doing that, Kolbo thought; both were giving minority applicants a systematic boost. As he wrote in the undergraduate case: "The illegality arises from the fact that *every* LSA applicant who is a member of one of the preferred racial or ethnic minorities receives consideration on account of race or ethnicity under terms more favorable than those for individuals who are not members of one of the preferred minority groups."

The undergraduate policy, Kolbo wrote, had problems on several levels. In addition to the grids and use of race in the point system, there was the practice of protecting seats for minorities. And Kolbo said the school had a "racially segregated" waiting list—that is, one that included only nonminorities. All told, it was "redundant proof of that institution's willful disobedience of the law."

Kolbo toned down his language in the law school case, but his point was essentially the same. He said the school still maintained a "special admissions program," a separate track that downplayed the importance of grades and test scores for minority applicants.

Beyond the specifics of the Michigan program, Kolbo had a more fundamental point to make. Powell's opinion, he argued, was just that—Powell's opinion. No other justice had signed on. Mirroring the Fifth Circuit's reasoning in *Hopwood,* Kolbo argued that Powell and the Brennan group had simply disagreed about the context in which race could be used. Brennan had thought it appropriate to correct for societal discrimination, Powell for diversity purposes. "The 'diversity' rationale of Justice Powell cannot plausibly be said to represent the holding of *Bakke* when it was explicitly or implicitly rejected by eight other justices," Kolbo wrote. He added that later Supreme Court decisions seemed to confirm that view.

———•———

THE BRIEFS WERE as notable for what they didn't say as for what they did.

For starters, Kolbo's brief made no mention of the requirement, clearly laid out by Justice O'Connor in her *Croson* opinion, that government bodies must consider whether they can accomplish their affirmative action goals through race-neutral means. Other critics of traditional racial preferences were advocating, as alternatives, so-called percent plans, which guaranteed admission to a state college for people who graduated at the top of their high school classes. After the *Hopwood* decision in Texas, for example, then-governor George W. Bush signed into law a system to admit the top 10 percent of each Texas high school class into any public university in the state. Other percent plans were in place in California and Florida. Because many of the high schools in those states were overwhelmingly black or Hispanic, the policies had the effect of ensuring that some racial minorities had the right to enroll at state universities.

The problem was that, to the team at CIR, the percent programs tended to be legally and morally murky, only marginally better than straightforward racial preferences. In Pell's view, the Texas plan was a dishonest gerrymander that relied upon the racial concentrations in the state's high schools to achieve ethnic balancing in its colleges.

There was also a practical problem: if the goal was a racially diverse class, the early evidence suggested that the percent plans didn't work as well as race-conscious admissions. The two states that had deployed percent plans to replace explicitly race-conscious systems—California and Texas—had both seen declines in minority admissions, most notably at their flagship schools. At the University of Texas at Austin, 20.3 percent of the students admitted to the undergraduate college in 1996—the last year race was used in admissions—were black, Hispanic, or Native American. After the *Hopwood* decision, state lawmakers moved quickly to implement a plan guaranteeing that students graduating in the top 10 percent of any public or private high school in the state could enroll at the state university of their choice. Nonetheless, in 1998 only 17.4 percent of the school's admissions offers went to African American, Latino, and Native American students.

The numbers in California were even more stark. In the wake of Prop 209, the state set up a plan that promised admission to students who graduated in the top 4 percent of their class. In an important difference from Texas, students were assured admission to the nine-school University of California system but not necessarily to the campus of their choice. The result was that undergraduate admissions offers to blacks, Latinos, and Native Americans across the system slipped from 17.9 percent in 1997 to 15.9 percent the following year. And at the most selective campuses, the percentages plummeted—from 23.1 percent to 11.2 percent at UC-Berkeley and from 20.0 percent to 12.7 percent at UCLA. Most devastatingly, at the state's most prestigious law school, Berkeley's Boalt Hall, only one black student enrolled in the fall of 1997, down from twenty the previous year.

Payton had his own constraints about what he could say. The *Bakke* decision left diversity as the lone potential rationale for university affirmative action. And it was a distinct strain of diversity. To Powell, the importance of diversity was its educational value. Universities, as he saw it, should have broad power to decide what the best learning environment was for their students. Most pointedly, schools could decide that white students benefited from having black and Hispanic colleagues. At the same time, Powell ruled out other diversity-related justifications. He had said that schools couldn't act for the purpose of ensuring more black doctors. To Powell, that smacked of "discrimination for its own sake."

And, of course, Payton couldn't argue that affirmative action was necessary to make up for centuries of discrimination across American society. When he first read the *Bakke* decision twenty years ago, it was Thurgood Marshall's passionate moral defense of affirmative action that Payton found compelling. But, as Payton was well aware, that wasn't the law.

———■———

ONE DEFECT IN Justice Powell's opinion was that the Harvard admissions policy he praised wasn't actually before the Supreme Court. Powell had seized upon an amicus brief filed by Harvard and three other prestigious universities. Those schools had outlined their admissions systems, but their descriptions hadn't been tested in court, leaving Powell with an incomplete picture of the way admissions actually worked there. The cursory nature of Powell's review of the Harvard plan might explain an internal tension in his opinion about the acceptable magnitude of affirmative action programs.

In one part of his opinion, Powell said race could be a "plus" for an applicant, one factor among many. Although he said all factors need not be given equal weight, he suggested that they at least would be close in importance. The race of a particular applicant "may tip the balance in his favor just as geographic origin or a life spent on a farm may tip the balance in other candidates' cases," Powell wrote, quoting from the Harvard policy. That language gave Kolbo grounds to contend that the Michigan preferences were simply too large relative to other admissions considerations to fit within Powell's framework. Race, Kolbo could argue, seemed to matter far more at Michigan than a rustic upbringing did.

Elsewhere in his opinion, Powell suggested that universities could seek a minority presence large enough that students wouldn't feel isolated. The Harvard policy, which Powell appended to his opinion in its entirety, said that "10 or 20 black students could not begin to bring to their classmates and to each other the variety of points of view, backgrounds and experiences of blacks in the United States." The policy went on: "Their small numbers might also create a sense of isolation among the black students themselves and thus make it more difficult for them to develop and achieve their potential. Consequently, when making its decisions, the Committee on Admissions is aware that there is some relationship between numbers and achieving the benefits to be derived from a diverse student body, and between numbers and providing a reasonable environment for those students admitted."

That description seemed to embrace exactly what Payton was seeking: the right to aim for a "critical mass" of minority students.

The problem, according to a growing body of research, was that racial preferences at the margins simply weren't enough to ensure significant numbers of black and Hispanic students at the most selective universities. In their landmark 1998 book, *The Shape of the River,* former Princeton president William G. Bowen and former Harvard president Derek Bok (both affirmative action proponents) analyzed data from five highly selective undergraduate colleges for their 1989 entering classes. Bowen and Bok found that the average combined SAT score for white applicants to those schools was 186 points higher than the average score for black applicants (1284 to 1098). Although the two men said the gap had narrowed over the years, they concluded that it wasn't likely to disappear any time soon. In the words of Columbia University law professor Samuel Issacharoff, a "credentials gap" separated the majority and minority applicant pools.

That gap meant that a top university would enroll only a handful of minorities if it relied solely on test scores and grades. Bowen and Bok concluded that a race-neutral admissions policy would reduce the share of African Americans from 7.1 percent to between 2.1 percent and 3.6 percent at the five schools they studied. A national simulation they conducted yielded similar results, with the greatest impact felt at the most selective schools, such as Harvard, Stanford, and Oberlin. At the law school level, Linda Wightman, an associate professor at the University of North Carolina at Greensboro, concluded from data on 1990–91 applicants that black admissions would drop by two-thirds under a system based solely on LSAT scores and even more with a system that considered grades along with test results. Even assuming that some rejected black candidates would have applied to, and attended, less selective law schools, African American enrollment would drop by half, Wightman found.[2]

Why was the credentials gap so large? The answer was a complex one that had fostered a fair amount of scholarly debate. One thing was clear: much of the explanation lay in inequalities of opportunity. White college applicants, on average, attended better elementary and high schools and were less likely to have grown up in poverty than their minority counterparts. Massie had tried to raise some of those issues at trial, and Friedman had acknowledged the truth of some of her contentions. But Friedman concluded that most of Massie's arguments weren't legally relevant. Indeed, even Massie acknowledged that the prevailing law barred the use of race to remedy societywide discrimination.

The credentials gap was the flip side of the large preferences that Kolbo decried. Kolbo was unquestionably right that, if the barometer was grades and test scores, Michigan was admitting minorities with considerably lower credentials than whites who were rejected. But if Michigan's goal of a "critical mass" was a valid one, it had no choice but to depart significantly from grades and test scores in admitting minorities. The real question, the most fundamental one in the case, was whether that trade-off was worth the cost.

Powell, by all appearances, failed to appreciate the magnitude of the credentials gap. By invoking the Harvard plan, his opinion suggested that universities could enroll significant numbers of minorities relatively painlessly. He gave no indication that he understood just how stark the choice was—or just how great the consequences of affirmative action were.

Chapter Eight

Bollinger's New Front

T ED SHAW HAD A GOOD FEELING as he walked out of the federal courthouse in downtown Cincinnati, the headquarters of the Sixth U.S. Circuit Court of Appeals, into the unseasonably hot, sticky spring air. The argument on his intervention appeal, he thought, had gone quite well.

Even before the attorneys stood up to make their arguments, the appeals court had sent subtle signals that it might allow Shaw and Massie into their respective cases. The makeup of the three-judge panel seemed to favor the would-be intervenors. Two of the three, Judges Martha Daughtrey and Karen Nelson Moore, were Clinton appointees with liberal reputations. (Daughtrey had dissented in 1994 when the Sixth Circuit voted twelve-to-four to revive anti-preference lawsuits by white police officers and firefighters against the city of Memphis. Moore hadn't been on the court for that case, but she joined Daughtrey in 1996 in dissenting from a ten-to-five ruling that limited minority lawsuits over voting districts.) The panel had seemed to confirm its leanings a few days before the argument, when it issued a series of stay orders barring Duggan and Friedman from moving ahead in their cases until the appeals court had resolved the intervention question.

In court, Shaw tried to focus the judges on what to him seemed obvious: at the end of the day, the people most affected by the outcome were his clients, a high percentage of whom would lose access to the top educational institution in the state. "If the plaintiffs win this case, the University of Michigan will go on. It'll just be much whiter," he argued. He invoked an old Polish phrase: "Nothing about us without us." He pointed out the Sixth Circuit precedent that he thought so clearly supported his case.

Kolbo's partner David Herr argued that the intervenors were seeking to add a slew of unrelated issues to the mix. He thought Massie was making especially frivolous claims, adding arguments about such wayward topics as gender discrimination. The upshot would be to complicate and delay the whole proceeding. "It will derail our case," Herr argued. His comments, including a reference to the intervenors as "strangers to this litigation," riled some of the BAMN supporters in the audience. In the elevator after the argument, a scruffy-looking Luke Massie, Miranda Massie's brother, confronted Herr and Kolbo. "You all are basically worthless, racist pieces of dog shit," Massie said.

Shaw thought Judges Daughtrey and Moore had seemed sympathetic, or at least open, to the arguments he was making. The third panelist was William Stafford, a district judge on assignment from the federal court in Tallahassee, Florida. Stafford, a Gerald Ford appointee, was harder to predict, but Shaw needed only two votes.[1]

———•———

BOLLINGER WAS FEELING FRUSTRATED. For all his coalition-building work, he had little to show for it. His efforts to rally business support had fizzled. Back in 1997, before the lawsuit was filed, he had convened a conference call involving more than a dozen corporate and university leaders. At the time, everyone sounded supportive. Yet somehow he hadn't been able to persuade a single chief executive or company chairman to come out publicly defending the university. Corporations were happy to extol the general virtues of racial diversity at colleges and to make broad statements of support for affirmative action. But not one would publicly acknowledge the necessary corollary—that race should be considered as an admissions factor. And businesses didn't seem to want to put their names alongside that of a university facing a multimillion-dollar lawsuit.

The political process was proving only slightly more fruitful. The Justice Department had decided to file a brief on behalf of the university at the district court. That was helpful, but Bollinger was looking for something stronger—something from the White House that would have a political impact. Months earlier, Bollinger had met briefly with President Clinton and asked for a public statement. The president was empathetic but noncommittal. Later, Michigan Law School dean Jeff Lehman had his own chat with Clinton in a receiving line after a speech by the president at the White House, and Clinton again offered words of support. But those private comments were as far as Clinton would go. His public position on affirmative action was a cautious one: "Mend it, don't end it." If Bollinger wanted political support, he would have to look elsewhere.

Bollinger decided to try the university's most famous graduate, former president Gerald Ford. Bollinger had worked with Ford on a couple of matters in the past and wondered whether the former president might be willing to voice support for affirmative action. After sounding out people close to Ford, Bollinger put in a call.

To Bollinger's delight, Ford agreed to write an article in support of affirmative action. Michigan officials quickly sent over a model op-ed that laid out some of the benefits of affirmative action. But Ford had something even more powerful in mind, and when the promised article arrived on a Sunday morning in August in the *New York Times*, Bollinger was overwhelmed. Not only did Ford endorse affirmative action, he specifically supported Michigan's policies. Ford praised the university for considering race as one of almost a dozen elements in the admissions process. "This eminently reasonable approach, as thoughtful as it is fair, has produced a student body with a significant minority component whose record of academic success is outstanding," he wrote.

Perhaps even more importantly, Ford cast his support for race-based admissions in poignant personal terms, telling a story from his days on the University of Michigan football team. Michigan was scheduled to play Georgia Tech during Ford's senior year in 1934. That year Michigan had a black player, Willis Ward, one of the finest all-around athletes ever to attend the school. Georgia Tech refused to take the field if Ward suited up. As the game approached, the Ann Arbor campus was in an uproar. In a detail that Ford modestly left out of his op-ed, he told his coaches that he wouldn't play if his friend Ward didn't. Ford relented only when Ward himself urged the future

Lee Bollinger struggled at first to win outside support for Michigan's admissions policies. The breakthrough occurred when he put in a call to the school's most famous alumnus, former president Gerald R. Ford, who wrote a *New York Times* column praising the university's affirmative action efforts.

president to play. Ward sat out, a decision that still saddened Ford sixty-five years later.

College diversity, Ford wrote, is necessary to ensure qualities that were missing during the debate over Willis Ward: tolerance and breadth of mind. "I don't want future college students to suffer the cultural and social impoverishment that afflicted my generation.... Do we really want to risk turning back the clock to an era when the Willis Wards were penalized for the color of their skin, their economic standing or national ancestry?"[2]

———◼———

SHAW'S INSTINCTS about the Sixth Circuit were confirmed a month after the argument. By a two-to-one vote, with Stafford dissenting, the panel said the students, both the minority high schoolers represented by Shaw's team and the broader array represented by Massie in the law school case, could intervene.

Daughtrey's opinion for the court tracked Shaw's brief in many respects. The university, she said, isn't likely to present evidence of its own past discrimination, and, as a consequence, may not adequately represent the interests of the minority students. Daughtrey suggested broad sympathies for the goals of affirmative action, hinting perhaps that she ultimately might vote to uphold the use of race in admissions. "There is little room for doubt," she wrote, "that access to the University for African-American and Latino/a students will be impaired to some extent and that a substantial decline in the enrollment of these students may well result if the University is precluded from considering race as a factor in admissions."

Shaw was thrilled. In the Texas Law School case, he had chafed when the Fifth Circuit forced him and his team to watch from the sidelines. Shaw thought the Texas attorney general had handled that case especially poorly. This time, Shaw and his NAACP Legal Defense and Educational Fund would be able to play a role. Shaw also had helped establish a legal precedent that would aid minority students in future legal fights.

The CIR team gave a collective sigh. The lawyers knew the ruling would add months to the fight, if not more than a year, as the intervenors put together their cases. It also would mean thousands of dollars in additional costs for CIR and countless hours of uncompensated work for Kolbo and the Maslon Edelman lawyers, all because of issues they were convinced had no relevance to the case. The group quickly decided not to appeal to the full Sixth Circuit or the Supreme Court. That probably would lead only to more delay.

Massie sprang into action. Suddenly, she had the opportunity of a lifetime, and she was determined to make the most of it. A day after the ruling, Massie mailed letters to three professors she hoped would testify about the legacy of race discrimination and the pervasive impact it still had on the university admissions process and campus life. No longer, Massie thought, was the case just about diversity. It was also about something she considered far more fundamental: equality.[3]

———

SUCCESS WAS COMING at a price for the Center for Individual Rights. As the organization entered its second decade, the unlikely marriage of Greve and McDonald was falling apart. The two founders increasingly squabbled over priorities, tactics, and each other's workload.

As often as not, Michigan was at the center of the controversy. Greve would storm through the office, complaining that the two cases were occupying a disproportionate amount of CIR's time and money. The Sixth Circuit's intervention decision only deepened Greve's concerns; the suits, it was now clear, were going to take at least five years and cost millions of dollars. Greve supported the litigation, but he had other priorities. The last thing he wanted was for CIR to become a one-issue organization. Greve wanted to press more federalism cases that would challenge the power of Congress. He also wanted to go after Title IX, the federal law that requires gender equity in college athletic programs. Greve complained bitterly that McDonald wasn't doing enough to find those types of cases.

For Greve, the issue of race had always been a secondary concern. His passion was reducing the role of government in private lives, whether the issue was banking regulation or race. Those libertarian instincts trumped his objections to race discrimination. Greve, in fact, argued that the federal civil rights laws shouldn't apply to private universities. Nonpublic universities, Greve thought, should be free to use affirmative action—or to discriminate against minorities. "Let each define its own mission," he wrote in the conservative journal *Policy Review*. "Let there be institutional choice and (for lack of a better word) diversity."

On several occasions, Greve asked McDonald and other CIR board members to promise they wouldn't pursue a discrimination lawsuit against a private university. A "private *Hopwood*," Greve argued, would be ideologically misguided and potentially even more of a financial burden than the Michigan cases. It also might turn off some of CIR's more libertarian donors. But McDonald and the other CIR directors refused. Some told Greve they agreed with him as a general matter: a suit against a private university, invoking Title VI of the Civil Rights Act instead of the Constitution's equal protection clause, wasn't a high priority. But board members didn't want to tie their own hands. CIR had always evaluated potential lawsuits on a case-by-case basis, and they saw no reason to change that policy.

The professional differences might have been manageable in another setting. But Greve was restless. He had always considered himself part activist and part scholar, and he felt his scholarly side was beginning to atrophy. The race debate had begun to seem particularly trite. Greve had taken part in countless debates and panel discussions on the topic, and the arguments from the other side now struck him as tired.

Greve was also feeling underappreciated. At the end of 1999, he told the CIR board he wanted a raise and a new title that would give him clear authority over McDonald. The board went along in part, giving him a small boost in salary and naming him chief executive officer. McDonald was relegated to a subordinate role. But it wasn't enough, and six weeks later Greve submitted his resignation.

To an outsider, McDonald might have seemed the obvious choice to take over the CIR reins. But McDonald's strengths lay in legal work, not in fund-raising or managing people, and he too seemed to have grown bored with the organization he founded. So the CIR board instead turned to Terry Pell, giving him the title of chief executive officer. McDonald agreed to stay on as director of litigation.

Pell brought a steadier, if less colorful, style to the CIR helm, as well as an unwavering commitment to the Michigan cases. For two-plus years, Pell had written extensively about the Michigan cases and traveled around the country for speeches and debates, shaping the way CIR presented the issue to the public. He had shepherded Gratz, Grutter, and Hamacher through countless media interviews, and he felt strongly that they were high-quality people who had suffered an injustice. And Pell was convinced that Michigan's admissions policies couldn't be squared with Powell's opinion in *Bakke*, much less the Constitution.

A few weeks after taking over as chief executive, Pell got a shock: CIR was on pace to close its fiscal year with a $500,000 deficit. A year earlier, the firm had been the beneficiary of a $1.4 million bequest. Under Greve's stewardship, the firm had spent more than half the money, expanding the staff to a dozen people and renting additional office space. Pell concluded he now had no choice but to do the opposite. He set about subletting office space and laying off staff.[4]

—•—

CIR's FEAR THAT intervention would mean long delays proved well-founded. With Shaw and Massie seeking time to marshal evidence, Duggan and Friedman quickly issued new scheduling orders extending their respective cases by almost a year. Eventually, both judges

AP/WIDE WORLD PHOTOS

Terry Pell, shown here talking to client Jennifer Gratz, took over the leadership of the Center for Individual Rights after co-founder Michael Greve resigned. Pell, a lawyer and philosopher, was ardent in his opposition to race-based admissions but fatalistic about CIR's prospects for success in the Michigan cases.

agreed to additional delays, ensuring the suits wouldn't be resolved before the fall of 2000, three years after they were filed.

The lawyers all had plenty of work to do, and much of it was tedious. Shaw's team spent months combing through documents in search of details that would show a historical pattern of discrimination against minorities at Michigan. His lawyers began by poring through the thousands of pages that school and CIR lawyers had already shared with one another. A team of nineteen researchers then began culling through decades-old university records, retrieving archived *Michigan Daily* articles, internal memoranda, and state government reports.

Kolbo used the delay created by his new opponents to renew his efforts to get more particulars from the university about its admissions decisions. When Krislov's office balked on student privacy grounds, Kolbo sought court intervention and eventually won the right to see a sampling of the application files from enrolled students. In a similar vein, Shaw's Detroit colleague Godfrey Dillard obtained a list of names and phone numbers of minority students so that an expert witness could gather data on their attitudes and experience.

With the lawyers spending much of their time behind the scenes, student activists turned their attentions elsewhere. BAMN members spearheaded a protest over what they said were racist security policies at the student union, then demonstrated when a CIR lawyer came to Ann Arbor for a symposium on gender and college sports. Students occupied the offices of a prestigious campus club to protest the organization's use of Native American traditions and relics. Bollinger, for his part, had to fend off criticism from the right over a course titled "How to Be Gay: Male Homosexuality and Initiation."

The postponement gave Judge Duggan time to enjoy a family accomplishment: his son's successful foray into elective politics. Leveraging a large campaign war chest and the backing of Wayne County Executive Ed McNamara, Mike Duggan captured the race for Wayne County prosecutor.

Massie had some outside business of her own, stemming from the anti-KKK protest in Ann Arbor in 1998. A judge had dismissed the misdemeanor charges against Driver and Massie's brother Luke, but Massie represented two other protestors who were going on trial. The first defendant, Tommy Doxey, was convicted of throwing rocks at police. At a press conference after the conviction, Massie called the undercover police officer who testified against Doxey "a highly trained liar." The second defendant, Robin Alvarez, was acquitted of inciting a riot.

Meanwhile, Massie's law firm was finding itself in financial straits, in large part because she was spending most of her time working pro bono for the student-intervenors. By the second half of 1999, the firm of Scheff and Washington was able to provide Massie with only an occasional paycheck. She had received $34,584 in salary in 1998, but for all of 1999 she earned just $21,771, and the first part of 2000 was proving little better. Before long, Massie discovered she wasn't able to pay all her bills. For the first time in her life, she started deciding which payment demands took priority and which she would have to ignore. (She learned that the phone company was far quicker to cut off service than the electric company.) She asked her parents for help and began relying on friends to pay for meals and plane tickets.[5]

———•———

IN AUGUST, on the twenty-first floor of a downtown Detroit skyscraper, Massie shepherded a nervous Agnes Aleobua through her deposition. Massie had listed Aleobua along with a handful of other students as potential witnesses in any trial. Kolbo and his team were skeptical the witnesses would say much of relevance to the legal issues in the case, but the lawyers felt duty-bound to interview each one to make sure. Kerry Morgan, a local attorney working with Kolbo, handled Aleobua's deposition. Responding to Morgan's questions, Aleobua described her on-the-spot admission to Michigan and her work for BAMN.

Morgan asked Aleobua whether she had encountered racism from professors in the classroom at Michigan. Aleobua's answer showed the depth of the gulf separating the various sides in the case. She couldn't point to any overt act of racism. But she described an encounter with a professor who had given her a C-minus on a paper on the history of Detroit, the lowest grade in the class. Aleobua talked to the teacher and got the grade raised to a B-plus. While others might have seen the encounter in a positive light, Agnes saw it as proof that the original grade was racially biased. "The original C-minus was not based on the merit of the paper, but on race and on political differences that the teacher had."

Later, Aleobua said she felt the school's financial aid office treated white and black students differently. Financial aid officers were rude and impatient, she said. "And if you're a black student that is depending on financial aid to go to college, and you're faced with an impatient person who is supposed to be helping you, it is a very, like, demoralizing situation," she said. But when Morgan pressed her, she acknowledged that she remembered talking to a white student who had also complained about the rudeness of the financial aid office.[6]

—•—

IN THE BACK SEAT of the Lincoln Town Car, Marvin Krislov looked down at his watch. He couldn't believe it: they were going to be late. Next to him, Lee Bollinger peered out the window at the sprawling, six-towered Renaissance Center in downtown Detroit and tried to ascertain which entrance would get them to the office of Harry Pearce, General Motors Corp.'s vice chairman.

Krislov had worked hard to set up the meeting, leveraging a contact in the GM general counsel's office. He had reason to hope that Pearce would be sympathetic to the university's cause. A lawyer by training, Pearce had started a program at the American Bar Association to help give minority attorneys access to major clients. He believed that African Americans in particular had suffered enormous injustices over the years and that affirmative action was needed to help level the playing field. And as the second-ranking executive at the world's largest automaker, Pearce was one of the most influential businessmen in the country. Still, Krislov wasn't sure whether Pearce would be willing to have GM itself take a stand in the Michigan case. On the forty-five-minute drive from Ann Arbor, he apologized in advance to Bollinger. "I'm not sure what will come of it," Krislov said. Bollinger said he thought it was worth a shot.

Now the two men were in danger of blowing the whole meeting. The driver pulled into what appeared to be a parking garage, only to discover it was a dead end. The car had to back out. Bollinger called one of his assistants to ask whether she knew how to get to Pearce's office. She didn't.

Bollinger and Krislov climbed out of the car and tried their luck on foot. They discovered that the inside of the massive building, with its array of walkways and elevators, was no easier to navigate than the outside. The two men asked several people for directions before someone finally offered to escort them to Pearce's office. They arrived fifteen minutes late, apologizing and hoping their gaffe wouldn't prove fatal.

Pearce was waiting for them with the company's general counsel, Tom Gottschalk, and chief diversity officer, Rod Gillum. Bollinger detailed the school's admissions processes and explained his concern that minority enrollment would plummet in the absence of affirmative action. He said a public show of support from GM would go a long way toward helping the university's cause.

Bollinger was a polished salesman, and Pearce didn't need much convincing in any event. In Pearce's view, affirmative action was not only morally right, it made good business sense. GM had a diverse customer base, and it needed a diverse group of corporate leaders to ensure it understood what those customers wanted. The company counted on Michigan and other universities to produce a pool of top-quality minority job prospects. "We absolutely support you," Pearce told Bollinger.

Bollinger decided to ask for the ultimate show of support: would GM file an amicus brief on Michigan's side? Pearce indicated the company would be willing. And for good measure, Pearce added, GM would try to persuade other companies to join the cause.

Bollinger and Krislov walked out of Pearce's office overjoyed. Almost three years after the first suit was filed, a major company finally was going to take a public stand backing the university. And it wasn't just any company. It was the single most influential business in Michigan and maybe even the country.[7]

—■—

ACROSS THE STATE, one of Bollinger's corporate connections was starting to pay dividends as well. Jim Hackett, chief executive officer of office-furniture manufacturer Steelcase Inc., was a 1977 UM graduate and a supporter of affirmative action. Bollinger had been talking to him about the case since 1997, when he visited Hackett in his Grand Rapids office to discuss a variety of business issues. Hackett had taken part in the conference call with other CEOs and university presidents before the suit was filed. He had asked the company's top legal officer, Jon Botsford, to look into the legal issues. Now Steelcase was finally ready to put its name on a brief supporting Michigan.

Botsford contacted Randy Mehrberg, a lawyer at Chicago's Jenner and Block who studied under Bollinger at Michigan Law School. Botsford asked whether Jenner and Block would handle the work on a pro bono basis. Mehrberg agreed and suggested they might try to expand the effort. "I know a lot of other like-minded companies," he said.

Momentum was on Michigan's side now, and General Motors's announcement in July that it was filing an amicus brief only fueled the enthusiasm. Mehrberg quickly enlisted another of his clients, 3M Co., whose top lawyer, John Ursu, had a network of contacts among corporate lawyers from his days as president of the Association of General Counsels. Ursu hit the phones and reported that he had several other interested corporations. Mehrberg added Jenner and Block clients Bank One Corp., Kellogg Co., and Sara Lee Corp., as well as Abbott Laboratories, where Mehrberg knew the general counsel. Michigan Deputy General Counsel Liz Barry helped persuade KPMG International to sign on. Procter & Gamble Co., whose board of directors included GM Chairman Jack Smith, joined as well. Companies that hadn't been approached began contacting Mehrberg on their own. Finally, an hour before Mehrberg's brief was to be filed, Microsoft Corp. agreed to join, becoming the twentieth Fortune 500 company in the group.

GM opted to file separately from the other companies. In a brief filed July 17, 2000, the automaker stopped short of arguing for the specifics of Michigan's policies—GM left that to the school. But GM presented a powerful argument that affirmative action programs at universities were vitally important for American businesses.

GM argued that, in an increasingly multicultural nation and a global marketplace, companies need workers with "cross-cultural competencies"—that is, the "abilities to work creatively with persons of any race, ethnicity, or culture and to understand views influenced by those traits." Corporate leaders with those skills will do a better job selling products to a diversified population, getting along with others in the workplace, and developing relationships with global business partners, GM said. And businesses need people to enter the workforce with those skills, the brief added. Playing catch-up would be not only expensive, but less effective. "Only schools, not businesses, offer a forum for cross-cultural contact among a society of equals, free of hierarchy."

A second benefit for businesses was that university affirmative action produced well-educated minorities for the workforce, GM said. A reduction in diversity on campus would lead to a reduction of diversity in corporate management. "An increase in stratification, which a reduction in the number of minorities graduating from top institutions will cause, may foment racial divisiveness."

Mehrberg, knowing that he needed to please twenty clients, put together a somewhat less detailed brief for what came to be known as the Fortune 500 group. The document read as much like a state-ment of interest as a legal argument. Seven companies attached to the brief descriptions of their own affirmative action efforts, which in several cases were intertwined with those at UM. 3M described a scholarship program it funded at Michigan and eight other universi-ties for promising minority engineering students. The manufacturing company also said it had a team of recruiters that specifically targeted minorities at Michigan and a handful of other schools for internship and employment opportunities. Steelcase explained that minorities made up 37 percent of its Cooperative Education Program, which gave engineering students at Michigan and other schools a chance to work at the company as part of their education. Kellogg said it con-tributed to a Michigan program that provided graduate fellowships for talented minorities.

All told, the briefs sent a clear message: the interests of corpora-tions were at stake in the case as well.[8]

———•———

MEANWHILE, BOLLINGER, almost by accident, had discovered a new front in his coalition-building efforts. While vacationing in Nantucket over the summer, he dined with journalist-author-historian David Halberstam, and talk turned to the lawsuits. Halberstam was sympa-thetic and suggested Bollinger get in touch with Jim Cannon, whom Halberstam said had political connections and might be useful in navigating the Washington scene.

At seventy-two, the courtly Cannon was a man of many hats. He was best known as President Ford's domestic policy adviser and later as his biographer. Before joining Ford's team, Cannon had spent two decades as a journalist, including a stint as national affairs editor at *Newsweek*. He later worked as the top aide to Senate Republican leader Howard Baker. Cannon also served as chairman of the U.S. Naval Academy's Board of Visitors, a civilian panel charged with over-seeing the institution and making recommendations to the president of the United States.

A few months after dining with Halberstam, Bollinger sat down for lunch with Cannon in the UM President's House, a stately white stucco-over-brick building and the oldest structure on the Ann Arbor campus. Bollinger laid out the issues in the lawsuits. Cannon quickly realized that he didn't have the type of political connections that could help Bollinger. But halfway through his host's presentation, Cannon was struck with a chilling thought: if a court were to bar the use of race in admissions, it would be devastating to the Naval Academy.

The academy, Cannon knew, would do almost anything to enroll qualified minority students. The school produced a thousand Navy and Marine officers a year, and administrators felt it was their duty to ensure that the group was racially diverse. Midshipmen, the thinking went, should leave the academy knowing how to relate to people from different backgrounds. And academy officials believed an integrated officer corps helped ensure morale and discipline among enlisted men and women.

Toward that end, the school went to great lengths to recruit able minority students. The academy relied heavily on a Navy preparatory school that gave potential midshipmen—mainly minorities and enlisted sailors of all races—an extra year of work to meet the academy's admissions standards. Cannon himself had once implored U.S. Representative Charles Rangel, a black Democrat representing Harlem, to help find African American students to enroll at the prep school. As he listened to Bollinger, Cannon thought to himself, "We're more guilty than they are." He described his concerns to Bollinger, explaining the consequences he foresaw for the Naval Academy.

Bollinger listened with rapt attention. For all the thought he had given to the issue of affirmative action, the military connection hadn't occurred to him. He had been focusing his attentions on building support among educational, corporate, and political leaders. Now that he heard Cannon describe the importance of racial diversity at the Naval Academy (and presumably the other military academies), it all seemed so obvious—and so powerful. Diversity wasn't just a matter of academic excellence or corporate success. It was, Bollinger now thought, a matter of national security. The parallel between Michigan and the Naval Academy wasn't perfect; a court conceivably could conclude that the national security justification made affirmative action legal at military academies but not at civilian institutions. But the importance of racial diversity at the military academies at the very least made it harder for opponents to contend that diversity wasn't a valid consideration under any circumstances. The argument would be especially potent if somehow Michigan could persuade the military itself to make it.

Bollinger thought the whole idea had the potential to transform the intellectual landscape of the fight. After the lunch, he filled in Krislov and asked him to start looking into the way the military academies used race in admissions.[9]

Chapter Nine

Duggan's Distinction

S HAW HAD A TOUGH TASK. To win his case, he needed to show that affirmative action at Michigan was warranted as a remedy for past racial discrimination against minorities. Under Supreme Court precedent, that discrimination had to have been perpetrated by the university itself, not by society as a whole. So it made no difference whether racism was the explanation for the segregated housing in the state or the disparity in quality among its high schools. Nor did it matter whether store security guards shot mistrustful looks at young blacks when they shopped or whether police were quicker to pull over minority drivers on the highway than whites. Shaw could win his case only by proving that the university, a self-styled leader in the integration and education of racial minorities, had actually done more to harm blacks and Hispanics than to help them.

As he laid out in his brief to Duggan, Shaw had some evidence that the university had engaged in, or at least permitted, discrimination against minorities. In the 1950s, Shaw wrote, Michigan President Harlan Hatcher rejected a student proposal to eliminate discriminatory clauses in the bylaws of campus fraternities and sororities. Until the 1960s, Shaw added, Michigan's on-campus residences were racially segregated, with students having the right to refuse to live with a student of another color.

Even after affirmative action began in the mid-1960s, bigotry permeated the campus, Shaw said. A 1980 study by university sociol-

143

ogy professor Walter Allen found that 85 percent of black students surveyed reported having encountered racial prejudice while at the school. Shaw went on to describe the racist "porch monkey" flyers and jokes that roiled the campus around the time Bollinger took over as law school dean in 1987. The brief described how a black student awoke one morning to find a note on her dorm room door with the words "two stupid bitches" and "niggar" [*sic*] along with two swastika symbols.

But Shaw still faced some daunting obstacles to his case. His most egregious examples of university-sanctioned discrimination, such as the segregated housing, were almost half a century old. In the interim, of course, Michigan had been actively recruiting minority students and giving them preferences in the admissions process. Whatever harm Michigan had done through its pre-1960s policies, Shaw was hard-pressed to argue that the school hadn't made amends by now. And the more recent incidents tended to be student-perpetrated. At most, the university could be criticized for not responding adequately. A final problem was that the university contended it was using affirmative action for diversity purposes, not remedial ones. Legally, it wasn't clear that Shaw could defend race-based admissions using a justification that the school itself had disclaimed.

Shaw argued in his brief that Michigan was complicit in creating a negative atmosphere for blacks, Latinos, and Native Americans. "The University's toleration of a hostile climate is itself a continuing effect of the University's long-standing discrimination against minorities on campus," he wrote. And even if the school "did not itself *cause* the hostile climate that is so detrimental to minority students, it still retains the power to take race-conscious steps to address it." He added that affirmative action leveled the playing field in the Michigan admissions office, counteracting other factors, such as alumni connections and high school curriculum, that tended to favor white applicants.

Shaw was well aware of the limitations of his case. He recognized that his evidence would have been inadequate had he sued the university for discriminating against minorities. But he thought it was enough to justify affirmative action for remedial purposes. In any event, Shaw felt his case provided crucial context. He wanted Duggan to know that discrimination against minorities was still a serious problem, even at Michigan.

—■—

THE FIRST BIG SHOWDOWN finally arrived on November 16, 2000, the date for Duggan's hearing on the pending summary judgment motions in the undergraduate case. Aleobua and her BAMN friends were expecting the worst. Michigan students had failed to persuade Duggan to hold the proceedings in Ann Arbor, as Friedman had done for a hearing in the law school case earlier in the year. The students were also angry that Duggan had tentatively scheduled trial to start in early December, coinciding with final exams. Fifty students and other activists decided to show their displeasure with Duggan, along with their belief in affirmative action. With signs and bullhorns, they rallied outside the Theodore Levin U.S. Courthouse, a fortress-like concrete structure that sat on the edge of downtown Detroit, next to an abandoned office building that once housed the *Detroit Free Press*.

Eight stories above, John Payton, Kirk Kolbo, and Ted Shaw arranged their respective notes in an elegant courtroom that was almost out of place amid the decrepit conditions outside. Three large windows, stretching almost to the thirty-foot-high ceiling, flooded the carpet with light, while three portraits of long-retired judges peered down at the assembling crowd. At 9:48, Duggan strode in and took his seat on the elevated bench, looking out onto the packed courtroom.

Kolbo was the first to argue. His goals for the hearing were modest. He felt he had made CIR's case as well as he could in his briefs. Now he just wanted to make sure Duggan didn't get so lost in the details of the byzantine admissions system that he missed the big picture. "The University of Michigan effectively operates a dual admission system based on race," Kolbo told the judge. "There is one high standard that applies to most applicants to the college.... And then there is a second different and lower standard that the university, through its admissions policies, has applied to a few select racial groups."

The few questions Duggan asked during Kolbo's presentation were polite and did little to indicate which way the judge might be leaning. Duggan pressed Kolbo to explain a passage in Powell's opinion from *Bakke* that indicated the justice thought race could be a factor in admissions. "I think," Kolbo responded, "it's quite easy to see what's not permitted under Justice Powell's opinion, a dual system like the University of Michigan operates. I think it gets a little bit tougher sometimes to understand exactly what Justice Powell *would* permit."

Kolbo pointed to a quote from the Supreme Court's *Croson* decision, the case John Payton had argued and lost. The high court spoke of a "dream of a nation of equal citizens in a society where race is irrelevant to personal opportunity and achievement." Kolbo closed by laying out what he saw as the stakes in the case:

> It seems to me, Your Honor, that there shouldn't be any mistaking the fact that when we let our government or our great universities treat people differently because of their race or skin color, what they do is they diminish this great creed. And ultimately, it seems to me, Your Honor, they risk losing it altogether, either through the course of time and complacency [or] habit of mind, replaced with a completely different proposition that all men are members of a racial group and to each according to his race.

—■—

PAYTON LISTENED CLOSELY to Kolbo. The two men had developed a professional respect for one another, having managed to litigate the case for three years with a minimal amount of friction. But Payton couldn't have disagreed more with Kolbo's comments about the relevance of race. Kolbo was saying that race shouldn't—and didn't—matter.

To Payton, a black man and a veteran civil rights litigator, the idea of a color-blind nation remained an aspiration. The present, unfortunate reality, he said when it was his turn to argue, was that race still mattered in America:

> In too many aspects of our lives, African Americans, Hispanic Americans, Native Americans are treated very differently by everybody else. And it doesn't matter what they are doing. It doesn't matter what their viewpoints are. They are treated alike because of their race or their ethnicity. And prejudice is often the reason for that. And, of course, prejudice often thrives on ignorance.

Duggan was deferential, as he had been with Kolbo, and the judge let Payton make his argument with few interruptions. Near the end of Payton's time, Duggan suggested he empathized with Jennifer Gratz and Patrick Hamacher. "How," Duggan asked, "do you deal with the fact that in achieving that admirable goal of diversity, you are, in fact, infringing on some individuals' rights to be treated the same?"

Payton acknowledged affirmative action might have "some impact on some small number of white students who may get in if there were a completely different system." But, he added, "that's the question that was decided by *Bakke.*"

———•———

ALONE AMONG THE three lawyers, Shaw wanted Duggan to hold a trial, covering both the history of racial discrimination against minorities and the value of diversity. When Shaw rose to make his case, Duggan said he was open to the idea of a trial on the first issue. But the judge bristled at the notion that he needed to hear testimony to decide whether diversity warranted the use of race in admissions.

"What's the factual issue?" Duggan demanded. "I've got all the record. Why can't I make the judgment about whether or not the, quote, value as given in this record rises to the level of a compelling interest?"

Shaw said he might want to cross-examine Michigan's diversity experts. Duggan cut him off, pointing out that even Kolbo accepted diversity had some value. "I don't think we need to have testimony on undisputed facts," the judge said.

Shaw decided to back off and return to the core of his case. "I don't think we should lose the fact that the University of Michigan throughout its existence and today is an overwhelmingly white institution," he argued moments later. "We're talking about an institution that has only for the last thirty years been making efforts to integrate its campus to provide diversity."[1]

———•———

JENNIFER GRATZ MISSED the hearing in Detroit. She was busy unpacking in her new home, San Diego. After graduating from Dearborn in 1999, she had taken a job with a suburban Detroit company that supplied software to credit unions. Her job was to go on site and help the credit union set up and use the software. The job meant a lot of travel, mostly to San Francisco, but she'd had no intention of leaving Michigan permanently until she fell in love with a San Diego man she met online. Now she was resettling in California, two thousand miles away from her family—and her lawsuit.[2]

———•———

THREE WEEKS AFTER the hearing before Duggan, the Ninth Circuit ruled on a legal question in the University of Washington Law School fight being pressed by CIR. The case was a procedural oddity because the university had stopped considering race after a 1998 state ballot initiative banned the practice. From the standpoint of the university's admissions policies, therefore, the legal fight had little if any practical significance. The lawsuit nonetheless was moving forward to determine whether the three white students, all rejected before passage of the measure, were entitled to any damages.

A unanimous three-judge panel of the Ninth Circuit said Powell's opinion in *Bakke* remained the controlling law.[3] "We, therefore, leave it to the Supreme Court to declare that the *Bakke* rationale regarding university admissions policies has become moribund, if it has," the court concluded. The court didn't resolve whether the law school's admissions policies fit within the framework laid out by Powell. But the panel made clear that at least some affirmative action was legal, explicitly disagreeing with the Fifth Circuit's reasoning in *Hopwood*.

Two appeals courts had now weighed in. The score was tied, and the need for Supreme Court intervention was growing.

———•———

ACROSS THE COUNTRY, the Supreme Court was wrestling with another equal protection case, one with the potential to profoundly affect the Michigan litigation.

The case was *Bush v. Gore*. Republican George W. Bush was trying to stop Florida ballot recounts that had the potential to swing the 2000 presidential election to Democrat Al Gore. One of the arguments Bush's legal team made was that the equal protection clause barred the use of different standards around the state for assessing what constituted a vote. Leading Bush's legal team at the Supreme Court was Ted Olson, the lawyer who had argued the University of Texas case for CIR.

The importance of *Bush v. Gore* to the Michigan litigants went well beyond the legal reasoning. During the campaign, Bush had strongly suggested his opposition to race-conscious admissions, notwithstanding a face-to-face lobbying effort by Bollinger. The Texas governor denounced quotas, saying during a debate that they "tend to pit one group of people against another." Bush backed what he called "affirmative access," including a Texas measure he had signed into law in the aftermath of the *Hopwood* decision. The new system guaranteed admission to any public university in the state for all Texas high school students graduating in the top 10 percent of their class. Vice President Gore, by contrast, was a staunch supporter of race-based admissions. "I don't know what 'affirmative access' means," Gore said during that same debate. "I do know what affirmative action means. I know the governor's against it and I know that I'm for it."

The next president could influence the Michigan cases in two ways. First, the new administration might weigh in publicly, seeking to sway the courts and the public. Speculation that Ted Olson would become Bush's solicitor general, the administration's top lawyer at the Supreme Court, only heightened the apparent stakes in that regard. Second, with three justices now over the age of seventy, the new president might have a chance to make new appointments to the Supreme Court. Both sides knew that a single vote at the high court could change the outcome of the case.

At 10 p.m. on December 12, staffers from the court's public information office handed out the first copy of the decision to journalists who had lined up in a marble hallway on the ground floor of the building. The jumble of opinions was a mess, much to the embarrassment of the correspondents who sought to make instant sense out of it on national television. As the night wore on, the answer became clear: the court had ruled five-to-four to bar any additional recounts, sealing George W. Bush's election as the forty-third president.[4]

—■—

DUGGAN HAD PROMISED a quick ruling when the hearing ended, and he delivered. Less than a month after listening to arguments, he issued his decision: Michigan's undergraduate admissions policy was constitutional.[5]

Duggan based his fifty-page opinion on Payton's diversity defense, saying he would decide in a second ruling whether Shaw's remedial justification provided an additional legal basis for affirmative action. The decision wasn't the complete victory that Payton had sought, but it was close. Duggan concluded that classroom diversity was a compelling government interest—a valid goal that would warrant the use of race in the proper circumstances.

His reasoning differed somewhat from that used by the Ninth Circuit a week earlier in the University of Washington case. Unlike the Ninth Circuit, Duggan said he wasn't sure that Powell's opinion represented the holding of the *Bakke* court. But Duggan reached the same result, using the path Payton provided. The judge said he was persuaded by social science evidence indicating that racial diversity indeed was an extraordinarily important ingredient on college campuses. The judge pointed to psychologist Patricia Gurin's conclusion that students "learn better in a diverse educational environment" and "are better prepared to become active participants in our pluralistic, democratic society once they leave such a setting." Duggan also was impressed by the importance that outsiders had ascribed to university diversity. The judge pointed approvingly to friend-of-the-court briefs filed by the Association of American Law Schools, the American Council on Education, the Clinton administration, General Motors, Steelcase, and other Michigan supporters.

Kolbo had opted not to challenge Michigan's social science evidence directly, leaving that task to an amicus brief by the National Association of Scholars, which disputed Gurin's methodology and findings. Kolbo also didn't put on his own case questioning the importance of a multicultural campus. As a group, the CIR lawyers thought diversity might well have some value in higher education— just not enough to warrant what they saw as race discrimination. In oral arguments, Kolbo had acknowledged that diversity was "good, valuable, and important." The problem, he argued, was that diversity was too amorphous and ill-defined to serve as a compelling interest. Kolbo also contended that diversity had no built-in time limit. Unlike remedial affirmative action programs, diversity-based ones weren't designed to end once they had compensated for past discrimination, he said.

Duggan wasn't buying it. He said he wasn't convinced that "what may be too amorphous and ill-defined in other contexts, i.e., the construction industry context, is also necessarily too amorphous or ill-defined in the context of higher education." Nor was Duggan especially bothered by the lack of a time limit on diversity programs. "[T]he permanency of such an interest does not remove it from the realm of 'compelling interests,' but rather, only emphasizes the importance of ensuring that any race-conscious admissions policy that is justified as a means to achieve diversity is narrowly tailored to such an interest."

On the question of narrow tailoring—that is, whether the school's admissions policies used race only as much as necessary—Duggan reached a curious conclusion. Both sides had told him that there was no material difference between the grids that were used for the pre-1998 entering classes and the point system that was used subsequently. The changes were "mechanical, rather than substantive," Payton said in a brief. Duggan saw it differently. The current policy, he noted, was constitutional, using race "as nothing more than the 'plus' spoken of with approval by Justice Powell in *Bakke.*" But the earlier admissions systems "cross that thin line from the permissible to the impermissible," he said.

The difference for Duggan lay in the mechanics that Payton and Kolbo both said weren't legally relevant. Duggan faulted the school for its prior practice of "protecting" seats for minority applicants. That practice, the judge said, made Michigan's admissions policies indistinguishable from the quota struck down in *Bakke.* "The fact that non-minority applicants may have had a chance at any 'leftover' spots at the end of the admissions cycle does not change this conclusion," Duggan wrote. "Under both systems, preferred minority applicants were insulated from competition from non-preferred applicants for a given number of seats." Duggan also blanched at the appearance the old system created and the "facially different grids and action codes based solely upon an applicant's race." As he understood the old system, white students could be automatically excluded from consideration without review by a counselor (even though, in practice, they rarely were), while black applicants were guaranteed individualized review. The effect "was to systematically exclude a certain group of non-minority applicants from participating in the admissions process based solely on account of their race," Duggan wrote.

While the prospect of applicants of different races being evaluated through different systems troubled Duggan, the notion that they were judged unevenly within the same system did not. In upholding the point system, Duggan dismissed Kolbo's contention that the rules created a double standard. Whenever a college uses a point system for admissions, "any factor that may result in points being added to an applicant's total score will necessarily have the effect of lowering that applicant's admission threshold," Duggan wrote. Ultimately, Duggan said, Gratz and her lawyers were really complaining that twenty points was too much for minority status, compared with the points allotted for other factors. "[A]s Justice Powell recognized in *Bakke*, universities may accord an applicant's race some weight in the admissions process and, in doing so, universities are not required to accord the same weight to race as they do other factors," Duggan wrote.

Despite Duggan's conclusion that the grids were unconstitutional, his opinion marked a victory for the university, ensuring that it could continue to use race in undergraduate admissions. Bollinger called the decision "an unequivocal ruling in our favor." He was so enthused that he told a reporter the university wouldn't even bother appealing the part of the ruling that went against it.

Gratz could take solace that Duggan had declared as unconstitutional the grid system that had excluded her. The ruling also meant she could seek damages, potentially by arguing that a degree from Ann Arbor would have improved her career prospects. "It's nice that Michigan has to admit that their policies were unconstitutional and that I was treated unfairly," she told the *Detroit News*. But, like her lawyers, Gratz was puzzled at the distinction Duggan had made between the old and new policies. She didn't understand how Duggan could ascribe meaning to a change the university itself acknowledged was purely cosmetic.

———■———

THE MICHIGAN TEAM didn't have much time to celebrate. Barely a week after Duggan's ruling, the lawyers were back in court, this time six floors below, in front of Friedman in the law school case.

Friedman originally hadn't planned on having a summary judgment argument session. He had been inundated with so many stacks of paper that he thought oral arguments would be superfluous. But after reading Duggan's ruling, Friedman realized he wanted a chance for some give-and-take with the lawyers.

The hearing, two days before Christmas, coincided with the arrival of an Arctic air mass and sub-zero temperatures. With the wind chill dropping as low as 40 below, Agnes Aleobua and thirty other BAMN activists decided to forgo their planned outdoor demonstration in favor of the relative warmth of the cherry-stained pews in the back of Friedman's courtroom. From there, they watched three and a half hours of polite but pointed debate.

Friedman had only a handful of queries for Kolbo. Early on, the judge sought to clarify Kolbo's position on the LSATs. Are they, the judge asked, a good predictor of law school success? Do they contain some cultural bias?

Kolbo wasn't taking any position on that issue. "It's not for us to tell the law school to use the LSAT or how much to use it," he said. But "as they have chosen to use the LSAT in their admissions process, then it is important and is critical that they do so without treating people differently on the basis of race."

From there, Friedman let Kolbo make his case. The lawyer argued that a trial wasn't necessary, echoing the contentions he had made a month earlier in front of Duggan. Diversity "may be a very fine goal, but it's so broad, so undefined, so amorphous that it simply cannot comport as a matter of law with a conclusion that it could ever be a compelling governmental interest," Kolbo said.

Even if Friedman disagreed on that point, Kolbo went on, the law school policy was unconstitutional because Powell's reasoning barred more than just fixed, rigid quotas. "Systematic and substantial double standards in the admissions process based on race can be just as effective and just as systematic a means of exclusion as the operation of a formal quota," Kolbo said. The lawyer added that, in the event of a trial, he was prepared to offer evidence debunking the university's social science case.

Payton had a tougher time when he stood up to make his argument. Friedman by nature wasn't an especially active questioner, but now, from the first moment, Payton found assertion after assertion courteously questioned by the judge. When Payton invoked Powell's opinion, Friedman asked where Powell got the legal support for his diversity rationale. When Payton suggested that virtually all law schools use race as a criterion, Friedman said he doubted that was the case at the Detroit College of Law, the school that had welcomed him despite his lack of a bachelor's degree or LSAT score.

Many of Friedman's queries followed a theme. Early on, he asked Payton whether the law school needed to use race to attain its goal of diversity. "Why can't they do it, for instance, by having a larger pool from which to select so that there's a better chance of getting a diverse student body?"

Payton had a ready response. Michigan, he said, is one of the best, most selective law schools in the country. "If you expand the pool by changing how selective you are, you change who you are as an institution."

Friedman wasn't satisfied. "But if diversity is so important, then maybe there's got to be a quid pro quo."

Payton had both a factual response and a legal one. Factually, he said, it's not clear that an expanded pool would have a significantly higher percentage of underrepresented minorities. And, legally, "I don't think that the Constitution says that we have to change from being the selective institution that we are."

If Payton thought he had satisfied Friedman, he learned otherwise a few minutes later, during Massie's presentation. First Friedman interjected when Massie used the word "elite" to describe top law schools. Massie saw the word as interchangeable with "selective," but Friedman didn't agree. "It's not the semantics, but when you talk about a public university being elite, there's just something—" he said, without ever finishing the thought.

Then Friedman asked Massie a question almost identical to the series he had posed to Payton. "You can't reach the same result without considering race?" And later, Friedman spelled out his thinking even more: "Don't they have some burden to devise a system that would be race neutral and that would also accomplish their goal of diversity? It may affect their selectivity. There's no question about that. It has to. If it didn't, then we wouldn't all be standing around here arguing."

As the lawyers were well aware, questions from judges can be deceiving. But Friedman's repeated return to the same topic suggested he was raising an issue that he saw as fundamental. He all but said he wouldn't mind if the University of Michigan lowered its admissions standards. And he said that might be the price the school had to pay if it really wanted a racially diverse body. Payton hadn't budged Friedman by suggesting that a less selective system might not produce a racially diverse class. The judge from the Detroit College of Law seemed to see little value in elitism at the University of Michigan.

Friedman harbored plenty of questions about Massie's arguments as well. He seemed incredulous when she said a black undergraduate student at Michigan, Erika Dowdell, would have trouble gaining admission to its law school.

The problem, Massie argued, was that racial bias pervaded the Ann Arbor campus to such an extent that it artificially depressed the grades of black, Latino, and Native American undergraduates. She told the judge she wanted a trial to lay out her evidence of racial discrimination and to show why affirmative action was necessary, even at the graduate level, to create a level playing field. When she finished her remarks, the students in the audience applauded.

———•———

FRIEDMAN TOOK A half-hour break to talk the case over with his clerks. He returned with some news: he wanted to hold a trial.

Some questions, such as whether diversity was a compelling interest, were matters of law, the judge said. He didn't need to hear from Pat Gurin in person to decide that question.

But the judge thought live testimony from witnesses would be useful on three other matters. To what extent did the law school actually use race in making admissions decisions? Was there a double standard in admissions, as Kolbo claimed? And was affirmative action necessary to "level the playing field," as Massie argued?

On one level, Friedman's decision to have a trial boded well for the university's policy. The first two issues he raised went to the issue of narrow tailoring; that is, they would matter only if the judge were to conclude that diversity was a legitimate interest that would warrant at least some use of race by the university. And a decision to hear evidence on the third issue was a victory for Massie, suggesting that the judge was taking her case seriously enough to warrant close scrutiny.

But Massie, for one, had seen enough of Friedman to be concerned. She left the courtroom with a bad feeling about which way the judge was leaning.

C h a p t e r 10 *T e n*

Preferences on Trial

F OR FIFTEEN DAYS in January and February, the lawyers—joined
by Aleobua and dozens of other students—made Friedman's
second-floor courtroom their new home. The room had a formal feel
with lush blue carpeting, polished wood benches, and twenty-foot
ceilings. Friedman had managed to make the room a little less impos-
ing by adding a few personal touches, including a model antique car
and a stuffed bald eagle, which the U.S. Fish and Wildlife Service
gave him after the endangered bird had been shot by a poacher. The
judge adorned his black robe with an ice cream cone pin his daughter
had given him.

To Kolbo and his colleagues, the case was so straightforward that it
required only three witnesses, none of them Barbara Grutter. At this
stage, Friedman was considering only the liability of the university,
not damages, and the CIR lawyers reasoned that Grutter's testimony
wouldn't be relevant.

Kolbo's first witness was Allan Stillwagon, the former Michigan
Law School admissions director pushed out by Bollinger in 1990
after he became dean. Stillwagon testified that when he was running
the admissions office, the faculty had set a goal of 10 to 12 percent
minority enrollment. That was important for Kolbo's contention that
the admissions policy operated as a quota. If Kolbo could show that
the current policy was just an extension of the Stillwagon-era system,
he could make the point that "critical mass" was simply a euphemism

for 10 to 12 percent. Stillwagon's testimony was followed by that of the current admissions director, Erica Munzel, who confirmed that the admissions office considered the race of applicants as part of a comprehensive review of their file.

The star witness for Kolbo's side was Kinley Larntz, a University of Minnesota statistician. In more than a day of math-heavy testimony, Larntz described how he calculated the "odds ratio" for applicants of various races—that is, their odds of being admitted to Michigan Law School relative to white applicants with similar grades and test scores. He told Friedman that the odds ratios for blacks, Mexican Americans, Puerto Ricans, and Native Americans were "enormous," among the largest he'd ever seen in his statistical research. Year in, year out, the conclusion was the same, Larntz said: minority applicants had a huge advantage over nonminorities.

Larntz had also put together a series of grids showing the number of applications and offers of admission for various grade and test score combinations, broken down by race. Kolbo elicited some more glaring examples from the grids to drive home his point. In 1995, two of the three black applicants with an LSAT score of 161–163 and a GPA of 2.5–2.74 were admitted; none of the seven white applicants with those numbers got an offer. For applicants with those scores and grades of 3.75 or higher, all three blacks were admitted, while only eight of ninety-three whites were.

Payton and his team began their presentation with Bollinger. As the president of the university, Bollinger wasn't going to provide much detail about the admissions process. But his testimony had symbolic value, showing that the man in charge believed in the school's affirmative action policies and could explain why he thought they were important.

Guided by Payton's questioning, Bollinger said a liberal education demanded exposure to people with different life experiences and backgrounds, Race, Bollinger said, was an indispensable part of the equation. "Given the history of this country, given the history of race relations in the United States and indeed in the world, both for good and for bad, it is simply part of life," he said.

Next up was Michigan law professor Richard Lempert, the chairman of the committee that drafted the policy. He acknowledged that his original draft referred to a numerical range of 11 to 17 percent.

Lempert said the committee never intended to set up a quota or floor. The draft simply said that in the past, the law school had seen the benefits of racial and ethnic diversity with minority enrollment at that level. Still, Lempert, Shaw, and most of the other committee members had concluded that any numbers could be misconstrued and should be removed.

Jeff Lehman, the dean of the law school, made his own case for the value of diversity on campus and also described a subtle change he had made in the admissions system. Until 1995 the law school had produced grids every year, much like those Larntz had created, showing the results of the admissions process by race. After Lehman took over, he asked that the grids be discontinued. In court, Lehman testified he feared that the grids would be misconstrued and that outsiders might think they were used to help make admissions decisions.

Kolbo's partner Larry Purdy tried hard on cross-examination to pin down the university officials to a number that was the minimum for achieving a critical mass of minority students. The witnesses stuck to their scripts, insisting that no particular number automatically constituted a critical mass. The closest Purdy came to eliciting a concession occurred in his questioning of Lehman.

"Depending on the individuals, Dean Lehman, could 5 percent underrepresented minority enrollment constitute a critical mass, in your opinion?" Purdy asked.

"It is conceivable to me but it is unlikely," Lehman responded.

The university also called its own statistician, Stephen Raudenbush, in an effort to discredit Larntz's testimony. Raudenbush argued that Larntz undermined his own results by ignoring useful data—namely, those grid cells in which either all or none of the applicants were admitted. In other words, Larntz was focusing only on those situations where race made a difference and ignoring those where it didn't.

Raudenbush said that an end to race-based admissions would decimate minority enrollment at Michigan. The current admissions policy had produced an entering law school class in 2000 that was 14.5 percent minority. Under a race-blind system, Raudenbush said, that number would have been only 4 percent.

—■—

RELATIONS BETWEEN PAYTON and Massie had grown increasingly tense behind the scenes. On day eight of the trial, the strain burst into public view.

For months, Payton had gone along as Massie piggy-backed on his work in the law school case. With his permission, she got in touch with four of his witnesses to ask whether they would help buttress the intervenors' case as well. Two of those witnesses, Lempert and Columbia University history professor Eric Foner, ultimately agreed to testify for her. But Claude Steele, a psychology professor at Stanford, wasn't interested. When the university decided a week into the trial not to call him as a witness, he decided he didn't want to testify at all.

Massie was badly disappointed. Steele had been one of the people she contacted the day after the Sixth Circuit let her into the case. Steele had studied a phenomenon known as "stereotype threat," which he said caused minorities to underperform on standardized tests. Each African American test-taker, Steele said, had to deal with the stereotype that says blacks have limited ability. A student sitting down at her exam table knew that a poor performance might reinforce the stereotype and might lead others to see her through that biased lens. As Steele wrote in a report he submitted to the court, "for those black students who care very much about performing well, this is an extra intimidation not experienced by groups not stereotyped in this way."

Massie decided she simply had to have Steele. She filed a subpoena in federal court in San Francisco, seeking a court order forcing him to testify. Payton, seeking to protect his reluctant witness, filed a motion asking Friedman to "quash," or nullify, the subpoena. Massie pleaded with Friedman to find a way to make Steele testify. The judge said that, with Steele in California and the trial already underway, the matter was out of his hands. "I have no ability to compel him to be here," the judge said.

"This is completely unfair," Massie said. "You're making it impossible for us to make our case."

"I don't think it is completely unfair," Friedman responded.

"It is."

"I think it complies with what the law is and the rules," the judge said.

CIR AND THE university together needed only five days to put on their respective cases. Massie took eight.

Early on, Friedman had indicated he wouldn't be rigid in keeping the testimony focused on the three questions he had raised before trial. Kolbo and Payton had each tried to bar several of the other's potential witnesses, arguing that they wouldn't address the questions at hand. Each time, Friedman permitted the testimony, saying he would simply ignore it if it didn't prove relevant. The design of the trial suited Friedman's personality. He liked hearing from witnesses and having a chance to ask them questions, even if their answers didn't bear directly on the issues he was considering. And in the case of Massie, Friedman already had been reversed by the Sixth Circuit for not letting the intervening students take part. Now he was going to err on the side of giving her wide latitude to make her case.

Even without Steele, Massie and her team had a lot to say. In emotional testimony, minority students described the damage inflicted by a segregated educational system. Erika Dowdell explained the decrepit conditions at Cass Tech and the insensitive remarks she had endured as a black student on the UM campus. Concepcion Escobar, a Michigan Law School student of Mexican and Apache heritage, described how her predominantly black public high school in Chicago had left her unprepared for college-level math and science classes. Chrystal James said she felt like a token as one of just two African American law students in her UCLA class in the wake of Prop 209. Tania Kappner, a California high school teacher, said her minority students had been demoralized by the abolition of affirmative action in the UC system. With a thirty-hour time limit for her case, Massie decided not to call Agnes Aleobua as a witness, concluding that her testimony would overlap with that of her Cass and Michigan classmate Dowdell.

Massie had her own expert witnesses. Three of them testified on the racial biases they found in various aspects of the LSAT. The dean of the education school at the University of California-Berkeley described the state's higher education system as becoming increasingly segregated. Hispanic and Native American educators testified about the particular obstacles faced by students of those races. Other witnesses described in detail the history of racial bias in America, the lingering effects of slavery and Jim Crow regimes, and the unhealthy academic climate on campuses that have only a handful of minorities.

———◆———

NONE OF MASSIE'S witnesses was more riveting than John Hope Franklin, a celebrated black historian who specialized in the history of U.S. race relations. For five hours the eighty-six-year-old Franklin told a transfixed audience stories from his life, at times talking ten minutes straight without interruption. He described the 1921 riot in which whites burned down the entire black section of Tulsa, Oklahoma, and then denied for seventy-five years that the incident had taken place. He detailed an incident on the night before he was to receive the Presidential Medal of Freedom in 1995. Franklin was hosting a party at a Washington club where he belonged, and he had walked into the lobby to see whether additional guests had arrived. A white woman approached him, tried to hand him a claim slip, and asked him to retrieve her coat. "She could have looked on the wall and seen my picture as the Man of the Year the previous year, but she didn't," Franklin said. "But maybe she thought that the Man of the Year was also a porter. I don't know."

Terry Pell was among the audience members who were captivated. One story in particular caught his attention. In 1939, Franklin traveled to racially segregated North Carolina to do some research at the state archives. The director of the archives set up a special room for Franklin just off the main reading room, so that he wouldn't be working alongside the white researchers. Because the pages who delivered requested materials would balk at having to serve a black man, Franklin was given a key to the stacks and told he would have to retrieve his own books. The arrangement suited Franklin fine. He happily began combing the shelves and then wheeling his book-laden dolly through the reading room and past the white patrons. After two weeks, the director said he was revoking the key. The white researchers were jealous and had begun requesting their own keys. "It was at that point that I realized the inconsistency and remarkable ingenuity, if I may put it, of racial discrimination," Franklin said.

Franklin presented the story as an example of racism against blacks, but as Pell sat in the courtroom, it struck him that he could have made an identical statement about the bias that affected Barbara Grutter, Jennifer Gratz, and Patrick Hamacher. The University of Michigan, Pell thought, was manipulating the rules no less than the North Carolina state archives did. As Pell saw it, the university's goal was racial balancing within its entering class, numbers it could cite when lobbying the state government for a budget increase. To get there, Michigan had set up two sets of rules—one for majorities and another for minorities—leaving itself enough flexibility to shift its standards if they failed to achieve the preferred balance.

Kolbo was confident that much of Massie's case would prove irrelevant. He and his team had no intention of challenging the history of racial discrimination or the pernicious effects of segregation. They simply thought those issues were legally irrelevant, given the Supreme Court's clear conclusion that societal discrimination didn't justify a race-based solution.

Kolbo also realized it would serve no purpose to attack the nervous students who had testified about their own experiences with racial bias. He and Purdy saved their attacks for the soft spots they saw in the expert testimony Massie had produced.

Purdy's cross-examination of Franklin elicited a remarkable acknowledgment from the witness.

Purdy asked: "You certainly oppose using different qualifications to permit athletes to come into a school from others that are non-athletes, correct? You oppose that?"

Franklin: "Yes."

Purdy: "You oppose using different qualifications for legacies. You don't think they should have a lower qualification to come to their school?"

Franklin: "I'll come to the end that you want me to come to, namely, that is, that I believe in using standards that are standards."

In case Friedman hadn't digested the full meaning of what the historian had said, Purdy returned to the point a moment later. "You've been clear, have you not," Purdy asked, "that you do not support the admission of less qualified minority applicants over more qualified Asian or white applicants?"

"That's right."

Purdy would later call his cross-examination the most satisfying of his career. The lawyer had done his homework and knew before asking that Franklin's support for affirmative action had its limits. Franklin advocated fair consideration for minority applicants, but he drew the line at preferential treatment. To Purdy and his partner Kolbo, that sounded a lot like their position.

———————

ON THE DAY of closing arguments before Friedman, so many students tried to attend that the judge asked the court security officers to work out an arrangement for rotating people in and out of the courtroom. He refused Massie's request to let additional spectators sit on the floor.

Kolbo and his counterpart Payton made clear that they saw little, if any, middle ground. Kolbo told the judge that Michigan used race as an enormous factor in admissions. "One can see it with the untrained eye. One can see it in the grids," he said. But he stressed that the size of the preference really wasn't crucial. It was the principle at stake. "The use of race to learn anything about someone, to learn about their qualifications is a step backward. It's … retreating away from that great American principle of equality."

For Payton, the choice was either to use race in admissions or to abandon the notion of a diverse campus. "We would not use race if we didn't have to in order to obtain the meaningful numbers of minority students that we need for our educational mission," he said. "We have to, and that fact simply cannot be avoided." Diversity was vital to the university's educational mission, he said. "'Compelling' is almost too tame a word. This is, in our judgment, an educational necessity."

Massie's argument was heavy on symbolism. She noted that in the hallway just outside the courtroom hung Norman Rockwell's famous painting of Ruby Bridges, a first-grade girl who desegregated the public schools in New Orleans in 1960. The painting shows a dignified little girl being escorted by four federal marshals past racist graffiti and a splattered tomato. "We'll move forward together, or we'll move back," Massie said. "We can make more steps toward equality and toward justice and toward democracy, or we can allow ourselves to be pushed backward, crippled, hampered, fall short of our common and individual potential."

Friedman listened intently to the lawyers, letting them make their case without interruption. As he left the bench, he told them the case was the toughest he'd ever had to consider.[1]

IN THE UNDERGRADUATE case, Shaw had low expectations for the second half of Duggan's decision. In Shaw's mind, the judge had always looked at the intervening students as something of an afterthought. In his opinion on diversity, Duggan hadn't even acknowledged the history of anti-minority discrimination at Michigan, much less relied on it.

Shaw's pessimism proved well-founded. On February 26, Duggan issued his second opinion, rejecting the idea that past discrimination against minorities provided a second justification for affirmative action. Much of Shaw's evidence, Duggan wrote, concerned practices that occurred years before the current undergraduate admissions policy was put in place. As for the more recent incidents of racism on campus, Shaw "provided no evidence that the University has been a 'passive participant,'" Duggan said. The judge added: "As the Supreme Court has acknowledged, there is no doubt that the sorry history of both private and public discrimination in this country has contributed to a lack of opportunities for African Americans. This observation, however, by itself, is not sufficient to justify race-conscious measures."

FRIEDMAN AND DUGGAN had a standing joke if the subject of the affirmative action cases came up when they saw each other around the courthouse. They would shrug their shoulders and laugh. "It doesn't matter what we do," they'd say. Their rulings would certainly be appealed, at least to the Sixth Circuit and probably to the Supreme Court.

But recognizing his role in the judicial hierarchy didn't stop Friedman from struggling over the law school case for weeks. He rolled the issues around in his head during his daily lunchtime runs, then jotted down notes upon his return to the office. He contemplated the case during the long car drives he loved to take. He debated his two law clerks, using the disagreement within his chambers to sharpen his own views.

When the trial started, Friedman had leanings on only some of the questions the case presented. For example, he wasn't sure how he would decide the fundamental question whether diversity was a compelling interest. By the time of closing arguments, he had heard enough testimony and run enough miles to be fairly certain what his conclusion would be: the law school policy was unconstitutional. Unlike Duggan, Friedman didn't believe that race could be a factor in admissions.[2]

Friedman considered his ninety-page opinion to be one of his proudest accomplishments. He rejected virtually the entirety of the university's case. Michigan Law School, Friedman wrote, "places a very heavy emphasis on an applicant's race in deciding whether to accept or reject." He said the school had a numerical target range of 10 to 17 percent minority enrollment. He accepted the conclusion of Larntz, Kolbo's expert statistician, that race was an "enormously important factor," while suggesting the testimony was almost over-kill. "One does not need to undergo sophisticated statistical analysis in order to see it; the statistical analysis simply confirms empirically what the grids suggest intuitively," Friedman wrote.

Turning to the *Bakke* decision, Friedman reached a conclusion where Duggan had equivocated. Friedman said Justice Powell spoke only for himself, not for a majority of the Court. And Friedman explicitly broke with Duggan by reading subsequent Supreme Court cases as a confirmation that Powell's diversity rationale wasn't the law.

Friedman acknowledged what Kolbo had conceded—that diversity had "important educational benefits." But to Friedman, what had value was "viewpoint diversity," not racial diversity. "While the educational benefits of the former are clear, those of the latter are less so," he wrote.

Payton had argued that viewpoint and racial diversity were, at least on college campuses, inseparable. It wasn't that Payton thought all racial minorities held the same views. To the contrary, Payton believed that a racially diverse campus could demonstrate that all minorities don't think alike. If law schools had only a token number of blacks and Hispanics, Payton contended, those students might feel they had to act as representatives of their racial group. "You need a critical mass of minority students so that individuals are free to be themselves," he said at the argument session.

Friedman, in his opinion, said the university was trying to "walk a fine line in simultaneously arguing that one's viewpoints are not determined by one's race but that certain viewpoints might not be voiced if students of particular races are not admitted in significant numbers." To Friedman, the important question was what students were hearing, not who was speaking. The judge pointed to testimony and articles from faculty members suggesting that black students rarely express ideas in class that couldn't as easily have come from a white student.

Friedman also concluded that the admissions policy wasn't "narrowly tailored" toward meeting its expressed goal of diversity. He wrote that "critical mass" was at once "ill defined" and "indistinguishable from a quota system." Unlike Duggan, he faulted the law school for putting no time limit on its use of race in admissions.

The judge questioned the school's decision to single out not just particular races, but subsets of those races, for preferential treatment. Friedman pointed to a statement that appeared for several years in the Michigan Law School Bulletin, indicating the admissions policy favored "students who are African American, Mexican American, Native American, or Puerto Rican and raised on the U.S. mainland." Why, the judge asked, would the school exclude blacks from other parts of the world, non-Mexican Hispanics, or Puerto Ricans raised on the island? "This haphazard selection of certain races is a far cry from the 'close fit' between the means and the ends that the Constitution demands in order for a racial classification to pass muster under strict scrutiny analysis," Friedman wrote.

The very nature of racial categories, the judge suggested, improperly stereotyped people. He wrote: "One cannot assume … that a particular African American applicant has been the victim of race discrimination or that a particular Mexican American applicant has grown up in an economically depressed neighborhood."

—■—

MASSIE FARED NO better, although Friedman agreed with some of the factual underpinnings of her argument. The judge acknowledged a "long and tragic history of race discrimination in this country." He said some of the "GPA gap" between minorities and whites was caused by the poverty that disproportionately afflicts blacks, Hispanics, and Native Americans. He also agreed with Massie on some of the causes for the lower LSAT scores among minorities. The judge said standardized tests are written in "academic English," creating special problems for students whose first language isn't English. And Friedman noted that minority students are less likely than their white and Asian colleagues to take LSAT preparation courses.

Friedman found other Massie contentions less plausible. He criticized a study by UCLA sociologist Walter Allen of the racial climate at four feeder schools for Michigan Law School. Friedman said the results of Allen's focus groups were skewed because supporters of affirmative action had encouraged participation by like-minded students.

The judge also said he couldn't conclude that the LSAT itself was racially biased. In a section that Massie would later find especially grating, he criticized the "sparseness of the evidence on this issue." Steele, the psychology professor whose testimony Massie had unsuccessfully sought to compel, had submitted an expert report on the subject, but Friedman said the document "describes his research only in the most general terms."

In the end, the underlying causes for low minority test scores and grades mattered little to Friedman. He said Massie's case suffered from a logical flaw. "It assumes all members of the underrepresented minority groups have suffered adversity entitling them to some degree of upward adjustment." Even more fundamentally, her case had a legal flaw, the judge added. Friedman said Massie was seeking redress for general societal discrimination, not wrongdoing specifically by the university. Massie had argued that the school, even with its affirmative action program, was still using racially biased selection criteria, but Friedman wasn't impressed. "[T]he law school may not consider the race of applicants in order to compensate for the effects of discrimination by others or by society generally," he wrote.

Friedman ended his opinion with a critique of the law school admissions system that seemed to draw from his own experiences and underscored his skepticism about "elite" schools. He expressed doubts about the usefulness of the LSAT—the test he himself never took—saying the evidence showed it was a poor predictor of law school success. "[O]ne must wonder why the law school concerns itself at all with an applicant's LSAT score," Friedman wrote. He even questioned Michigan's reliance on undergraduate grades, and he cited with skepticism the preferences given to sons and daughters of alumni. Reducing the importance of those factors, Friedman wrote, might lessen the need for explicit consideration of race. "Whatever solution the law school elects to pursue, it must be race neutral," the judge said. "The focus must be upon the merit of individual applicants, not upon assumed characteristics of racial groups."[3]

——•——

FRIEDMAN'S RULING HIT the UM Law School admissions office near the height of its application cycle, as workers were sifting through the 4,000 applications the school had received. As of March 27, the date of the judge's decision, the school had extended 826 offers and needed to extend at least 300 more to round out the 2001–2002 first-year class of 350 students. Most urgently, the admissions office estimated it needed to make another 100 offers in the next ten days to fill its summer section, which was to begin May 29.

Friedman's decision brought the process to a halt. Although his order didn't preclude the school from making offers, it said the admissions office couldn't consider race in the process. School officials didn't quite know what to make of the order. The entire admissions process was set up to include race as a factor. The application form asked students to identify their race and offered them a chance to submit an essay describing the contributions they would make to the diversity of the class. Moreover, a race-neutral system would force the school to re-determine where the cut-off line would be between admitted and rejected applicants, a distinctly nonlinear problem that would have to take into account such factors as the different "yield rates"—the percentages of accepted applicants who enroll—among various races.

Law school officials concluded the only prudent course was to stop making decisions on pending applications. Stacks of envelopes containing acceptance letters would have to stay in the office. Admissions counselors would continue to read applications and jot notes on them but could make no final decisions. The school would just have to hope that either Friedman or the Sixth Circuit issued a stay in short order.

Friedman refused. In an April 3 opinion, the judge scoffed at Payton's contention that a requirement of race neutrality would throw the admissions office into disarray and put the school at a competitive disadvantage. Speaking of the summer class, Friedman wrote: "With their extensive experience in reviewing law school applications, defendants should have no difficulty identifying 100 excellent candidates within this time frame"—now just four days—"without considering race." The law school admissions process remained frozen.[4]

Part Three

On Appeal

(April 2001–December 2002)

C h a p t e r   E l e v e n

A Court Divided

FOURTEEN YEARS AFTER a Democratic-controlled Senate rejected Ronald Reagan's Supreme Court nomination of Robert Bork, that bitter fight still cast a long shadow, one that stretched to Cincinnati, home of the Sixth U.S. Circuit Court of Appeals.

Bork was a champion of "judicial restraint," the view that the Constitution protected only those rights specifically enumerated in the document. He was an outspoken critic of such landmark decisions as *Roe v. Wade*, which guaranteed abortion rights. To Bork, the "right to privacy" that underlay *Roe* was nowhere to be found in the Constitution; it was a product of judicial activism. Alarmed liberals rallied to defeat his 1987 nomination, enraging Bork's backers, who accused opponents of distorting the nominee's record. Four years later, liberal groups tried to derail another Republican Supreme Court nominee, Clarence Thomas, who was facing allegations that he sexually harassed a woman who worked for him. The Senate voted to confirm Thomas 52-48.

By 1995, the political parties had reversed their roles. Democrat Bill Clinton was in the White House, and the Republicans, still smarting from the Bork and Thomas fights, controlled the Senate. Clinton's two Supreme Court nominees, Ruth Bader Ginsburg and Stephen Breyer, stirred little controversy. But Republicans exacted their price on the president's appeals court nominees, subjecting them to unprecedented scrutiny and, in some cases, years-long delays.

The Sixth Circuit felt the ramifications of the judicial war as much as any court in the country. When the first President Bush left office in 1992, two of his nominations to the appeals court died without ever receiving a Senate vote. Of Bill Clinton's eight judicial selections for the Sixth Circuit, the Senate confirmed only five, leaving one nominee dangling for a record four years without a hearing or vote.

At the time the Michigan cases reached the Sixth Circuit, the makeup of the court was at an ideological tipping point. Of the eleven active judges on the court, six were Democratic appointees, five Republican. Five seats were vacant, and three more vacancies were likely in the next year because a trio of judges were scheduled to take senior status. (Senior judges are semi-retired jurists who continue to serve on the three-judge panels that handle most cases but can't vote on the matters that reach the full or *en banc* court.) The eight openings would give the new President Bush a chance to move the court to the right over the next several years, assuming he could get his nominees through the Senate. More immediately, however, the impending conferral of senior status on the three judges—Alan Norris, Richard Suhrheinrich, and Eugene Siler—had the potential to tilt the en banc court in the opposite direction. All three were Republican appointees, and their departures would leave the court with a six-to-two Democratic tilt.

If the Sixth Circuit was divided ideologically, it was splintered geographically. The court had jurisdiction over four states, running from Michigan in the north through Ohio and Kentucky to Tennessee in the south. The court officially was based in Cincinnati, but only one judge made that city his home. The others were scattered in almost a dozen cities around the circuit, generally seeing one another only when a group of them gathered every few weeks to hear arguments. The lack of proximity meant the judges did much of their communication electronically, relying on faxes to one another rather than face-to-face discussions.

———•———

THE SIXTH CIRCUIT'S first action on the various appeals underscored that the court, at least for the time being, leaned to the left. Acting on a motion from the university, a unanimous three-judge panel stayed the injunction Friedman had issued, freeing the law school to resume admitting applicants and, at least for the time being, to use race in the process. The court said Friedman's injunction "disrupts the selection of the 2001–02 first-year law school class." The law school would have had to come up with a new admissions policy, a time-consuming task that would have left hundreds of applicants in limbo and prompted many of them to accept offers elsewhere, the court said. "This harm cannot be undone and therefore is irreparable."

The ruling was a boon for the university in more ways than one. In addition to providing immediate relief for the law school admissions office, the decision was a good omen for the university's appeal itself. The makeup of the panel that issued the stay order seemed to favor Michigan. The three judges all had moderate-to-liberal track records. Two of them, Martha Daughtrey and Karen Nelson Moore, had been on the panel that two years earlier let student supporters of affirmative action intervene. The third was Boyce Martin, the court's chief judge. Like Moore and Daughtrey, Martin in the past had favored affirmative action; in 1994 he joined Daughtrey in voting to uphold racial preferences used by the Memphis police and fire departments. If Moore, Daughtrey, and Martin stayed with the cases until the final ruling—an official announcement would come two weeks before the argument—the university would have a significant advantage.

The lawyers weren't privy to the details of how the panel was assembled, and the court itself provided no explanation. Judges for a federal appellate panel usually were selected randomly—as they were when Daughtrey, Moore, and District Judge William Stafford had been assigned to the intervention appeal. The rules got more complicated when an appeals court was called upon to handle later issues connected to the same case. Under the Sixth Circuit's internal operating procedures at the time, a panel of judges could declare itself a "must panel," ensuring that future appeals in the same lawsuit would be assigned to the same group of judges. When the original panel included a district judge sitting temporarily, the other two judges decided whether to recall the district judge or instead to seek a third, randomly selected appellate judge.

From the outside, Martin's participation appeared to be the product of that last scenario. Daughtrey and Moore apparently were part of a "must panel" and, with Stafford now back in Florida, the clerk's office had randomly selected Martin to be the third judge. The Michigan team had every reason to feel fortunate.

As Kolbo and his colleagues discussed how to deal with the unfavorable panel assignment, someone suggested asking the court to hear the two cases en banc—that is, to skip over the three-judge panel stage and bring the matter before the full, eleven-judge court. It would be an unusual maneuver; litigants typically seek en banc review only after a three-judge panel has heard a case. But if it succeeded, the move offered a number of tactical advantages for Kolbo and CIR.

First, of course, it would take the appeals out of the hands of the Martin-Daughtrey-Moore panel and put them with an en banc court that was more evenly divided along ideological lines. Second, bringing the cases before the full court now, rather than waiting six months to a year for the three-judge panel to rule, would expedite matters, relieving some of the financial burden the case was imposing on CIR. And finally, an immediate en banc motion might do something a later petition wouldn't—permit the participation of Judges Alan Norris and Richard Suhrheinrich, two conservatives who were planning to take senior status over the summer and thus would become ineligible for en banc cases. CIR was especially familiar with Suhrheinrich and his views because the judge's former law clerk, Curt Levey, was the firm's public affairs director.

The CIR team decided it had little to lose. Kolbo filed a petition asking the court to hear both cases en banc, saying the disputes were of "exceptional importance." Kolbo wrote: "Each year that passes without resolution of these cases means that many students applying to these schools have effectively lost forever a right to have their applications in the freshman or first-year classes of these schools (or other affected schools) considered in a racially nondiscriminatory manner."

Three weeks after filing the motion, Kolbo received what struck him as a peculiar reply from the Sixth Circuit. The court said it would postpone any decision on the en banc petition until the parties had filed their briefs. Kolbo showed the order to his partner Herr, who specialized in appellate practice. Herr thought the order created unnecessary logistical headaches. The litigants, for example, might have to send their briefs to their outside printers twice—once to make copies for the first three judges and again to make additional copies for the rest of the en banc court. "It's illogical," Herr told Kolbo.[1]

———■———

MIRANDA MASSIE WAS in court again, but her appearance had nothing to do with affirmative action. She was in eviction court. Scheff and Washington, teetering on the brink of financial collapse, had all but stopped paying her. Massie owed her landlord $1,500 in back rent and late fees on her $420-a-month apartment.

Fortunately for Massie, she was able to befriend the lawyer representing the landlord, and he agreed to cut the amount she owed to a little more than $1,000. She got the money from her parents and paid off the debt. Soon thereafter, Massie's parents began giving her $1,000 a month to help her pay her mounting bills.[2]

———■———

MASSIE WASN'T THE ONLY person facing eviction. On May 24, the Michigan Senate voted 33-2 to expel David Jaye, one of the lawmakers who had helped connect CIR with Gratz, Grutter, and Hamacher in 1997. His detractors pointed to his three drunken driving convictions—two while in office—and allegations that he hit his fiancée on two occasions and stored lewd photos on his Senate laptop.[3]

The expulsion was the first in the 164-year history of the body. Defiant to the end, Jaye called the whole episode "a witch hunt, a railroad job."

———■———

THE EFFORTS BY Marvin Krislov and others to win corporate endorsements were continuing to gather steam. Thirty-two companies signed the latest version of the "Fortune 500" brief at the Sixth Circuit. New support came from almost every major sector in the American economy. American Airlines Inc., Boeing Co., Coca-Cola Co., Ernst & Young LLP, Fannie Mae, and Pfizer Inc. all joined the effort. The United Auto Workers also filed a brief, giving Michigan its first union backing.

The military front was proving less fruitful, although Bollinger had scored one early success. Shortly after his meeting with Cannon, Bollinger had put in a call to General Colin Powell, the first black chairman of the Joint Chiefs of Staff and a supporter of affirmative action. Soon thereafter, Powell announced on a Detroit radio talk

show that he hoped Michigan would win its fight. While not specifically addressing race-conscious admissions at the military academies,
Powell issued a sweeping endorsement of affirmative action in higher
education generally. "I think a great public university and great public
institutions should reflect the public," he said. "And when they don't
reflect the public, they should do something about that, and that's
called affirmative action."

Hoping to build on that success, Krislov made the military issue
one of his top priorities. The first step seemed straightforward: gathering details about the academies' admissions policies and the impact
of affirmative action there. But Krislov soon discovered that the
military academies weren't any more forthcoming about their admissions policies than many civilian universities. A paralegal working
under Krislov in the Michigan general counsel's office pored through
public minutes from academy board meetings but found little in the
way of specifics. Krislov telephoned his old political contacts in the
Clinton administration but couldn't find anyone willing to talk about
the admissions policies. He spoke with Michigan Undergraduate
Admissions Director Ted Spencer, who had worked in the Air Force
Academy admissions office before coming to Michigan. Spencer
confirmed that the academy looked at race in admissions, but his
efforts to obtain documentation failed. Jim Cannon tried to tap his
Republican and Navy acquaintances but struck out as well. The group
even tracked down retired superintendents of the military academies
but could do no better than to get off-the-record acknowledgments
that race was a factor in admissions.

George W. Bush's election as president further complicated
Krislov's task. Krislov had always figured that the military argument
was one that would be made by the government—namely, the White
House and Defense Department working through the solicitor general. That had seemed a realistic possibility as long as Clinton or Al Gore
was in the White House. Bush's skepticism about race-based admissions, however, meant the university might now be fighting a defen-
sive battle, trying to persuade the new administration not to oppose
Michigan's policies. So even if Krislov could document the use of race
at the academies, he wasn't sure who would argue for its importance.

In the months before briefs were due at the Sixth Circuit, representatives from the solicitor general's office met with attorneys from

both sides of the Michigan case. Payton and the university's lawyers urged the administration to consider the potential impact that a ruling against affirmative action might have on the military's ability to maintain a racially integrated officer corps. The government attorneys listened intently, but the administration ultimately decided to duck the fight at the appeals court level and not file a brief.

With little to show for his efforts, Krislov put the military issue on the back burner. He was convinced that the topic was enormously important, carrying the potential to swing the balance in the case. But he wondered whether he would ever manage to put the argument together.[4]

———■———

FOR FOUR YEARS, Lee Bollinger had been the public face of the University of Michigan's fight for affirmative action, both on campus and nationwide. He had delivered speeches, participated in symposia, and granted countless media interviews. He had testified at trial and crisscrossed the country attempting to drum up support for the university. He devoted hundreds of additional hours of work behind closed doors, helping shape the university's legal strategy and develop its case. His leadership amounted to a bold statement to the public that Michigan was proud of its affirmative action policies. Under Bollinger, Michigan wasn't apologizing for using race in admissions, as other schools had done. Nor was Michigan hiding what it was doing, as it seemed to have done when Carl Cohen began conducting his research.

Bollinger's prominence was a boon not just for the university, but also for himself, thrusting him into the leadership of higher education nationwide. With every editorial board meeting he attended or *60 Minutes* interview he granted, Bollinger inched toward becoming the foremost spokesperson for American universities. His defense against the lawsuits came at a time when higher education lacked a nationally known voice. Bollinger began to fill the void.

He was also proving to be a skilled and in some ways visionary university administrator. Since 1997, Michigan had raised almost $1 billion from individual and corporate donors, bringing in more money from alumni than any other public university for three of Bollinger's four years. The university broke ground on a $100 million life sciences center (and dedicated another $130 million for start-up staffing and equipment). New buildings cropped up all over campus, including a drama center with a 450-seat theater. Bollinger even enticed the Royal Shakespeare Company to come to campus and perform four plays. Under his leadership, undergraduate applications were at record levels. Friends believed he was popular enough to have mounted a run for governor had he been inclined.

Bollinger's combination of qualities got the attention of the committee seeking a new president at Harvard. Early in 2001, Bollinger became one of two finalists for the position, an extraordinary accomplishment for a man who had never attended the university. (The university hadn't had a president without a Harvard degree since 1672.) In March, Harvard ended weeks of public speculation by announcing its selection of former Treasury Secretary Lawrence Summers.

The Harvard search threw a scare into more than one Michigan regent. The nervousness lingered even after Bollinger said publicly in May that he had no intention of being a candidate in future presidential searches. Two other Ivy League schools, Princeton and Columbia, were still seeking new presidents. In fact, Princeton was already trying, unsuccessfully, to woo Bollinger.

The regents knew that both schools offered higher salaries to their presidents than Michigan did. In Columbia's case, outgoing President George Rupp earned more than $560,000, compared with Bollinger's $326,000. Some of the regents wanted to launch a preemptive strike and offer Bollinger a long-term, more lucrative extension of his contract.

But the board, composed of five Democrats and three Republicans, increasingly was in disarray. In June a group of Democratic regents negotiated a tentative agreement with Bollinger that, by some accounts, would have made him the highest paid president in the country. The Republican regents balked when they learned of the plan, objecting that they had been kept out of the loop. Republican Andrea Fisher Newman also argued that, with the state facing a budget crisis, the university should seek funding from private sources to boost the president's salary. Supporters of the accord decided not to bring it up for a formal vote. For the next several months, the board was all but paralyzed, unable to reach agreement on a new contract for Bollinger. In late September the regents finally made Bollinger an offer, slightly lower than the June proposal. The five-year deal included $500,000 a year in salary, plus annual raises, and $500,000 in deferred compensation. It would have made Bollinger the highest paid public university president.

But by then, it was too late. Bollinger, no longer willing to wait for the fractured board, was deep in discussions with Columbia, the last of the three Ivy League schools with presidential vacancies. Columbia offered a number of enticements. Bollinger, an aficionado of culture and the arts, would get to live in New York, as would his artist wife. He would return to the university where he had earned his law degree. He would get the long-term financial security he sought. And Bollinger would be taking the reins of one the nation's most prestigious universities.

For all Bollinger's loyalty to Michigan, where he had spent all but two years of his career in academia, the opportunity at Columbia was too good to turn down. On October 3, Columbia announced that Bollinger was its choice. Bollinger told his colleagues at Michigan he was leaving at the end of the year.

Bollinger's departure announcement hit the general counsel's office especially hard. After three years of working with Bollinger on affirmative action and other matters, Krislov had developed a close relationship with the man who hired him. Krislov was sad to lose that connection and anxious about what the change would mean for the lawsuit defense. Still, he knew a majority of the regents supported the affirmative action fight and probably would seek a like-minded successor. Krislov also was convinced the cases had become far bigger than any one person, even one with the stature of Bollinger.[5]

——•——

AS THE OCTOBER 23, 2001, date for arguments in the two cases at the Sixth Circuit approached, racial tensions escalated in an unlikely place—the Sixth Circuit itself. The catalyst was the case of John W. Byrd, a white man on death row for killing a store clerk in 1983. Byrd, scheduled to die on September 12, filed a last-ditch appeal with the Sixth Circuit, seeking a new hearing on his claim that his accomplice was the real killer.

The panel considering the appeal consisted of two white judges, Richard Suhrheinrich and Alice Batchelder, and one black jurist,

Nathaniel Jones. Suhrheinrich and Batchelder both thought that Byrd had had his day in court and lacked any right under federal law to file a new appeal. Suhrheinrich said as much in his opinion for the court, but, for reasons unclear, also said he would agree to stay Byrd's execution until September 18 to give Judge Jones "additional time to consider the matter." Jones, who wanted a longer stay, immediately began tracking down judges, hoping to find a majority of the en banc court who agreed with him. Suhrheinrich, meanwhile, changed his mind and sought to withdraw the eight-day stay that same afternoon, leaving the procedural status of the case in doubt.

The following day, September 11, the Sixth Circuit clerk's office issued an order staying the execution until October 8 and saying a majority of the court's active judges supported the longer stay. What exactly prompted that order would be a matter of much debate. Jones would later say that he had spoken with a majority of the active members of the court, though not all. Boyce Martin would say he instructed the clerk's office to issue the order, using his authority as chief judge to manage the court's caseload. Martin was in Washington that day for meetings with Chief Justice William Rehnquist and other judges. The group was at the Supreme Court when hijacked airplanes slammed into the World Trade Center in New York and the Pentagon in Washington, D.C.

Whatever the genesis of the order, it infuriated death penalty advocates on the court, particularly Danny Boggs, a feisty and brilliant judge appointed by Ronald Reagan. Boggs fired off an opinion saying that the first stay (the one written by Suhrheinrich) made no sense, given that a majority of the panel had rejected Byrd's claims. And the extension until October 8 created a procedural mess, Boggs said, given that Byrd hadn't requested it and some members of the court hadn't even been notified of the possibility it would be issued. Boggs speculated that the majority might have granted Byrd a stay if all he had filed was "a hot dog menu."

Boggs's opinion triggered a flurry of responses and counter-responses. Jones wrote to say that the full court was simply acting as it often did in urgent situations. "The exigencies of the circumstances required the prompt entry of the Order to preserve the status quo," he said.

That "is simply a lie," Boggs shot back. He said Suhrheinrich's stay had already postponed the date of execution to September 18. "This type of secret undocumented decision-making by exclusive in-groups is the way decisions are made in totalitarian countries, not usually in the United States," Boggs added.

Jones tried to get Boggs to withdraw the "lie" reference, calling it "unwarranted, unprofessional and wrong." When Boggs refused, the court's three other black judges, Senior Judge Damon Keith and Judges Guy Cole and Eric Clay, decided they'd had enough. The three circulated a letter calling Boggs's comments "patronizing and condescending." The three men considered accusing Boggs, the son of a white father and a Cuban American mother, of racism. But after consulting with Martin and other judges on the court, they chose to leave that charge implicit.

Ultimately, the Sixth Circuit would order a hearing into Byrd's claim of innocence. A federal magistrate judge rejected the contention, and on February 19, 2002, Byrd was executed.

His death ended his legal saga but not the animosity the case had engendered at the Sixth Circuit.[6]

——•——

ON OCTOBER 19, four days before the scheduled date for arguments, Kirk Kolbo received a call at his office at Maslon Edelman Borman & Brand. It was the clerk's office at the Sixth Circuit. Kolbo was told the court had just issued an order granting his long-dormant motion for an en banc hearing. The court also was postponing the hearing until December 6.

Kolbo, having spent the last several weeks preparing for possibly the biggest argument of his career, was stunned and baffled. The Sixth Circuit had sat on his motion for five months, apparently either forgetting or ignoring it. Over the summer, Kolbo even sent a letter reminding the judges of the pending motion, but the court still didn't act. For the court to suddenly grant the motion on the eve of the argument was bizarre, to say the least.

In Washington, Terry Pell was convinced that something unseemly was afoot at the appeals court. The en banc order came after Judges Norris and Suhrheinrich had taken senior status, which meant they could now serve only on three-judge panels. The court that would hear the Michigan cases now seemed to lean sharply toward the university, with six of the nine remaining judges having been appointed by Democrats. Pell was pleased that the full court was going to consider the matter—en banc consideration probably would expedite matters and ultimately might improve prospects for Supreme Court intervention—but he was suspicious of the circumstances.

A few blocks away, in the high-priced offices of Wilmer Cutler Pickering, John Payton was both perplexed and irate. The clerk's office had neglected to call him or even to fax the order. Payton, who had spent countless hours preparing for the October argument, learned about the postponement only when he got a call from a reporter. Not one to mince words, Payton phoned the Sixth Circuit's clerk, Leonard Green, to complain.

Massie and her friends at BAMN decided to go ahead with the rally they had planned for October 23 in Cincinnati. Hundreds of young people from around the country marched from the University of Cincinnati campus to the downtown plaza across the street from the federal courthouse. As students pumped their fists into the air, Shanta Driver exhorted them to keep fighting. "You will lead us into the future," she said, "a future in which the dream of integration in America is realized."[7]

—•—

FROM THE DAY Jennifer Gratz and Patrick Hamacher's lawsuit was filed, everyone involved knew the two Michigan cases had the potential to reach the U.S. Supreme Court. Not only were the issues important, they practically begged for Supreme Court review. The legal status of university affirmative action was unquestionably murky.

As the lawyers prepared for the December 6 argument, circumstances seemed to conspire to ensure the Sixth Circuit wouldn't be the last stop for the Michigan cases. In particular, a split had developed among federal appeals courts around the country on the question of racial preferences, meaning that the law on affirmative action varied depending on one's locale. The legal disarray heightened the need for Supreme Court intervention to create a uniform national rule.

At the time of the Gratz-Hamacher lawsuit, only the Fifth Circuit had weighed in, having struck down the University of Texas Law School's admissions system in 1996. In December 2000, the San Francisco–based Ninth Circuit added a voice in disagreement, saying in the University of Washington Law School case that college racial diversity was a legitimate goal.

For several reasons, the Washington case itself wasn't a good candidate for Supreme Court review. The admissions policy at issue there went out of existence after state voters outlawed university racial preferences through a 1998 ballot initiative. The only thing still at stake in the lawsuit was whether the rejected white students could win damages. In addition, the Ninth Circuit didn't actually decide whether the law school complied with Powell's diversity standard, so that issue wasn't ripe for Supreme Court review. Not surprisingly, the high court on May 29, 2001, said it wouldn't consider CIR's appeal of the Ninth Circuit ruling.

Four weeks later, the Supreme Court turned aside an appeal by the state in the Texas Law School fight, marking the second time the high court had refused to get involved in that case. As with Washington, the Texas case presented some procedural obstacles. For starters, the state wasn't arguing that the Fifth Circuit was wrong to strike down the law school's admissions policy, only that the appeals court shouldn't have taken the additional step of outlawing all race-conscious admissions policies.

In August 2001, the Atlanta-based Eleventh Circuit ruled in a non-CIR case, striking down the admissions policy at the University of Georgia.[8] The Eleventh Circuit used a less sweeping rationale than the Fifth Circuit, assuming that Powell's opinion set out the controlling principle but saying the Georgia policy nonetheless was unconstitutional because it wasn't narrowly tailored. The Eleventh Circuit faulted the university for mechanically awarding a bonus to every minority applicant while ignoring other aspects of diversity, such as unique experiences and perspectives that some applicants offered.

The Georgia case appeared to be tailor-made for Supreme Court review. It had none of the procedural defects that had marred the Texas and Washington case appeals. And the Eleventh Circuit ruling exacerbated the circuit split. Two courts had now ruled against affirmative action and one for it. But in November, the University of Georgia announced it wouldn't appeal the ruling, saying it wasn't the best test case for defenders of affirmative action.

Suddenly, Michigan was the only game in town if the Supreme Court was going to get involved.

KOLBO AND HIS PARTNER David Herr arrived in Cincinnati four days
before the Sixth Circuit argument, now scheduled for Thursday,
December 6, at 1:30 p.m. Both men had long ago learned that they
preferred to avoid the stress that came with traveling on the day
before a big hearing. That was especially so now that winter had
arrived in Minneapolis, bringing flight delays with it.

Kolbo had never argued in front of the Sixth Circuit, and Herr
had argued only before a three-judge panel of the court. They wanted
to get a sense of what was in store. On Monday morning, Kolbo and
Herr walked the four blocks from their hotel to the Potter Stewart
U.S. Courthouse, an aging concrete edifice in the heart of downtown Cincinnati. The two men introduced themselves to the court
clerk and discussed such logistics as where they could gather before
the argument began. Over the next several days, Kolbo and Herr
attended a series of arguments in other cases, hoping to get a sense
of the judges. On the surface, at least, it seemed a gracious court. The
judges were polite and let the lawyers make their arguments with few
interruptions. There were no outward signs of the ill will that had
infected the Byrd death penalty case.

Unlike Kolbo and Herr, who were splitting their argument time,
Payton would be the lone courtroom voice for the university. On
the morning of the argument, he stepped outside into a cold rain
and walked across the street from his hotel to the courthouse. The
argument would be held on the fourth floor in the Sixth Circuit's
largest courtroom, a stately, dark-wood paneled room adorned with
portraits of former judges. Payton had argued in the room before,
but he wanted to see the exact setup, particularly where the court
staff had placed the video camera that would record the session so
that it could be fed into the room set up to handle the overflow
audience.

Two miles north of downtown, at the University of Cincinnati,
Agnes Aleobua and her BAMN colleagues were making preparations of a different sort. Hundreds of people, mostly students from
around the Midwest, gathered in the tentlike pavilion for a "speak-
out" in support of affirmative action. Many, like Aleobua, had left
home in the early morning hours to trek to Cincinnati. Student

after student took the microphone, urging their colleagues to be vigilant in their defense of affirmative action. Aleobua had become the group's media star and spent much of the morning giving interviews. Clad in a Polartec sweatshirt with a blue bandana atop her head, she told each reporter that affirmative action had given her the chance to shine at Michigan. She described how the university's diversity was nothing more than "tokenism," designed to ensure one or two African American students in a classroom of thirty. She said that true affirmative action should bring minorities into the nation's power structure and not simply comfort whites by putting a few black faces on campus. With her determined brown eyes and clear delivery, Aleobua had become an effective public-relations counter to Jennifer Gratz and Barbara Grutter. She was the symbol of the benefits of affirmative action.

The students moved outside into the drizzle, where they lined up with signs and banners to march the two miles to the courthouse. Aleobua took the megaphone and led the way down Vine Street through Cincinnati's impoverished Over-the-Rhine neighborhood, where eight months earlier the police shooting of an unarmed black man had sparked riots. Walking past pawn shops, discount stores, and boarded-up buildings, they chanted, "Affirmative action is on the way! Long live the fight of MLK! They say Jim Crow! We say, 'Hell, no!'" People came out of shops to join the parade. The cold rain only added to the exhilaration, giving the students the sense that, like the civil rights activists of the 1960s, their commitment to the cause of equality took priority over their physical comfort. As the group turned a corner, the courthouse came into sight. The students jumped up and down and pointed. "We won't take resegregation! Equal quality education!" They gathered in Fountain Square, next to the courthouse, and rallied for another hour.

By 1 p.m., the bustling courtroom was packed with hundreds of people, including Lee Bollinger, now in his final weeks as Michigan's president. Aleobua tried to persuade a court security officer to let her use her overflow-room ticket for admittance to the courtroom. The officer politely refused. At least two other students snuck in using counterfeit tickets they had manufactured at a local copy shop.

In the audience, some of the judges' law clerks speculated aloud that the court would split six-to-three, with all six Democratic appointees voting for the university and the three Republican judges siding with CIR. The real question, one said, was whether the judges would resort to sending each other "nastygrams" the way they had in the Byrd case.[9]

Martin v. Boggs

A T 1:30, THE NINE appellate judges filed into the room, and David Herr moved to the lectern. He would be the first to argue, making the case on behalf of undergraduate applicants Gratz and Hamacher. Under the back-and-forth procedures set up for the consolidated argument, the court first planned to consider the white students' challenge to the undergraduate policy that Judge Duggan had upheld. That would be followed by Shaw's appeal on behalf of his group of minority student beneficiaries, arguing that Duggan should have approved the policy not just as a means to diversity but also as a remedy for the history of racial injustice at Michigan. Finally, the court would consider the law school case, where the university and Massie's group of intervenors were both seeking to overturn Judge Friedman's decision invalidating the admissions policy. All told, the session would take about two hours.

Chief Judge Boyce Martin took his place in the center chair. With his Kentucky drawl, the Louisville native welcomed the audience and apologized for the cramped quarters. "We've seldom seen a crowd like this," Martin said.

Herr's main goal was to impress upon the judges how mechanical the undergraduate racial preference was, how it automatically gave each minority applicant 20 points out of a possible 150 regardless of whether they had suffered any hardship as a result of their race. He quickly got bogged down in a series of exchanges about Duggan's decision not to issue an injunction barring the university from reviving its pre-1998 policy. By the time Herr extricated himself from the discussion, he had spent almost ten minutes—half his allotted time—on a relatively trivial matter.

Judge Ronald Gilman, a moderate Clinton appointee, eventually moved the conversation to a more salient point: whether the 1998 changes made by the university were enough to make the admissions policy constitutional. He said the school had stopped at least one of its questionable practices, that of reserving slots so that minorities who applied later in the admissions policy would have spaces available to them.

"The reserved seats sound more like the UC-Davis plan that was struck down in *Bakke,* whereas this 150-point plan is one that does not have a separate admissions committee," Gilman said.

"Well, it has the same effect," Herr replied. "And this court has recognized that you don't have to call it a quota. You don't have to call it protected seats. It functions the same way."

———•———

PAYTON HAD A very different plan for his argument. Rather than discussing technicalities, he wanted to persuade the court on the big issues: that classroom diversity was important and that there was no way to achieve it without considering race in the admissions process. He would focus on the current admissions program, the 150-point system, even though the university had filed its own appeal of Duggan's ruling that the grids were unconstitutional.

Almost immediately Judge Alice Batchelder, a Reagan appointee, hit Payton with a question. "Why limit it to just three minority races?" she asked. Payton answered that blacks, Hispanics, and Native Americans would be underrepresented without affirmative action.

Boggs asked whether Payton's diversity argument had any limits. "Would it be constitutional for a university to decide that it didn't have enough Southern Baptists, so it should admit more of those and admit less Episcopalians and Jews, for example?"

It was a classic Boggs question. The Reagan appointee loved to spar in court with lawyers, to try to hem them in and show the fallacies of their position. (Boggs's fondness for sharp minds extended to his law clerks. He gave every prospective clerk a general-knowledge test, asking them, "Who wrote *The Jew of Malta?*" and instructing them to "name three quarks.") Boggs was an almost certain vote against the university, yet he was an important figure in the case if only because of his potential to shape the debate and influence other judges.

Payton was ready with his answer. Religion, he said, was different because public institutions that favored a particular sect would run up against the ban on the establishment of religion under the Constitution's First Amendment.

How about politics? Boggs asked. Could the university consider that in weighing applicants?

Absolutely, Payton said.

Martin and Boggs turned the discussion to the twenty-point preference. How did the university decide how many points to give minorities?

Payton gave a characteristically direct reply: twenty points is the amount because "we think we wouldn't get sufficient diversity without giving it the value that we give it."

Gilman contrasted the undergraduate policy with the Michigan law school's more "holistic" approach, which didn't give a fixed number of points. Didn't that show the undergraduate admissions policy failed the "narrow tailoring" test set out by Justice Powell in *Bakke?*

The question was a telling one. Gilman, it was becoming clear, was in the middle. He wasn't looking to bar all uses of affirmative action by universities. Nor was he willing to endorse the university's methods without tough scrutiny. His vote might well be up in the air.

Payton said the law school received only 3,500 applications a year, few enough that a single person could read each one. By contrast, the undergraduate college received 14,000 applications and needed more rigid rules to sort them all out. Both policies complied with *Bakke*, Payton said, because they had no separate admissions track for minorities and no quotas.

Boggs was skeptical. To him, the point system was no different from a quota. Doesn't the university have an expectation that the twenty points "will result in the admission of an approximately determined number" of minorities? Boggs asked.

That's not the case, Payton said.

"So if one year you woke up and this system led to 3 percent minority admissions, you wouldn't have any heartburn at all?" Boggs asked.

The question forced Payton into one of the stickiest parts of his argument—how to distinguish a "critical mass" from a quota. If "critical mass" set a floor for the number of minorities to be admitted, how was it different from the reserved-seat system overturned by the Supreme Court in *Bakke*?

Payton acknowledged that 3 percent probably wouldn't be enough. He argued that Powell's opinion in *Bakke* made clear that having "token numbers" of minority students wasn't enough to ensure true diversity.

Boggs wasn't convinced. "I'm sympathetic with that as a public policy reason, but for exactly the reasons you gave, it sure sounds like you are trying to get about a certain number."

"Clearly we care," Payton acknowledged. "But caring about a critical mass is different than saying we want a rigid quota of 16 percent or whatever the number is."

"Do you agree that the twenty points, though, is connected to whatever that critical mass is?"

"Yes."

"If it were ten points, you know, or your clients know as professionals, there would be a roughly lower number?"

"Yes."

"If it were forty points, your clients know that it would be roughly some higher number? Is that fair?"

"Actually, I agree with your first proposition, but the second one is wrong," Payton replied. "We have a pool of minority applicants that is so small that that causes us, in effectuating these policies, to end up admitting virtually all of the qualified applicants."

As Payton's time wound down, he finally heard from Clinton appointee Martha Daughtrey. "How do you know a critical mass when you see it?" she asked simply.

For Payton, the question went to the core of the case:

You know when students in your student body don't see themselves and each other as representatives or symbols, but as individuals. And you know when the students have their stereotypes about each other, which we all bring, ... undermined by the encounters they have with the other students that they see. And you know when students find differences and similarities about each other that enrich their own understanding of others and themselves.

—■—

HERR WASN'T IMPRESSED with Payton's answer to Daughtrey.

"If you can't answer that question in three or five or ten seconds," he said when he stood up to give his rebuttal, "it's a sign that it's too amorphous a concept to exist in the world of narrow tailoring. It just doesn't work."

Judge Moore, a Clinton appointee, disagreed. "If a critical mass is too amorphous, then how can it be a quota?"

The question was a chance for Herr to explain why that apparent contradiction was actually a strength of his case. Herr didn't need to make the case that "critical mass" was both too amorphous and too rigid, even though he thought it was. He needed only to convince the court that it must be one of the two—either so definite that it amounted to a quota or so vague that no judge could determine whether it met the narrow-tailoring requirement.

Herr instead responded that the university implicitly admitted it was using a quota when it switched from the unconstitutional grid system to the 150-point scale after CIR filed suit. The new system "doesn't look quite as much like a quota but functionally is the same," he said.

Gilman later returned to what for him was the key to the case: Powell's opinion in *Bakke*. How, Gilman asked, did the Michigan system compare to the "plus" that Powell had said universities could give minority applicants?

Herr said the problem was the bluntness of the instrument Michigan used—namely, giving twenty points to every minority applicant regardless of other factors.

With Herr's time running out, Judge Eric Clay, one of two blacks on the panel, finally weighed in. Clay wanted to know whether the university might be violating the Constitution by favoring white students through preferences for children of alumni or for applicants from certain regions.

Herr had a ready answer for that one. He said if a university were to indirectly discriminate in favor of white students, a black applicant could sue under federal civil rights laws.

—■—

NEXT UP WAS Ted Shaw of the NAACP Legal Defense and Educational Fund, arguing that affirmative action was warranted as a means to make up for past discrimination against minorities. "The institution does not have to sit by silently and quietly while there are problems on campus, which perhaps others have been responsible for but that affect the climate of the community on the campus with respect to race," he said.

Shaw's presentation had the feel of a halftime show at a sporting event. The judges, who had aimed rapid-fire questions at Herr and Payton moments earlier, slowed their pace. They interrupted Shaw far less frequently, as if they were disengaged from what he was saying. Much like Duggan, the judges on the Sixth Circuit were signaling that they weren't interested in upholding the Michigan admissions policy for the reasons Shaw advocated.

Shaw pressed on. He argued that the first affirmative action programs at Michigan unquestionably were efforts to remedy past discrimination.

Midway through the argument, Boggs interrupted Shaw to ask how much affirmative action would be warranted if the court were to accept the attorney's theory. "How much remediation? Either what's the goal or how do you measure it?" Boggs asked.

Shaw refused to tie himself to any "mechanical numbers." At the end of the day, "what we want is an institution that ought to be able to consider race as long as race continues to be a problem on campus and as long, as I indicated a moment ago, as the problem of race on the campus could dissuade students from enrolling at the University of Michigan."

———■———

THE FLOOR WAS Payton's again, this time to argue for overturning Judge Friedman's law school opinion.

Boggs asked Payton a hypothetical question. Suppose Barbara Grutter were to ask the dean of the law school whether she would have been admitted if she were black. "Wouldn't he have to honestly say either 'yes' or 'pretty darn almost certain'?" Boggs asked.

It was a pivotal question, perhaps even the central one in the case for Boggs. As he saw it, two otherwise identical applicants would be treated differently solely because of their race. That was racial discrimination to Boggs, and there existed a heavy burden on the university to prove it was justified.

Payton could have responded by challenging the question itself. He might have said that the real issue wasn't whether Barbara Grutter would have been admitted if she were black, but whether Barbara Grutter would have been admitted in the absence of an affirmative action program. The law school said she still wouldn't have been accepted.

But Payton, with his characteristic bluntness, opted to address the question head-on:

> If Barbara Grutter were black, she would thereby have a completely different set of life experiences. And then the answer to your query would be yes. ... Race matters in the United States. If we had someone who was a black woman, who had otherwise an application that looked like Barbara Grutter's, that would be a different person with different life experiences that would have a different contribution to our class.

Boggs pressed on: "But under your system, would it not be a given, with what her stats were, which I think is 3.8 and 161, she would have been admitted whether she had grown up in the inner city or Grosse Point?"

"That's probably right," Payton acknowledged. "And the reason for that is that race affects the black woman you just described whether she was in Grosse Point or in the inner city."

Boggs then returned to his earlier line of attack. Couldn't a university say the same thing about Southern Baptists, that their experiences are probably different from the majority of the people at the law school?

Payton said admissions officers probably would take the background of a Southern Baptist into account.

Boggs turned to the analysis by Kinley Larntz, Kolbo's statistical expert, who had put Michigan's applicants into cells based on grades and test scores and concluded that black applicants often had dramatically greater chances of admission than whites in the same cell. "Is there any other kind of factor that, if you applied it to that cell, it would come anywhere close to those numbers?" Boggs asked.

Payton said the numbers didn't reflect the holistic manner in which admissions officers review applicant files. "When you look at the full file, you get the richness of the person that was reviewed and offered admission," he said.

———————

MIRANDA MASSIE WAS a lawyer, but she had a political point to make. She had only five minutes to state her case and she planned to make a splash. She pointed to a stack of Federal Express boxes that she and her colleagues had carried into the courtroom.

"I come before you with, over there on the table, some 50,000 petition signatures representing 50,000-plus Americans who have reaffirmed our national commitment to *Brown v. Board of Education,*" she told the judges.

From his seat, Shaw cringed. Over time, he had come to like Massie personally and admire her energy and commitment. But trying to present petitions to a federal appeals court was a clear violation of court rules. While judges often generally welcome outsiders who presented legal arguments as "friends of the court," a petition smacked of political pressure. Appellate judges must make their determinations based on the law and the record in the case before them. No appeals court could properly consider Massie's submission. Shaw braced himself for the court's reaction.

Chief Judge Martin cut Massie off. "I don't think petitions are what decide lawsuits," he scolded. "We decide the case on the law and the facts, and we want it very clear that we are not policymakers. We are not a legislative body. We are not the executive branch. We are the judiciary. ... So the petitions are not of any benefit in our decision-making. I think we prefer to hear from you the law of why what the University of Michigan is doing is appropriate and authorized under the Constitution."

Massie had been expecting the rejection. She responded that the Supreme Court "reshaped the notion of citizenship" when it decided *Brown,* making the petitions relevant. It was a tenuous connection— and hardly one that could justify the stunt she had just pulled—but it at least functioned as a segue to her core contentions.

"*Bakke* doesn't make sense outside the context of *Brown* and other anti-discrimination and anti-segregation cases," Massie continued.

"Justice Powell's rationale was a diversity rationale, but reading his opinion it is perfectly clear that it [was] shot through with broader notions about integration and equality. Because otherwise racial diversity isn't compelling. It's only compelling if it's connected to integration."

Even more so than Shaw, Massie was a sideshow. Her role, as she saw it, was not so much to provide legal arguments as to make the moral case for affirmative action. The university wasn't about to argue that it remained complicit in racial discrimination through its reliance on test scores and grades. Massie sought to fill that void.

Only Boggs engaged Massie. "How do we know when we've gotten to integration and equality?" he asked.

Massie responded that the goal was a "rough proportionality" between the percentages of minorities in the population at large and at the law school. "Until we reach a point where we have rough proportionality, there isn't any question that we haven't gone far enough. We think the University of Michigan needs more affirmative action, not less."

———•———

IT WAS FINALLY Kolbo's turn. As with Herr's argument earlier, Kolbo's primary aim was to underscore the size of the racial preferences the law school used and argue that the system was indistinguishable from a quota. Kolbo recognized those arguments were tougher to make against the law school, with its subtle consideration of race, than against the undergraduate admissions office and its point system. He urged the judges not to be swayed by appearances.

Martin asked about an affirmative action plan Powell specifically endorsed in *Bakke*—the system used by Harvard's undergraduate admissions office. "Didn't the testimony of the dean at the time, in Michigan, say that that was the plan that they had adopted?"

"Oh, yes," Kolbo said. "Michigan has taken the position that they have the Harvard plan. We don't think that's true."

Martin asked how the plans were different.

Powell didn't endorse "the functional equivalent of a quota," Kolbo said. "We believe that is what the law school operates."

Boggs jumped in to buttress Kolbo's point. "Isn't the problem with that, counsel, that we simply don't know what the Harvard plan, whatever that was, or Justice Powell's application of it, meant quantitatively? You can read Powell's decision and you can say it means a tiebreaker … or it can mean something so large that every qualified, minimally qualified, person gets in. And we have no way of getting directly out of Powell how big that amount is. Isn't that the real problem here?"

"That's exactly right, Judge Boggs."

Martin wasn't so sure. He suggested to Kolbo that Powell's opinion might represent the controlling law.

Even if Powell's opinion is the law, Kolbo said, the Michigan Law School program went way too far. He pointed to the grids constructed by Larntz. "These grids are far more eloquent than I can be. They tell the story. And what we have here is a double standard in admissions. Justice Powell didn't approve of that."

Boggs asked what would happen if the numbers weren't so stark.

Kolbo said he could imagine a tougher case. But "it's not even close here," he said. "Nothing but race can explain how it is that cell after cell is at 90 percent, 100 percent admission rates for designated minorities and 0, 5, 10 percent admission rates for the vast majority of the white students and Asian students. That's a double standard."

Maybe, Gilman suggested, that's what Powell was endorsing in *Bakke*. Powell said race could be a plus. "And if it didn't make some difference, it wouldn't be a plus."

"A plus could be as heavy as you want under that analysis," Kolbo answered. "I don't think that is what he intended. And I think he made that clear by stating that applicants with different races must be able to compete on the same footing."

As Kolbo's time expired, the judges let him step back and address the big picture, answering Payton's arguments about the value of diversity:

It is simply not enough to say that there is educational advantage to diversity, that it is a good thing. That doesn't answer the question. And it doesn't answer it to say that there is academic freedom to engage in race discrimination. The courts have never recognized a right, a First Amendment right, to engage in the practice of race discrimination. Certainly not by governmental entities.

———■———

PAYTON WAS CONFIDENT when he left the hearing room—and with some justification. Only one judge, Boggs, seemed a clear vote for the white students. Martin, Moore, and Clay all appeared to be leaning toward the university. Four judges—Daughtrey, Batchelder, Siler, and Guy Cole—had asked only a question or two apiece. If Democratic appointees Daughtrey and Cole voted for the university, Michigan would win the case.

The most intriguing vote would come from Gilman. He clearly was interested in a narrow ruling, one that neither endorsed nor rejected all affirmative action plans. The issue for him was whether the Michigan admission policies could be squared with Justice Powell's opinion in *Bakke*. How he would answer that question was anyone's guess.

That night Kolbo, Herr, Pell, Cohen, Grutter, Gratz, and Gratz's fiancé and parents met for dinner in a downtown restaurant. (Gratz had recovered from being called a "racist bitch" by a heckler as she left the courthouse.) This was Cohen and Herr's first opportunity to spend time with the two women whose names would forever be attached to the lawsuits. Both men were impressed. Gratz and Grutter, they thought, were smart, decent women who would have added a great deal to the University of Michigan. Herr saw his two white plaintiffs as modern-day versions of Rosa Parks. CIR had chosen its clients well, despite the rush to file suit that had so concerned Pell.

The diners rehashed the day's events and optimistically discussed which judges might vote to strike down the policies. Cohen was among the few pessimists, predicting the court would rule six-to-three for the university.

Pell was realistic. He felt all along that the Sixth Circuit was stacked against his side and would probably rule for the university. But the ultimate goal was to get in front of the Supreme Court, where Pell believed he had the votes to roll back racial preferences.[1]

———■———

IN THE EYES of some observers, Payton had been the star of the Sixth Circuit hearing. He was eloquent and quick on his feet, and he held his ground in the face of a barrage of hostile questions. He did well enough that Carl Cohen, whose fervent opposition to preferences had instigated the conflict, sought out the lawyer afterward to compliment him on his performance.

But with the cases likely headed toward the nation's highest court, Bollinger and his colleagues at the university concluded that Payton wasn't the right person to lead the final stage of the fight. Although the consensus at the university was that Payton had put on a strong case at the trial court level, the reviews of his Sixth Circuit briefs were mixed. Perhaps more importantly, Bollinger and Law School dean Jeff Lehman were former Supreme Court clerks who had developed firm views about the type of lawyer likely to succeed there. The Michigan officials decided they needed an appellate specialist, an attorney with deep knowledge of the justices, their tendencies, and the unique nuances of Supreme Court practice. Bollinger and his colleagues wanted the lawyer who would give them the best chance to win at the Supreme Court, and they concluded that wasn't Payton.

In the weeks before Bollinger's departure at the end of December, he, Lehman, and Krislov interviewed three candidates, all of them white. Their top choice was the only woman in the group, Maureen Mahoney, a former deputy solicitor general and a partner at Latham and Watkins in Washington. Mahoney, a forty-seven-year-old blonde with an angular jaw and determined blue eyes, was known for her brains, writing skill, and sheer doggedness in pressing her client's case. She had come highly recommended by Michigan Law School professor Ronald Mann, who had worked with her in the solicitor general's office and thought she was one of the best Supreme Court attorneys he had ever seen.

Mahoney offered a measure of Supreme Court expertise missing from Payton's résumé. She clerked for then-Justice Rehnquist in the 1979–1980 term and later argued eleven cases before the high court, winning ten. While a handful of other Washington attorneys had even longer track records—one of the lawyers interviewed by the university had argued more than forty times at the Supreme Court—Mahoney's experience nonetheless put her in elite company. Her victories included high-profile fights over the use of statistical sampling in the U.S. Census and the legal status of Haitian refugees.

Mahoney also had a status that some thought might give her special credibility with moderate-to-conservative justices: she was a Republican. She was no ideologue and wasn't especially active on

With the cases headed for the Supreme Court, Michigan beefed up its legal team with Maureen Mahoney, an ex-clerk to Chief Justice Rehnquist with a history of success at the nation's highest court. Her involvement led to weeks of behind-the-scenes wrangling. Bollinger and other officials initially tapped Mahoney to be the lead attorney, but some questioned the wisdom of replacing John Payton, a black civil rights attorney.

political matters, but Mahoney had donated money to Republican candidates and appeared on television talk shows defending the *Bush v. Gore* decision. And, of course, she had clerked for Rehnquist, a conservative.

Mahoney had wanted to be a lawyer since she was eight years old. She graduated Phi Beta Kappa from Indiana University, then went on to the University of Chicago Law School, earning a position on the law review and graduating with honors.

Her year as a clerk to Rehnquist would always be one of the high points of her career, even though the term featured no block-buster cases. Mahoney developed a close relationship with Rehnquist that continued well after she left her clerkship. Seven years later, Mahoney, then in private practice, got a phone call from Rehnquist asking her to serve as counsel in a Supreme Court case where one side lacked a lawyer. Mahoney won the case, performing so well at argument that the justices reportedly passed notes praising her performance and discussing her background.

In 1991, Mahoney took a position as deputy solicitor general under Ken Starr, who later would become a household name for his investigation of the Bill Clinton–Monica Lewinsky scandal. A year later, President Bush nominated Mahoney for a position as a federal judge in northern Virginia, only to see her nomination die in the Senate without a hearing. She returned to Latham and Watkins, where she established herself as a top appellate lawyer.

Mahoney had been thrilled when she got Krislov's initial call asking whether she was interested in representing the university. Her conservative credentials aside, Mahoney thought affirmative action had its place in higher education. A rule barring any use of race by admissions offices, she thought, would have dramatic negative consequences. Her interests, however, were more professional than ideological. At bottom, Mahoney saw herself as an advocate who relished taking on—and winning—challenging cases, regardless of who the client was. The affirmative action cases were nothing if not challenging. For Mahoney, they represented the new pinnacle of her career.

Shortly before his departure at the end of December, Bollinger decided to retain Mahoney to take the lead in the litigation and, if the Court granted a hearing, argue for the university. But there was a hitch. Although Bollinger would continue to consult on UM's defense strategy from Columbia, in a few days he no longer would have the final say on Michigan's litigation decisions. Starting in January, that right belonged to Joseph White, a former Michigan Business School dean who had been tapped to serve as interim president while the regents conducted a nationwide search for a permanent successor.

Soon after taking over, White met in Ann Arbor with Payton and his partner John Pickering. The two lawyers urged the new president not to make the change. Around the same time, White held an informal meeting with the board, his first. Several regents objected to the planned change, arguing that it was wrong, not to mention ironic, to take a major affirmative action case away from a black civil rights lawyer who had performed well. White said he would think about it.

Meanwhile, three prominent black lawyers—Ted Shaw, Harvard law professor Charles Ogletree, and Duke law professor Jim Coleman—arranged a meeting with Bollinger at Columbia. The group had heard talk that Michigan was considering replacing Payton and was specifically looking for a woman in an effort to appeal to Justice O'Connor. Much like the regents at the meeting with White, the three attorneys told Bollinger they were troubled by the shift, particularly if Michigan was operating under the misguided notion that a woman would somehow hold special sway with O'Connor. Bollinger acknowledged that the current plan was to have Mahoney argue the cases in the event of a hearing. Diplomatic as always, he assured his visitors that he wanted Payton and Wilmer Cutler on board to work on the briefs.

For more than a month, officials debated the move behind the scenes, Payton's backers arguing that he deserved to keep control of the cases and Mahoney's supporters contending she would maximize their chances of success. At one point, one Mahoney advocate was convinced White would reverse Bollinger and leave Payton in charge.

In the end, White settled on an unusual compromise: Michigan would hire Mahoney but not in the role originally envisioned for her. Instead, she would take the lead only in the law school case, where she would work closely with one of her strongest backers, Dean Jeff Lehman. Payton would remain in charge of the undergraduate case. Publicly, the two would share the title of co-lead counsel as the cases headed toward the Supreme Court.[2]

———•———

FOR THE OTHER attorneys and litigants, the first part of 2002 was a time to enjoy vacations and turn their attentions to matters they had put to the side while they focused on the affirmative action appeal.

Massie went to trial in Ann Arbor on another lawsuit involving UM. Representing a music student who said she was sexually harassed by a professor, Massie won a $250,000 verdict that she hoped would bring some financial relief to her struggling law firm. The university dashed any hopes she had of a quick payout by vowing to appeal.

As winter turned to spring, Payton and Kolbo began checking the Sixth Circuit's website each morning. The court made a practice of posting new opinions each morning, and the lawyers figured that might be the first word they got about a ruling.

What none of the lawyers knew was that the Sixth Circuit was in an uproar again. The decision to hear the case en banc had been the culmination of a series of charges and countercharges among the judges that rivaled the Byrd case.

———•———

AT THE CENTER of the feud were Boyce Martin and Danny Boggs, men with offices 100 feet apart who never spoke to one another unless they happened to pass in the hallway. Martin and Boggs, the Sixth Circuit's only judges in Louisville, had once been squash partners. Ideology, personality, and circumstances had driven them apart over the years, and now they were bitter adversaries.

The controversy grew out of Martin's presence on the three-judge panel that had been scheduled to hear the cases. After the intervention decision, Judges Daughtrey and Moore needed a replacement for District Judge William Stafford, who had returned to Florida and wasn't available. Daughtrey and Moore had declared themselves a "must panel," meaning all future appeals would come their way. Under the Sixth Circuit's rules, the proper next step was for Daughtrey and Moore to ask the clerk's office to make a random appointment.

By most accounts, that step never happened in the Michigan cases. Months later, Boggs would say Martin had simply placed himself on the panel, bypassing the random selection process. Moore would implicitly confirm that interpretation, explaining that the chief judge routinely chose replacements to fill vacancies on panels for the sake of court efficiency. Martin, however, would say he was sure he had selected himself randomly, probably by drawing his own name out of a bowl, although he didn't have a specific recollection of doing so.

Kolbo and CIR added a new wrinkle in May when they asked the court to consider the case en banc. The previous December the Sixth Circuit had implemented a new policy for handling so-called initial en banc petitions—that is, requests to skip the three-judge panel stage. The impetus for the change was the frequency of frivolous en banc motions from prisoners acting without lawyers. By its terms, the new policy applied to all cases, except those designated as "unusual" by the clerk and chief judge. Under the policy, when an initial en banc petition was filed, the clerk's office sent out an order delaying resolution until the briefs were filed. The judges on the panel then were to decide whether to deny the petition or, if they saw some legitimate argument for en banc review, circulate it to the full court for consideration.

The new policy explained the unusual order Kolbo received three weeks after he filed his en banc request. Rather than declaring the cases to be "unusual," the clerk's office, with Martin's approval, simply sent Kolbo the same standard order used for prisoner cases. Kolbo's en banc motion, the order said, would be held in abeyance until the briefs were filed.

The court, in fact, took no action on Kolbo's petition for another four months, neither denying it nor circulating it to the panel so that

Boggs and other judges would learn of its existence. The motion wasn't even distributed to Moore and Daughtrey until late August. By that time, Norris and Suhrheinrich had taken senior status, making them ineligible for any en banc proceeding. The three-judge panel then held Kolbo's petition for seven more weeks, neither denying it nor circulating it to the full court.

The petition finally came to the attention of the full court in October. Three weeks before the scheduled hearing, a U.S. government attorney told Senior Judge Ralph B. Guy Jr. he had heard the Michigan cases were being "taken care of." Disturbed by the allegation, Guy investigated and concluded there was yet another problem, namely that Daughtrey and Moore shouldn't have declared themselves a "must panel" and should have left the case entirely to the random selection process. In an October 15 letter to Martin, Guy said he thought the cases now should be reassigned by blind draw, adding that he planned to share his thinking with the rest of the court.

Martin consulted with several colleagues and concluded he now needed to seek a vote on the long-pending en banc petition, even though Guy's letter hadn't mentioned that issue. Martin circulated the petition along with a note explaining that a "question ... has been raised regarding the composition of the panel."

Martin's memo reached Boggs just as he was preparing to leave town. Not yet appreciating the unusual path the cases had taken, Boggs gave the matter little thought and didn't even cast a vote on the petition. His colleagues, however, quickly concluded they wanted to hear the cases en banc.

In the months after the argument, Boggs began to piece together what had taken place. He concluded that Martin must have simply placed himself on the three-judge panel in contravention of the court's internal operating rules. And Boggs was at a loss to explain the panel's delay in acting on the en banc petition—unless Martin was trying to keep Suhrheinrich and Norris from taking part in the case.

With the memory of the Byrd death penalty case still fresh, Boggs was seething. And he was determined not to sit by silently.[3]

IN THE EARLY morning of May 14, the Sixth Circuit announced its first decision. On a five-to-four vote, the court upheld the law school's admissions policy. The judges had broken down almost along party lines. The lone exception was Gilman, who had split from his fellow Democratic appointees and voted to strike down the policy.

Chief Judge Martin's majority opinion addressed only the university's arguments, not those made by Massie for the intervening students. Martin took a technical approach toward Powell's reasoning in *Bakke,* relying on a 1997 Supreme Court decision that laid out guidelines for interpreting splintered high court rulings. Powell's logic "is *Bakke's* narrowest rationale," Martin said. "Accordingly, Justice Powell's opinion constitutes *Bakke's* holding and provides the governing standard here." Martin, in effect, tossed the ball back to the Supreme Court. Addressing the contention that later high court decisions cast doubt on *Bakke,* Martin wrote that "the Court of Appeals should follow the case which directly controls" and leave to the Supreme Court "the prerogative of overruling its own decisions."

Martin chose not to incorporate Payton's evidence about the importance of campus diversity. Privately, Martin thought some of Michigan's social science evidence was questionable. He also thought a long discussion of it would reduce the chances of Supreme Court review. One of Martin's goals was to frame the case so that the high court would agree to hear it, and he thought the best approach was to keep his opinion narrow, focusing on the differing interpretations that federal appeals courts had given *Bakke.* The trade-off was that Martin passed on a chance to use his opinion to make the case for diversity, to consider the type of evidence that might prove crucial if the Supreme Court were to get involved.

Martin's opinion turned to the question of narrow tailoring. The law school, he said, "does not employ a quota for under-represented minority students." It "does not reserve or set aside seats." It "operates a single admissions system" that puts all candidates in the same pool. "Thus, the Law School's admissions policy avoids the critical defect of the Davis admissions program," Martin wrote.

Martin compared the Michigan policy to the Harvard plan embraced by Justice Powell. Martin noted the statement in Harvard's policy that "10 or 20 black students" wouldn't be enough to provide genuine variety and prevent a sense of isolation.

Martin said he wasn't concerned that the law school's policy resulted in a range of minority enrollment from 10 to 17 percent. "[O]ver time, reliance on *Bakke* will always produce some percentage range of minority enrollment," he wrote. "And that range will always have a bottom, which, of course, can be labeled the 'minimum.'" The judge dismissed CIR's argument that Michigan was using an unconstitutional double standard. The evidence "demonstrates just what one would expect a plan like the Harvard plan to demonstrate—that race and ethnicity, as 'plus' factors, play an important role in some admissions decisions."

Finally, Martin rejected the assorted concerns Judge Friedman had raised. The law school, Martin said, had adequately considered race-neutral alternatives. Neither enhanced recruiting, nor a lottery system, nor a shift in focus to "experiential diversity" would ensure significant numbers of minority students, he said. And Martin rejected the contention that "critical mass" was vaguely defined; Friedman's "apparent insistence that 'critical mass' correspond with a more definite percentage" was "fatally at odds with *Bakke*'s prohibition of fixed quotas."

———————

A CONCURRING OPINION, written by Judge Clay and joined by Moore, Cole, and Daughtrey, covered some of the ground that Martin skipped. Clay said that the Gurin report proved what Powell had asserted about the educational value of diversity. Other scholarship backed Gurin up, Clay added.

Clay also made the emotional case that Martin's workmanlike opinion lacked. Clay blasted a suggestion by dissenting Judge Boggs that the law school could focus on socioeconomic status, instead of race. It is "insulting" to suggest that wealthy blacks aren't touched by the long history of racial oppression in America, Clay wrote. "A well-dressed black woman of wealthy means shopping at Neiman Marcus or in an affluent shopping center may very well be treated with the same suspect eye and bigotry as the poorly dressed black woman of limited means shopping at Target." Adopting Massie's arguments, Clay said *Brown* was as relevant to the Michigan case as *Bakke*. "Diversity in education, at its base, is the desegregation of a historically segregated population."

Clay's opinion was laden with contempt for Boggs. The dissent's arguments against diversity were "myopic, baseless conclusions," Clay said. Boggs's acknowledgment that race matters "constitutes a thinly veiled offer of dubious sincerity, to say the least." His refusal to consider the history of discrimination in the educational system evinced "narrow-mindedness."

———■———

To Boggs, the issue was simple. "This case involves a straightforward instance of racial discrimination by a state institution," he began his dissent. The authors of the Fourteenth Amendment "decided that our government should abstain from social engineering through explicit racial classifications." The fundamental problem, Boggs said, lay in Michigan's definition of diversity. The law school, he said, was considering race for the sake of race, not to ensure a diverse set of experiences. "Thus, to the Law School, ten under-represented minority students, each a child of two-parent lawyer families, are considered to be diverse, while children whose parents are Chinese merchants, Japanese farmers, white steel workers or any combinations of the above are all considered to be part of a homogenous (and 'over-represented') mass," he said. The law school's goal also lacks a logical stopping point, he added. It would "justify an infinite amount of engineering with respect to every racial, ethnic and religious class."

Even if diversity were a legitimate goal, the preferences the law school used were far from narrowly tailored, Boggs went on. "Its admissions officers have swapped tailor's shears for a chainsaw." The goal of a critical mass was effectively a quota, he said. And Michigan had failed to prove that an "empirical link" tied the goal of a critical mass to the values of diversity, Boggs noted, dismissing the Gurin report as "questionable science." The school, he said, should have tried race-neutral means, such as directly seeking out students with unique experiences or track records of overcoming hardships. As written, the policy was unfair to the Barbara Grutters of the world, he said.

Gilman issued a short dissenting opinion of his own. Saying the court didn't need to reach the compelling interest question, Gilman said the policy failed the narrow tailoring test. A Michigan applicant's race or ethnicity gets "grossly disproportionate weight," he said. The critical mass goal is "functionally equivalent to a quota." The policy is far closer to the set-aside program struck down in *Bakke* than to the racial "plus" that Powell thought permissible, Gilman said.

—•—

THE DECISION ALSO contained a bombshell.

It came from Boggs, who let out months of pent-up outrage over the irregular handling of the case. In a 3,000-word "procedural appendix," Boggs detailed the path the case took in reaching the nine-judge en banc court. Boggs described what he called "a series of decisions in contravention of our rules and policies." He said Martin had selected himself for the three-judge panel when the rules of the court unequivocally required a random selection. "It is absolutely clear that the applicable procedures for potential 'must panel' cases were not followed to determine whether and how these cases should be heard as a 'must panel,'" Boggs wrote. Boggs described the delay in circulating the en banc petition to the full court, saying Suhrheinrich and Norris might have been able to take part had the proper procedures been followed.

Boggs stopped short of directly accusing Martin of trying to engineer the outcome of the case, but made it clear he suspected as much. He all but absolved Moore and Daughtrey of any wrongdoing, saying he had "no reason to doubt" that they hadn't known about the petition before August 28. That left Martin as the sole culprit. "These facts speak for themselves," Boggs said, "however each of us may choose to characterize them." He said he had decided to put the matter on the public record "for such remediation as may be possible."

By any measure, Boggs's decision to go public was an extraordinary step, reminiscent of Judge Friedman's opinion on the case reassignment issue at the trial court level. Not only had Boggs revealed the inner workings of the court, he had questioned its very legitimacy in the Michigan cases. The outcome, Boggs was suggesting, might have been different had Martin not bent and broken the court's rules.

Several of Boggs's colleagues privately had urged him not to publish his appendix, and Martin himself had asked three other judges to intervene. Boggs wasn't swayed. "Legitimacy protected only by our silence is fleeting," he wrote. "If any damage has been done to the court, it is the work of the actors, not the reporters."

Batchelder wrote separately to voice her support for Boggs. "Unless we expose to public view our failures to follow the court's established procedures," she wrote, "our claim to legitimacy is illegitimate."

———■———

ALTHOUGH MARTIN BY nature wasn't one to hold his tongue, he chose not to respond to Boggs's allegations in writing. More than a year later, Martin told a visitor that debating Boggs would have been like getting into "a pissing match with a skunk." Martin was irritated that Boggs had never asked to sit down and discuss the matter before going public. The chief judge thought that arguing with Boggs would only serve to legitimize Boggs's breach of protocol in going public.

Moore and Clay rose to Martin's defense. Moore in her opinion called Boggs's opinion "shameful." She said Martin and other court officials had simply followed their established rules and customs. No one was trying to engineer a particular result, she said. "Judge Boggs's opinion marks a new low point in the history of the Sixth Circuit," she wrote. "It will irreparably damage the already strained working relationships among the judges of this court, and ... serve to undermine public confidence in our ability to perform our important role in American democracy."

Notably, Moore didn't dispute Boggs's assertion that Martin had bypassed the random selection process when he added himself to the three-judge panel. She instead said that Martin "has frequently substituted himself in a variety of matters, of varying degrees of importance, throughout his tenure as chief judge, in order to avoid inconveniencing other circuit judges." Moore continued: "Thus, it was not unusual for him to place himself on the panel in July 2000."

Clay called Boggs's opinion "an embarrassing and incomprehensible attack on the integrity of the Chief Judge and this Court as a whole." He said it was "ludicrous" to think that on an overworked court, the chief judge might single out one case and scheme to ensure a particular outcome.

Together, the opinions made clear that any appearance of civility at the December argument was a façade. The profound mistrust that had infected the Sixth Circuit's consideration of the Byrd case had only worsened with the affirmative action dispute.

—■—

READING THE DECISION from his desk in Washington, Terry Pell thought he saw a lot to like. He hadn't really been expecting to win at the Sixth Circuit, with the court seemingly stacked in the university's favor. A five-to-four decision was in many ways a victory; winning Gilman's vote was clearly a coup. And the ruling came in the case that was widely viewed as the more favorable of the two to the university, with the undergraduate decision still to come.

Pell, already contemplating his team's appeal to the Supreme Court, also thought the majority opinion by Chief Judge Martin was full of holes, starting with Martin's decision not to discuss the importance of diversity. If the high court agreed to hear the case, Pell was sure the justices wouldn't base their ruling on a technical discussion of the holding of the *Bakke* decision. Race-based admissions instead would rise or fall on the justices' own assessment of the value of racial diversity on college campuses. Martin, given a forum to persuade the court on that issue, chose not to weigh in.

In Ann Arbor, the reaction was one of tempered celebration. Fifty BAMN members and other supporters of affirmative action gathered outside the student union building to hear Jesse Jackson say he was "alarmed at how close the decision was."

Even as they cheered the decision, the members of the Michigan legal team couldn't help but look ahead to the next step. CIR would certainly ask the Supreme Court to consider the case, and the university would have to decide how to respond. Should Michigan go along with the request or try to argue that the high court shouldn't intervene? The Sixth Circuit ruling had only heightened the need for the Supreme Court to get involved. Federal appeals courts now were evenly split, with two tending to support affirmative action and two either fully or partially opposed. The issue had become a classic candidate for Supreme Court involvement, and the university would be hard-pressed to argue otherwise.

Boggs's "procedural appendix" only underscored the explosiveness of the issue. At two levels of the court system, the Michigan affirmative action cases had sparked extraordinary, bitter battles among the judges. The stakes were so high that men and women who had sworn to uphold the Constitution were accusing one another of breaking their internal rules of procedure to get a piece of the action. If lower-court judges were so anxious to play a role, surely the Supreme Court, after twenty-four years of silence on the issue, would want to get involved.

Payton, for one, was eager to make his first trip to the Supreme Court since losing the *Croson* case in 1989, even if he had to share the lead role with Maureen Mahoney. He was proud of the record he and his colleagues had put together in defense of Michigan's policies. He thought the cases represented as good an opportunity as affirmative action was going to get. Ever confident, Payton was convinced that the Supreme Court would uphold the use of race in admissions, given the chance.

Bollinger, too, was keen on seeing the nation's highest court take up the issue. "If I were a justice," Bollinger told the *Detroit News* the day the Sixth Circuit ruling came down, "I would want the Court to speak to this issue."[4]

——■——

ANY DOUBTS ABOUT Michigan's commitment to its admissions policies in the post-Bollinger era disappeared on May 28 when the regents named University of Iowa president Mary Sue Coleman to take the helm at Michigan, becoming its first female president. In her seven years at Iowa, she managed to almost double both research funding and private donations. Coleman, a biochemist by training, won the Michigan regents over with her intelligence, vision, and friendly smile.

The issue of race-based admissions didn't have quite the gravity in Iowa City that it had in Ann Arbor, in large part because Iowa accepted almost 90 percent of its undergraduate applicants. Coleman nonetheless had been an affirmative action advocate at Iowa, saying it was especially important in such an overwhelmingly white state to ensure that students learned to work with people from other backgrounds and cultures. Years earlier, she had attended a presentation by Krislov and approached him afterward to offer words of support. Coleman knew she had a lot to learn on the subject of affirmative action, but there was no question where she stood.[5]

Looking to the High Court

O F THE 8,000 REQUESTS for review the Supreme Court receives
each year, only seventy or eighty—roughly 1 percent—are ever
scheduled for argument. Most of the filings are so-called petitions
for certiorari ("cert petitions," for short), which the high court in its
discretion may deny without considering on the merits. By unwritten
tradition, the Court agrees to consider a case only if at least four of
the nine justices want to schedule arguments.

Pell, Kolbo, and the CIR team knew their appeal of the Sixth
Circuit's law school decision stood a far better chance than the average cert petition. The indisputable importance of the issues, combined with the two-two split among federal appeals courts, made the
case a prime candidate for high court review. As the attorneys debated such matters as how to frame the precise question they would ask
the Court to resolve, Kolbo couldn't help but think that the justices
would indeed agree to hear the dispute. Justice Ruth Bader Ginsburg
seemed to bolster that view a few weeks after the Sixth Circuit ruling. Taking questions after a speech, Ginsburg said the high court
probably would take up the issue of race-based admissions "sooner
rather than later." Kolbo's partner David Herr nonetheless was pes-
simistic, putting the chances of a hearing at somewhere between a
third and a half.

Kolbo's August 9, 2002, cert petition in the law school case asked
the court to decide "whether our Nation's principles of equal protec-

tion and non-discrimination mean the same thing for all races." The diversity justification, Kolbo wrote, would "give the Nation its first *permanent* legal justification for racial classifications." Michigan's admissions system was nothing more than race discrimination, something that was "anathema to the outcome and principles" of *Brown v. Board of Education* and other cases, he said.

The filing put the university in a delicate spot as officials mulled their response. From the early days of the case, Bollinger had portrayed the fight as one not just for Michigan but for all of higher education. But with the cert petition, Michigan's interests diverged somewhat from those of other higher education institutions. A decision by the Supreme Court not to review the law school ruling would mean that Michigan had won that fight; Michigan Law School could continue to use race in admissions and wouldn't have to pay any damage awards. But other institutions, or at least those outside the four states where the Sixth Circuit had authority, would be left to fend for themselves. And in the Fifth Circuit, the *Hopwood* decision would still reign, barring any use of race by universities in three Southern states.

Complicating Michigan's decision was the lingering presence of the undergraduate case, the one widely perceived to be less favorable to the university. Should the high court refuse to hear the law school case but later agree to consider the undergraduate dispute, Michigan might be at a disadvantage, having to defend the more difficult case by itself.

But as Labor Day approached, the Sixth Circuit still hadn't ruled in the undergraduate matter. In Louisville, Martin was struggling with the case. Immediately after the December argument, the Sixth Circuit judges had tentatively voted five-to-four to uphold the policy, dividing the same way they had in the law school case, and Martin had assigned himself to write the majority opinion. But as the months went by, he started to have doubts. The more Martin looked at the undergraduate policy, the more he thought it might not comply with *Bakke.* He decided the best course was to do nothing, not even circulate his draft opinion to the other judges, until the Supreme Court made a move.[1]

———■———

Kolbo and Pell had their own tactical concerns. As much as they wanted the Supreme Court to hear the law school case, they were even more eager that the justices look at the undergraduate policy, with its mechanistic point system. The problem was that, unless the Sixth Circuit ruled soon, the undergraduate case wouldn't be ready for the high court in time for a decision in its 2002–2003 term. In light of Chief Judge Martin's handling of the law school case, the CIR team wondered whether some further shenanigans had indefinitely bottled up the undergraduate decision.

One of Pell's staffers, Curt Levey, offered a possible solution that would put both cases before the high court. Levey, an attorney, knew the Supreme Court had a rule that let the justices take on a case even before the appeals court ruled. The Court didn't often grant "cert before judgment," but Levey thought the approach was worth considering.

Kolbo's team at Maslon Edelman dug through some old cases. The Court apparently hadn't invoked the cert-before-judgment rule since the 1974 Watergate tapes cases, *United States v. Nixon* and *Nixon v. United States*.[2] But the Maslon lawyers did come across an intriguing, even older example. Shortly after agreeing to hear *Brown v. Board of Education,* the Supreme Court granted cert before judgment to hear arguments in a case that raised closely connected issues. The parallel seemed perfect. CIR could argue that, just as with *Brown,* the Court wouldn't be able to see the full picture of university admissions without hearing both cases. Kolbo, Pell, and the other attorneys decided they had little to lose. Kolbo and Herr got to work writing a second petition.

They were nearing completion when Kolbo received a surprising phone call from Payton. The Michigan team, Payton said, had been looking at the same Supreme Court rule. The university planned to oppose cert in the law school case, notwithstanding Payton's confidence in Michigan's chances. But if the high court wanted to hear the law school case, Michigan intended to urge consideration of the undergraduate dispute as well. Given a choice between both cases or just the law school fight, Michigan, like CIR, had developed a preference for giving the high court a fuller picture of the way race factored into university admissions.

Payton asked Kolbo whether, in the event of a cert grant, the two sides might file a joint request urging review of the undergraduate case as well. Kolbo told Payton about the new petition he was crafting and said he was glad to hear of Michigan's position. But Kolbo said he was too far along to turn back. He and his friends at CIR wanted to get Gratz and Hamacher's case before the high court as quickly as possible.[3]

———•———

MAHONEY WAS A staunch supporter of the decision to oppose cert in the law school case. As she saw the issue, universities in forty-seven states—all but the three in the Fifth Circuit—still could consider race in admissions. If the Supreme Court intervened, the Court might well bar the practice nationwide. Michigan had won the law school case at the Sixth Circuit, and Mahoney thought that victory was worth trying to preserve.[4]

Mahoney took the lead on the brief opposing cert. Her October 29 filing sought to walk a fine line. She couldn't deny the importance of the issues, nor the fact that four federal appeals courts had reached different conclusions on university affirmative action. Mahoney gently suggested that the justices would be better served by waiting for additional lower court opinions. She noted that the Sixth Circuit was the first panel to see evidence of the educational benefits of diversity, glossing over the fact that Martin's opinion for the court hadn't discussed that issue.

Mahoney used the brief to foreshadow the central components to her argument. *Bakke* has served America well, she told the Court. Citing past opinions written by Justices O'Connor and Scalia, Mahoney said the Court traditionally has been reluctant to overturn decisions "woven into the fabric of our 'national culture.'" Overturning *Bakke,* as it had been interpreted by universities, "would be enormously disruptive."

In a second brief, Payton laid out the university's response to CIR's petition in the undergraduate case. Payton first reiterated the position Mahoney had taken in the law school brief: Michigan believed the Supreme Court should stay out of the fray for now. But if the court chose to hear one dispute, it should consider both, Payton wrote. Hearing the cases together "would allow this Court an opportunity to provide more helpful guidance to lower courts and to colleges and universities charged with complying with this Court's decisions than would be possible if only one admissions system were before the Court."

———■———

FROM NEW YORK, Shaw watched the procedural maneuvering with great interest. He had filed his own cert-before-judgment petition in the undergraduate case, urging the Court to consider, additionally, his arguments about past discrimination by the University of Michigan. Shaw knew his petition was unusual, but it wasn't unprecedented. And he thought the idea of putting both cases before the Court was a promising tactic.

Shaw had always felt more confident about the law school admissions policy than the one at the undergraduate level. At the law school, Shaw had been in on the ground floor, helping to draft the policy while serving as a Michigan faculty member. The hallmark of the policy was flexibility, considering race but still treating each applicant as an individual. Shaw was confident the law school was complying with *Bakke.* The undergraduate point system, by contrast, was more numbers-driven. Shaw thought it was legally defensible, but he also believed the school would have been wiser to come up with a method that seemed less mechanical.

Shaw nonetheless was eager for the Court to see both cases. One reason was the particularly deep context for diversity at the undergraduate level. The majority of UM students entered college with virtually no experience in a racially integrated environment. As Payton had pointed out repeatedly throughout the litigation, Michigan was an extraordinarily segregated state. More than 90 percent of the white undergraduates at the university grew up in predominantly white neighborhoods; more than 80 percent went to high schools that were almost all white.

A second reason was tactical. Two cases would give the Court a chance to uphold the use of affirmative action while putting limits on it. The Court might opt to split the difference, upholding the law school policy (and declaring diversity to be a compelling interest), while striking down the undergraduate system. That outcome, from Shaw's perspective, would be a major victory, upholding the principle of race-based admissions and perhaps even providing a road map for universities to avoid future constitutional challenges.[5]

———■———

MAHONEY'S ARRIVAL ON the team had reinforced General Counsel Krislov's conviction that the military issue was a potential case-turner at the Supreme Court. Mahoney knew the Court cared deeply about issues that affected the U.S. government, regardless of what position the solicitor general took. Mahoney also thought the military academies were a wonderful illustration of the linkage between higher education admissions and leadership roles throughout society. "If there's any way to do this, Marvin, you need to do it," she told him early on.

Jim Cannon, the man who first raised the military academy question with Bollinger, likewise was determined to make something out of the issue. With almost naïve optimism, he scheduled a meeting with Mitch Daniels, a friend who was director of the Bush administration's Office of Management and Budget. Daniels was happy to listen, but the meeting produced nothing tangible. Undeterred, Cannon arranged an appointment with David Chu, the undersecretary of defense for personnel, hoping to convince the Pentagon to file a brief supporting Michigan. Meeting with Chu, his deputy, and several lawyers, Cannon made little progress. "We're not sure the case will affect us," one attorney said. Besides, the lawyers reminded Cannon, the Defense Department wasn't an independent entity that could file its own brief. Ultimately, the Pentagon was obligated to go along with the Bush administration's position on the issue.

Cannon pressed on. If the military wasn't going to make the case for diversity in the armed services, he figured, he would simply do it himself: he would find a lawyer, raise funds, and put his own name on a friend-of-the-court brief. Cannon visited his friend A. B. Culvahouse, chairman of the 900-lawyer firm O'Melveny & Myers. Culvahouse brought in Walter Dellinger, the firm's top Supreme Court lawyer and the former acting solicitor general. Cannon told Dellinger that an all-white officer corps would be a disaster. Cannon described how the service academies were the gateways to the officer ranks and how race-based admissions were essential if the academies were to be racially diverse. With characteristic modesty, Cannon finished by saying he wasn't sure whether the Supreme Court would want to hear from him.

Like Bollinger and Mahoney before him, Dellinger was instantly struck by the potential force of the argument. He saw it as a way to get the high court past the "zero point," to accept that outlawing racial preference, in at least one important context, would have devastating consequences. Dellinger assured Cannon that the Court would be extremely interested.

Unfortunately, Dellinger said, he was already committed to filing an amicus brief supporting Michigan for the Law School Admissions Council, which administers the LSAT and coordinates the admissions processes at 200 law schools. But Dellinger promised to help Cannon find a lawyer and encouraged him not to give up.

—■—

KRISLOV WASN'T AS worried about getting a lawyer for a military brief so much as he was worried about finding clients. In November, he signed up a man who was a little of both.

Joe Reeder was an accomplished Washington attorney, working at the firm of Greenberg Traurig, who also had a web of military connections and a storehouse of knowledge about the services. In the Clinton administration, Reeder served as undersecretary of the Army, the service's number-two civilian post, with responsibility for overseeing the admissions criteria at West Point and the ROTC programs around the country. Reeder had a reputation as a man who could get things done. Once he made up his mind to do something, he was like a pit bull, refusing to quit until he completed his mission.

Reeder also could be a tough man to reach on the phone, as Krislov had learned over the course of several weeks. Krislov first called Reeder at the suggestion of Reeder's partner Bob Charrow, a health-care attorney who represented the university on other matters. The problem was that Reeder wouldn't call Krislov back. After several failed attempts, an exasperated Krislov said to Charrow, "You make him call me back." Reeder still didn't phone Krislov, but a few days later Charrow at least was able to send word that his partner was interested in joining the team.

Krislov eventually learned that Reeder believed deeply in a diverse officer corps, having seen its importance first hand. Reeder, a West Point graduate and Army Ranger, served in the Vietnam War in a battalion that had no black commissioned officers. First Lieutenant Reeder did have several black noncommissioned officers serving under him, and he found their presence invaluable for ensuring morale and discipline. Not only were the African American sergeants and corporals simply among the best in the business, they had special credibility with black soldiers. The black noncoms could give dangerous assignments without risking an accusation of racism, Reeder discovered. And they had especially high expectations for the black troops, an attitude that tended to bring out the best in the soldiers.

When Reeder finally did call Krislov, the Michigan general counsel got his first taste of Reeder's brisk, military style. Calling from his wireless phone, Reeder said he had only a minute to talk but, yes, he would help. They would work out his exact role later.[6]

———•———

UNBEKNOWNST TO ANY of the attorneys, amid the marble halls and ornate offices of the Supreme Court, one justice was considering a step with the potential to devastate Michigan's case.

The justice was John Paul Stevens, the Court's oldest member at eighty-two. The bow-tied, genial Stevens was an intriguing figure on the Court, particularly on affirmative action cases. He had voted against the University of California in the *Bakke* case on narrow, statutory grounds. Since that time, Stevens had gradually moved to the left while the Court inched in the opposite direction. Stevens now was, arguably, the most liberal member on the Court. He had voted in favor of affirmative action in the most recent cases before the Court. His was a vote Michigan was counting on. Without Stevens, winning the case would be almost impossible for the university.

As he would disclose months later in a speech, Stevens was troubled by the law school case because one of the named defendants, Dean Jeff Lehman, was a former clerk to the justice. Every year, each justice hires three or four young lawyers, most of them just a year out of law school, to assist in analyzing the cases and drafting opinions. The law clerks hold their posts for only a year but many, including Mahoney, develop close and lasting relationships with their justices.

Stevens worried that he might create an appearance of impropriety by ruling in a case in which his former clerk had an interest. In 1978, Stevens had recused himself from a private-sector affirmative action dispute because a close friend had designed the employer's policy in question and because Stevens himself had once done legal work for the company. Stevens wondered whether a similar step might be in order in the Michigan law school case.

Stevens consulted his fellow justices. The issue of ex-clerks was a familiar one, given that clerks tended to move on to high-powered jobs that brought them back into contact with the Court. The justices had long ago concluded that none of them should have to step out of a case simply because a former clerk was representing one of the parties. A rule to the contrary would leave the Court frequently operating with only seven or eight justices, depriving the public of a full panel. In the affirmative action cases, it would mean that Chief Justice Rehnquist also would have to disqualify himself because of Mahoney's participation. The question now was whether Lehman's involvement as a defendant in the law school case (as well as an attorney on the defense team) was different from the work of the countless former clerks who had practiced before the Court.

Meeting at one of their regularly scheduled, private conferences, the other justices were unanimous and firm: Stevens shouldn't disqualify himself. Stevens agreed, deciding to stay in the case, and Michigan survived a threat it didn't even realize had existed.[7]

———■———

ALONG WITH THE CIA, the Supreme Court is one of America's great leak-proof institutions. Other government bodies in Washington regularly give advance word of their actions, but at the Court secrecy is practically a religion. Employees must follow an ethical code that bars them from discussing the Court's internal deliberations. The justices' law clerks are forbidden from taking case memos or draft opinions outside the building, out of concern that a copy might land in the hands of an outsider. Breaches are so rare they become the stuff of lore. (In a notable recent example, Edward Lazarus wrote a book about the Court in 1998, drawing from his experiences as a clerk to Justice Harry Blackmun, who had retired four years earlier. The other justices responded by further tightening their confidentiality rules.)

So as the various lawyers sat in their offices on the morning of December 2, they could only speculate as to what the Court would do. They knew from the clerk's office that the justices had considered the three pending cert petitions at their closed-door conference the previous Wednesday. The Court was scheduled to issue a list of hundreds of orders at 10:00 a.m. It was likely that the orders list would include the Michigan cases, but even that wasn't a sure thing.

The press would be the first to know. At a few minutes before ten, two dozen reporters crammed into the anteroom of the Court's public information office. With both affirmative action and an important gay-rights case pending before the Court, the media crowd was larger than usual. Wire service reporters stood directly in front of the wooden desk by the door, facing two court employees. Representatives of daily newspapers, radio, and television waited a few steps behind or to the side, knowing that their colleagues would soon be dashing to their computers and desk phones. (Mobile phones were banned in the office.) At 10:00, Public Information Officer Kathy Arberg and her assistants began handing out the twenty-page list, and reporters furiously flipped through it.

Seconds later, news outlets flashed the first headlines: the Court would hear the appeals by the Center for Individual Rights in both the law school and undergraduate cases, though not Shaw's separate petition. What promised to be a landmark fight would forever be known by two names: *Grutter v. Bollinger* and *Gratz v. Bollinger.*[8]

Part Four

The Supreme Court

(December 2002–June 2003)

Chapter Fourteen

The Most Powerful Woman in America

THE NINE JUSTICES who would hear the *Gratz* and *Grutter* cases were known commodities. Each had been on the Supreme Court for at least eight years, marking the longest stretch of continuity since 1823. Although only two justices had specifically considered the question of university admissions, each of the nine had a well-developed judicial philosophy. Neither side's lawyers had to do much guesswork to figure out where to start counting their votes.

Gratz and Grutter's support began on the right with sixty-six-year-old Antonin Scalia, the Court's standard-bearer for conservatives since his appointment in 1986. The Court's first Italian American, "Nino" Scalia was an avid poker player and hunter (the latter hobby one he occasionally enjoyed with Vice President Dick Cheney) and was notorious among his colleagues for his fast driving. Brilliant and acerbic, Scalia used biting prose and a sharp tongue to argue for bright lines in the law. He believed jurists are constrained by the words of the Constitution and the intent of its authors. He thought the Constitution provides fixed guarantees, not evolving ones that vary with the personal preferences of the justices. The equal protection clause, as Scalia saw it, gives the same rights to whites as to blacks. Scalia had consistently voted against affirmative action and, because he had no reservations about toppling prior decisions he thought were wrong, was a sure vote to overturn the prevailing interpretation of *Bakke*.

A second vote against racial preferences almost certainly would come from the Court's only black justice, fifty-four-year-old Clarence Thomas. Born dirt-poor in Pin Point, Georgia, Thomas learned the lessons of hard work and self-help from the grandparents who raised him. Those qualities—and affirmative action—led him to Yale Law School. In 1991, George H. W. Bush, in what detractors would call the ultimate example of affirmative action, nominated the forty-three-year-old Thomas to replace Thurgood Marshall on the high court. Liberals were aghast at the notion of the conservative Thomas replacing a civil rights icon, all the more so when sexual harassment allegations surfaced against the nominee. Thomas nonetheless won confirmation on a 52-48 vote. Once on the Court, Thomas confirmed expectations that he would oppose racial preferences, saying they stigmatized minorities. "So-called 'benign' discrimination teaches many that because of chronic and apparently immutable handicaps, minorities cannot compete with them without their patronizing indulgence," Thomas wrote in 1995 in *Adarand*.

Chief Justice William Rehnquist, seventy-eight, was another preference opponent, having voted against affirmative action at virtually every opportunity in his thirty-one years on the Court. Rehnquist, the son of a wholesale paper salesman, finished first in his class at Stanford Law School and rose through the ranks of Republican politics before Richard Nixon tapped him for the high court. Rehnquist was a history buff who moonlighted as an author, publishing books on Supreme Court procedures, impeachments, and civil liberties in wartime. (The impeachment book was brought back into print after Rehnquist presided over the 1998 trial of President Bill Clinton.) With a deep, resonating voice, Rehnquist was a commanding presence in the Supreme Court's center chair. He strictly enforced argument time limits, more than once cutting off a long-winded lawyer mid-sentence. As chief justice, Rehnquist enjoyed an important administrative power. If an initial vote by the justices indicated that he was in the majority, Rehnquist could assign the opinion to the justice of his choice. That way, he could help keep the majority intact, while ensuring the strongest possible opinion.

A fourth good prospect was sixty-six-year-old Justice Anthony Kennedy. A mild-mannered, likeable California native, Kennedy was a devotee of Shakespeare, opera, and Supreme Court history.

He was Ronald Reagan's third choice to fill a 1986 vacancy, getting the nod only after the Senate rejected Robert Bork and after Douglas Ginsburg's name was withdrawn amid questions about past marijuana use. Kennedy's middle-of-the-road stances on abortion and school prayer had disappointed many conservatives and made him an occasional swing vote on the court. But Kennedy had been solid in his opposition on racial preferences. In the *Metro Broadcasting* case, he blasted the notion of broadcast diversity as "trivial" and said the majority would "move us from 'separate but equal' to 'unequal but benign.'"

The university could point to four likely votes of its own, at least for the general validity of affirmative action, if not for the specifics of the Michigan policies. One was Ruth Bader Ginsburg, sixty-nine, one of only two Democratic appointees on the Court. The shy, hard-working Ginsburg was well acquainted with hardships and discrimination. During her second year of law school in 1957–58 her husband, third-year student Martin Ginsburg, contracted testicular cancer and had to undergo surgery and extensive radiation treatments. Undaunted, Ginsburg made sure Martin could graduate, copying notes from his classmates and typing his third-year paper, all the while rearing the couple's toddler and attending to her own studies. She graduated a year later, only to discover that she couldn't find a law firm job in New York. Ginsburg later became the nation's foremost courtroom advocate against gender discrimination, arguing and winning a series of Supreme Court cases. As a lawyer for the ACLU, she had filed a brief in support of the medical school in *Bakke.* Three decades later Justice Ginsburg wrote that racial discrimination persisted in America. "Congress surely can conclude that a carefully designed affirmative action program may help to realize, finally, the 'equal protection of the laws' the Fourteenth Amendment has promised since 1868," she wrote in *Adarand.*

A second likely vote for the university was sixty-three-year-old David Souter, a New Hampshire–born bachelor with a wry sense of humor and a tendency toward a spartan lifestyle. (He refused to wear an overcoat, even in the coldest weather, and owned a black-and-white television.) Nominated by George H. W. Bush in 1990, Souter was dubbed by the media as the "stealth justice" because of his sparse track record. For conservatives, he turned out to be an even bigger disappointment than Kennedy, favoring abortion and gay rights and voting to limit government support for religion. Like Ginsburg, Souter dissented from the 1995 *Adarand* decision and the tough legal test it laid out for federal affirmative action programs. He was a likely vote for Michigan, though not a sure one. In explaining his reasons in *Adarand,* Souter noted with approval that programs designed to remedy the lingering effects of past discrimination would impose only a temporary burden. As Pell and Kolbo were eager to point out, the Michigan program, by contrast, appeared to be a permanent one.

Stephen Breyer, the other Democratic appointee, was the newest member of the Court and therefore had the shortest track record. Married to the daughter of a British lord and educated at Stanford, Oxford, and Harvard, Breyer had the Court's most aristocratic résumé. His 1994 nomination was complicated by his status as a Lloyd's of London investor. Breyer, sixty-four, nonetheless maintained the demeanor of a less privileged man. Every year to celebrate Read Across America Day, Breyer donned a striped hat and read Dr. Seuss's *The Cat in the Hat* to a group of Washington, D.C., grade school children. Professorial on the bench, Breyer loved posing multipart hypothetical questions to draw out the positions of the lawyers. As often as not, those questions indicated that he was struggling to decide how to vote. On race, Breyer had supported affirmative action, joining the dissenters in *Adarand.* Like Ginsburg and Souter, he also backed the power of state legislatures to carve out congressional districts for black politicians.

John Paul Stevens was the fourth probable vote for the university. In his twenty-seven years on the Court, Stevens had developed a reputation as a maverick. Alone among the justices, he declined to take part in the pool system for analyzing cert petitions, instead instructing his clerks to evaluate each of the 8,000 petitions every year themselves. Stevens was a friendly face on the bench for like-minded lawyers, often intervening to help struggling attorneys make their case. Even into his eighties, the Chicago native was full of energy, enjoying golf, tennis, and bridge and insisting on preparing the first draft of his opinions.

Stevens had come a long way since his vote against the University of California-Davis program in *Bakke.* His vote in that case was on statutory grounds; he said that since Title VI precluded preferences, he didn't need to decide whether the Constitution permitted affirmative action. In a 1983 case involving discrimination claims by minority police officers, Stevens made an important clarification. He said he was bound by a conclusion five justices had reached in *Bakke:* that Title VI restricted affirmative action only to the extent the Fourteenth Amendment did. Thus, Stevens concluded, he was free to discard his interpretation of Title VI and focus on the equal protection clause as the sole limiting force on affirmative action. In the 1990 *Metro Broadcasting* case, Stevens made clear that he was now solidly on the side of university affirmative action. The public interest in student-body diversity at professional schools, he said, "is in my view unquestionably legitimate."

———

THE FINAL, CRUCIAL VOTE would come from Sandra Day O'Connor. It would be a familiar role for the seventy-two-year-old, dubbed by the *New York Times* as "America's most powerful jurist." O'Connor was at the center of the Court on virtually every high-profile issue. Whether the question was church-state separation, abortion, federal government power, or the election of a president, O'Connor almost inevitably was the swing vote.

O'Connor's story in many ways was the quintessential American tale. Born in 1930, just as the Great Depression set in, she grew up on the Arizona–New Mexico border on an arid, 160,000-acre ranch known as the Lazy B. She learned how to ride horses, handle farm equipment, and euthanize injured animals. Her best friends were the farm's uneducated cowboys, whom she admired for their dignity and work ethic. Her father was a perfectionist who chastised his fifteen-year-old daughter one day when she arrived late with the cowboys' lunch after changing a flat tire. "You should have started earlier," he said. "You need to expect anything out here." Sandra's mother, a subscriber to the *New Yorker* and *Vogue,* taught her daughter a love for style and culture. Both parents stressed education, and they sent her away to live with her grandparents in El Paso to attend a private girls' grade school.[1]

O'Connor eventually made her way to Stanford Law School, where she graduated third in her 102-member class. (Classmate William Rehnquist, whom she briefly dated, was first.) Like Ginsburg,

As with many hot-button issues, Sandra Day O'Connor was the justice in the middle at the Supreme Court on affirmative action. Four of her colleagues— John Paul Stevens, David Souter, Ruth Bader Ginsburg, and Stephen Breyer (left)—broadly supported affirmative action. Four others—William Rehnquist, Antonin Scalia, Anthony Kennedy, and Clarence Thomas (right)—were skeptical.

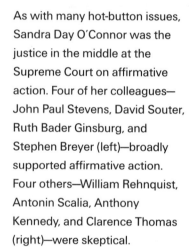

O'Connor initially struggled to find a job in the male-dominated legal world; only one California law firm would hire her even as a legal secretary. She finally landed a position as a deputy county attorney in San Mateo, California. O'Connor later returned to Arizona, where she got involved in Republican politics. She ran for the state legislature, won, and became the first woman in the United States to hold the title of state Senate majority leader. She served two years on a state court before Ronald Reagan fulfilled a campaign pledge by making her the first female justice.

O'Connor quickly discovered that her new job required her to be a role model as well as a jurist. Five hundred letters a week poured in during her first term, many from young girls, and for a time O'Connor tried to answer them all. She accepted one speaking invitation after another, including one at the law firm that had offered her the secretarial position. O'Connor even organized a morning aerobics and yoga class at the Court for female employees.

Her judicial philosophy reflected her background as a legislator as she delved into the details of government policies. O'Connor eschewed the sweeping, bright-line rules favored by colleagues like Scalia. She preferred to evaluate each dispute on its facts, deciding no more than what was necessary to resolve the case. She frequently made fine distinctions: a city-sponsored nativity scene was constitutional if it was part of a larger nonreligious holiday display, but not if it stood by itself. A state could require a minor to get parental or judicial approval before getting an abortion, but it couldn't insist that a married woman notify her husband. O'Connor's approach to the law, coupled with her position at the ideological center of the Court, meant that she frequently was the one to decide whether a particular law or practice was constitutional.

Nowhere was O'Connor's influence more important than on questions of race. In her two decades on the Court, she had written some of its most important race-relations decisions, including *Croson, Adarand,* and *Shaw v. Reno,* a 1993 ruling that allowed a challenge to a North Carolina redistricting plan and its two bizarrely shaped majority-black districts. O'Connor was skeptical of affirmative action but, in typical fashion, refused to rule it out altogether. She believed the proper level of review for affirmative action plans was strict scrutiny. But she seemed to mean it in *Adarand* when, quoting from an earlier case, she said that "we wish to dispel the notion that strict scrutiny is 'strict in theory but fatal in fact.'" O'Connor said the ultimate question in that case was whether the set-aside program was "narrowly tailored." She told a lower court to revisit the case and consider whether government officials considered using race-neutral means to assist minority companies and whether the program had some sort of time limit.

On the question of diversity, O'Connor's published thoughts suggested some uncertainty. In 1986, she suggested Powell's *Bakke* opinion was the law of the land, saying that "although its precise contours are uncertain, a state interest in the promotion of racial diversity has been found sufficiently 'compelling,' at least in the context of higher education, to support the use of racial considerations in furthering that interest." But then in *Metro Broadcasting* in 1990 she wrote that diversity among broadcasters "is simply too amorphous, too insubstantial, and too unrelated to any legitimate basis for employing racial classifications." She added: "Like the vague assertion of societal discrimination, a claim of insufficiently diverse broadcasting viewpoints might be used to justify equally unconstrained racial preferences, linked to nothing other than proportional representation of various races."

What was clear was that O'Connor, now in the twilight of her career and busy dispelling retirement rumors, was the pivotal vote. All sides knew they would need to focus on the woman from the Lazy B ranch.

———■———

IN MID-DECEMBER, Krislov flew to Washington for a pair of back-to-back meetings he had arranged to discuss the game plan for the outside briefs supporting the university. The university rented a 1,500-square-foot conference room a few blocks from the Capitol to accommodate the seventy-five lawyers and policy advocates Krislov was expecting.

The first session was a smaller affair, attended by a dozen people and dedicated to the military brief idea. Payton, Mahoney, Reeder, and Cannon all were on hand, along with a pair of staffers from the office of Carl Levin, Michigan's senior U.S. senator. Levin was an attorney and the top Democrat on the Senate Armed Services Committee. He also was a big supporter of the University of Michigan and its defense of affirmative action.

Also attending was Virginia Seitz, a lawyer with Sidley Austin Brown & Wood. Sidley was another of Washington's top law firms and the home to one of the most accomplished Supreme Court practitioners, Carter Phillips. Soon after the high court agreed to hear the case, Mahoney had called Phillips to ask whether he would handle an amicus brief. Phillips agreed, but when he learned that the university wanted him to work on the military brief, he concluded that his partner Seitz was better suited to take the lead. Seitz, a former clerk to Justice William Brennan and a Rhodes scholar, was well-versed on the equal protection clause through her work as a labor and employment lawyer. The plan was for Seitz to take charge of researching the issues and writing the brief. Reeder would help her on the brief and work to recruit military leaders to sign it.

The group gathered around the head table in the front of the room. The talk focused on what the brief had to say to be effective. First, of course, it would need details on how race was used in admissions at the four service academies. The team still lacked much in the way of documentation, but Cannon and Reeder knew from first-hand experience that affirmative action programs were in place. "Whether or not you can find it, it's true," they insisted. "If it's out there, we'll find it," Seitz promised.

The brief, everyone agreed, also had to cover the history of race relations in the military. That would include the racial tension that all but paralyzed the military in the Vietnam War, when barely 3 percent of the Army's officers were black.

The conversation turned to ROTC programs at universities. Krislov and Payton had always thought of ROTC as a minor supporting detail in their case: because Michigan was racially diverse, it produced more black and Hispanic military officers. The argument was useful, but it wasn't different in kind from the contention that university diversity meant more minority accountants, engineers, and lawyers.

Reeder told the group that ROTC programs were even more important to the military than the academies. More than half the military's officers come from ROTC, Reeder said. If the services had to choose between the two, "in a heartbeat, they'd get rid of the military academies," he said.

At once, Krislov and Payton realized that Reeder was offering a powerful new component to the argument. ROTC programs were a direct link from the University of Michigan's admissions policies to the nation's military readiness. By itself, the service academy argument had a limitation; the Supreme Court might simply distinguish between the academies and nonmilitary institutions, leaving open the possibility that affirmative action might be justified if national security were at stake. ROTC programs bridged that gap: the military was relying on universities like Michigan to help develop its minority officers. National security *was* at stake.

As the discussion wound down, other people began arriving for the second meeting Krislov had planned. In the days following the Supreme Court announcement, the general counsel's office had been besieged by calls from supporters wanting to file briefs. Krislov concluded that a mass meeting was the only way to coordinate the various efforts. He wanted to ensure that each interest group knew what was happening at other organizations with similar perspectives. Three religious groups, Krislov figured, would help Michigan far more by combining forces on one excellent brief than by submitting three mediocre filings.

At the meeting, Krislov, Payton, Mahoney, and university attorney Jonathan Alger made brief presentations about the case, then split the crowd into breakout groups. While higher education officials talked to one another, representatives for the legal profession did the same across the room. In the end, every lawyer went home with a client to represent, and Krislov declared the session a success.

Seitz returned to her downtown office assuming that she would need a small army of her own to make the military brief happen. She quickly put together an action plan, several pages long, laying out the various topics that needed to be researched. It was a long list, but Sidley had plenty of resources. Seitz assembled a group of eight to ten associates and told each to spend a week finding as much as possible about a particular topic. One lawyer took each of the four service academies and started looking into the admissions policies. One was assigned to investigate the prep schools that fed the academies, while another looked into the ROTC aspect of the case. Seitz asked two other associates to research the history of race and military, with one focusing just on Vietnam. Still another attorney looked into legal questions affecting the military. Seitz herself set to work on a preliminary draft, beginning to realize the potential her brief had to influence the outcome.[2]

———◆———

FOR TWO YEARS the Bush administration had managed to stay out of the fray. Justice Department and Education Department attorneys had met with representatives from both sides on several occasions, but the government remained studiously neutral, declining to take sides at the Sixth Circuit or during the cert petition stage.

Politically, that stance made some sense. Affirmative action created risks for the administration whatever it did. In the 2000 election, Bush had captured 35 percent of the Hispanic vote, the best showing by a Republican since 1984. Would a strong stand against affirmative action cost him that support in 2004? On the flip side, if Bush were to appear less than fervent in his opposition, would he alienate his conservative base? And would he appear inconsistent, given his campaign stance against "quotas" and in favor of "affirmative access"?

With the Supreme Court now set to consider the merits of the two cases, staying out was less of an option. The federal government, acting through the solicitor general's office, had participated in every affirmative action dispute the Supreme Court had ever considered, except for one 1993 case that raised only procedural issues. The Michigan cases were looming as potentially the most important affirmative action cases of a generation. For the Bush administration to sit silently, fearing the political repercussions, would be a nonaction of historic proportions.

As the administration began its deliberations, outside forces raised the political stakes. At a December 5 birthday party for 100-year-old Senator Strom Thurmond, Senate Republican Leader Trent Lott of Mississippi uttered a remark that would set off a political and racial furor. Lott praised Thurmond's presidential campaign of 1948, when Thurmond ran on a segregationist platform. "I want to say this about my state," Lott said. "When Strom Thurmond ran for president we voted for him. We're proud of it. And if the rest of the country had followed our lead, we wouldn't have had all these problems over all these years, either." The audience laughed and applauded.

At best, Lott's remarks were profoundly insensitive. Bush decided he needed to distance himself from his fellow Republican. A week after the party, Bush said in a speech that Lott's comments were "wrong" and "do not reflect the spirit of our country." Bush stopped short of calling for Lott's resignation. The senator nonetheless soon found himself with little support, and on December 20 he stepped down as Republican leader.

The Lott imbroglio fueled speculation that the White House would duck the Michigan fight. But Bush was already moving toward a conclusion that he needed to take a stand. And, based on preliminary conversations with a handful of trusted advisers, the president was leaning toward a position that would satisfy almost no one outside the White House.

———■———

PELL AND KOLBO figured they had at least one strategically placed friend in the administration. He was Ted Olson, who was rewarded for his victory in the *Bush v. Gore* case with an appointment as solicitor general.

Olson was a lawyer with a gentle public demeanor who nonetheless took office with as much partisan political baggage as any solicitor general in history. Controversy had surrounded Olson since the 1980s when, as an official in Ronald Reagan's Justice Department, he was accused of lying to a congressional panel. An independent counsel's three-year-long investigation ended without an indictment, although her report called Olson's congressional testimony "disingenuous and misleading."

He returned to private practice, where he threw himself into a variety of conservative causes. Olson represented President Reagan in the Iran-Contra investigation and the state-run Virginia Military Institute in its unsuccessful effort to remain all-male. Olson joined the board of directors of a right-of-center magazine, the *American Spectator.* His wife, Barbara Olson, wrote a scathing biography of Hillary Rodham Clinton.

Perhaps Olson's biggest success came while working with CIR in Cheryl Hopwood's discrimination lawsuit against the University of Texas Law School. Arguing before the Fifth Circuit, Olson cast the matter in absolutes, demonstrating the depth of his opposition to

racial preferences. "Racial discrimination, in any form, causes damage," he said. "It stigmatizes people. It causes feelings of inferiority.
It sparks resentment." The Fifth Circuit concluded that race-based
college admissions were unconstitutional.

Democrats reacted aggressively to Olson's nomination as solicitor general, grilling him about his role in a $2 million campaign at
the *American Spectator* to dig up dirt on the Clintons. The Senate
eventually confirmed Olson by the narrowest of margins, 51-47. The
criticism died down after Olson took office and got to work. Olson
adopted the solicitor general's long-standing practice of defending all
federal statutes and programs, even if they went against the administration's policy preferences. Olson argued in favor of a federal law
guaranteeing family and medical leave for workers. He disappointed
preference opponents by arguing at the Supreme Court in favor of a
federal affirmative action program for minority highway contractors.
On the way out of the courtroom in that case, he met Ward Connerly
for the first time.

"Nice argument," Connerly said. "I wish you were on the other
side."

"Next time," Olson promised.[3]

On September 11, 2001, Barbara Olson died aboard the hijacked
airliner that crashed into the Pentagon. Ted Olson coped with the loss
by talking. He granted interview after interview to tell stories about
his late wife and, in the process, tying the Bush administration in a
personal way to the tragedy.

As the government's top litigator, Olson had a complicated role.
The solicitor general answered to the president, yet by tradition
enjoyed considerable independence. Known informally as the "tenth
justice," he (no woman has ever held the post) was a judicial officer
with a special duty of candor toward the Supreme Court and, consequently, a unique credibility with the justices. The solicitor general
took sides in cases at the high court but often was more interested
in the legal principles that would be established than the outcome
of the dispute at hand. In the words of former solicitor general
Simon Sobeloff: "My client's chief business is not to achieve victory
but to establish justice." As if to underscore his competing loyalties,
the solicitor general had offices in two branches of government, at
both the Justice Department and the Supreme Court. (Only the vice

president, with offices in the White House and Senate, could claim a similar distinction.)

In the vast majority of Supreme Court cases involving the U.S. government, the solicitor general made the final call regarding the administration's position, usually after hearing from affected federal agencies. But with so much at stake politically, the Michigan disputes were no ordinary cases. Olson could make his recommendation, but the ultimate decision would rest with the president.

In late December Olson, Deputy Solicitor General Paul Clement, and Attorney General John Ashcroft met at the White House with a group of the president's top aides, including Domestic Policy Adviser Jay Lefkowitz and White House Counsel Alberto Gonzales. Backed by Ashcroft and Clement, Olson made his case forcefully: the administration should oppose any use of race in admissions and seek to overturn the prevailing view of *Bakke.*

Olson's position was that a clear stand against racial preferences was not only right constitutionally, but also smart as a matter of tactics and coherence. As he put it, any argument that stopped short of seeking to overturn *Bakke* would make little sense. Olson was particularly disdainful of an alternative being discussed: focusing solely on the narrow tailoring question and urging the court not to resolve the compelling interest aspect of the case. The upshot would be that diversity would survive as a justification for preferences. To Olson, that approach was akin to fitting a suit without knowing who was wearing it; before deciding whether Michigan's policy was narrowly tailored, the Court would have to decide exactly what interest the policy was supposed to be serving.

Olson also contended that the administration needed to show the justices it was willing to take the political heat from a stance against any racial preferences. CIR was asking the Court to wipe out the admissions practices at hundreds of schools. Olson couldn't see how the Court, particularly Sandra Day O'Connor, would be willing to take that step unless the Bush administration first led by example. The Supreme Court liked to have things made easy for it.

Lefkowitz and Gonzales were noncommittal. The White House officials already sensed from Bush that the president wasn't inclined to go as far as Olson wanted, and they asked Olson whether various alternatives might work. Olson stuck to his position: the administra-

Solicitor General Ted Olson, the Bush administration's voice at the Supreme Court, had once argued a case against racial preferences at the University of Texas. Olson wanted the administration to take an unequivocal stand against racial preferences, but the White House refused to go that far.

tion needed to argue against the status of diversity as a compelling interest.

Soon after the meeting, Olson sent the White House a draft brief calling on the Court to overturn *Bakke* and bar any use of race in admissions.

Lefkowitz and Gonzales responded in a matter of days. The president, they told Olson, didn't want to go that far. The brief would have to be scaled back.[4]

———■———

THE HIGH COURT'S DECISION to hear both cases created a practical problem for Kolbo. At the lower court level, the cases had generally proceeded along separate schedules. Briefs on major issues were never due simultaneously in both cases. At the Supreme Court, Kolbo had the same January 16 deadline—just forty-five days after the Court granted cert—for the two fifty-page briefs he needed to file. Since Kolbo had decided he would take the lead in drafting both briefs (as well as arguing both cases on April 1), he had a lot of work ahead of him.

Kolbo didn't want the two filings to be clones. He decided to write the *Grutter* brief in its entirety first before turning his attention to *Gratz*. Kolbo first made sure the Court understood just how big the scope of racial preferences was at the law school. He devoted page seven to a grid, similar to those Michigan Law School had once produced, showing how minorities stood a far better chance of admission than whites and Asian Americans with identical grades and test scores. "The Law School's own admissions data and witnesses demonstrate the 'staggering magnitude' of its racial preferences," Kolbo wrote, quoting from Judge Boggs's dissent.

Kolbo said he wasn't asking the Court to overturn *Bakke*. There was, he said, nothing to overturn because the splintered *Bakke* court didn't produce any holding that authorized the use of race in admissions. Citing the high court's post–*Bakke* decisions, Kolbo argued that diversity was too vague a concept to meet the strict criteria the justices had laid out for use of race by a governmental entity. "Its adoption as a compelling interest would give the Nation its first *permanent* justification for racial preferences, and one that is indistinguishable from simple racial balancing," Kolbo wrote.

In the *Gratz* brief, Kolbo ratcheted up his attack on the University of Michigan itself, accusing the institution of "defiant resistance to this court's precedents." He added: "In defending its rigid, mechanical racial preferences on the asserted ground that they comport with Justice Powell's strictures on the use of race in admissions as set forth in his opinion in *Bakke*, the University in fact mocks that opinion."

Kolbo saved room to attack some of the logical underpinnings of the university's case, including the notion that the high court should defer to the educational judgment of school administrators. That position "is simply inconsistent with the notion that strict scrutiny must be applied to the use of race," Kolbo wrote. Strict scrutiny, he said, means skepticism—"the bedrock proposition that all official actions that treat a person differently on account of race or ethnicity are inherently suspect."

———

IN PRESIDENT BUSH'S VIEW, diversity was a valuable goal, but racial preferences were a cop-out, at least when used on such a large scale. Bush told his staffers that, based on what he had seen at the University of Texas while he was in Austin, he thought universities weren't doing enough to make themselves attractive to minorities. Nor were they searching hard enough for alternatives to preferences, Bush said.

In meetings in the Oval Office, Bush said he wanted to balance the competing goals of diversity and equal protection. He wouldn't rule out the use of race altogether—Bush said race might be an appropriate factor as a tie-breaker—but he wanted to sharply restrict the practice.

As the deadline approached for the Bush administration to file, the president met almost daily with White House aides, sometimes in formal group settings, other times one-on-one, occasionally playing devil's advocate as his staff made recommendations. The inner circle included White House Counsel Alberto Gonzales, Domestic Policy Adviser Jay Lefkowitz, and National Security Adviser Condoleezza Rice, who had previously served as provost at Stanford University. Bush also spoke with Secretary of State Colin Powell, Vice President Dick Cheney, Chief of Staff Andrew Card, and Senior Adviser Karl Rove.

Conspicuously out of the loop was Olson, the attorney charged with making Bush's argument at the high court. Since the December meeting with Gonzales and Lefkowitz, Olson had visited the White House a handful of times, but never for a formal briefing with the president on the Michigan cases. Rumors swirled at the White House that Olson was so annoyed he might resign or withhold his name from the two briefs that were being prepared. White House officials knew they needed to do something to make sure Olson was on board.

Cheney, one of Olson's closest allies in the administration, put in a call to the solicitor general. It's the president's right to make these decisions, Cheney reminded his friend.

Olson decided to stay on the job and put his name on the briefs. And he concluded that he should be the one to argue the case before the Supreme Court.

—■—

THE AFTERNOON BEFORE the administration's briefs were due, George W. Bush stepped into the Roosevelt Room of the White House and stood in front of a waiting group of television cameras, reporters, and photographers. Sporting a maroon tie and an American flag lapel pin, Bush said that he supported diversity, "including racial diversity in higher education." But, he went on, "at their core, the Michigan policies amount to a quota system that unfairly rewards or penalizes prospective students based solely on their race."

Bush pointed to the size of the preference at the undergraduate level—twenty points compared with twelve for a perfect SAT score.

But the president also suggested that the amount of preference really didn't matter. At the law school, the problem was simply that admissions officers passed over students with higher grades and test scores to admit minorities, he said. "This means that students are being selected or rejected based primarily on the color of their skin," Bush said. "The motivation for such an admissions policy may be very good, but its result is discrimination, and that discrimination is wrong."

Bush hailed the percent plans that were in place in California, Florida, and Texas. "In these states, race-neutral admissions policies have resulted in levels of minority attendance for incoming students that are close to, and in some instances slightly surpass, those under the old race-based approach," Bush said.

———■———

THE PRESIDENT'S SIX-MINUTE SPEECH left some crucial questions unanswered. What was Bush's position on *Bakke?* Should diversity be a compelling interest? Could universities ever use race as a factor in admissions? Bush clearly was aligning himself with Jennifer Gratz and Barbara Grutter. Much beyond that, the speech was vague. In truth, the administration's lawyers—specifically, Deputy Solicitor General Paul Clement, Domestic Policy Adviser Jay Lefkowitz, and Associate White House Counsel Brett Kavanaugh—were still negotiating some of those crucial details in the thirty-one hours they had left before the two briefs were due. Clement served as Olson's representative, urging a more definite stance against racial preferences.

The briefs' central focus was the efficacy of so-called race-neutral alternatives—particularly the percent plans of Florida, California, and Texas. The administration argued those plans were successful in bringing minority enrollment numbers to about the same levels as under the previous, race-conscious systems. Because those systems worked, the briefs contended, Michigan had a duty to use them, rather than race-conscious admissions.

As for the other questions in the case, the administration relegated them to footnotes that were crafted in the final hours before the deadline—and scrupulously avoided giving clear answers. The *Grutter* brief told the justices they need not decide whether Powell's opinion was good law. The Court "should instead directly resolve the constitutionality of race-based admissions standards by focusing on the availability of race-neutral alternatives," the brief said in footnote four. Nor did the administration take a position whether diversity *should* be a compelling interest. Although the administration said it was a "paramount government objective" to have universities that were open to all races, the briefs simply didn't answer whether diversity was so important as to be a constitutional value.

Likewise, the briefs ducked the closely related issue of the potential use of race in the event race-neutral alternatives failed. In footnote seven of the Grutter filing, the administration said the Court need not decide that issue. The fact was, the note said, race-neutral methods worked.

———■———

THE BUSH ADMINISTRATION's brief introduced a shade of gray into what previously had looked like a black-and-white case. Both Kolbo and Payton had always asked the judges they encountered to make a fundamental choice: to decide whether universities could consider an applicant's race for the sake of diversity. Kolbo argued that diversity didn't rise to the level of importance that would warrant the explicit use of race, while Payton contended it did.

The president's briefs told the Court it didn't need to make that decision. The administration argued that diversity was attainable through less offensive means. With a little finesse, the administration said, the Court could have it both ways.

To be sure, the administration's position was far closer to CIR's than to Michigan's. The bottom line for the government was that universities were rarely, if ever, justified in using race in admissions. But the administration followed an especially messy path to reach that result. Under the government's reasoning, Powell's opinion in *Bakke* would be left as a meaningless shell, possibly the law but nonetheless irrelevant because of the availability of percent plans. Even if diversity was a compelling interest, the administration said universities still couldn't use race in admissions to achieve that goal.

At the same time, the Bush briefs left open the possibility that universities could return to the Supreme Court, arguing that percent plans didn't actually work as well as advertised. Much like the Harvard plan in *Bakke*, the percent plans hadn't actually been tested in a courtroom. No expert witnesses had ever discussed whether the

Texas, Florida, and California systems were effective or whether a similar plan would be workable in Michigan. No judge had sifted through documents that described the impact on state-run universities. The Supreme Court had only the Bush administration's word for the proposition that percent plans were an effective alternative.

The underlying data were far from clear. As the administration correctly noted, minority admission and enrollment percentages in Texas and California, after initially dropping, had rebounded and in many cases approached the levels under the old race-conscious systems. At the University of Texas's flagship Austin campus, minority undergraduate admissions, which had fallen from 20.3 percent of the class in 1996 to 17.4 percent in 1998, rose to 19.8 percent in 2003. In the University of California, underrepresented minorities comprised a slightly higher percentage of the student body in 2002 than in 1997, the last year race was explicitly used. Black and Hispanic undergraduate enrollment at the University of Florida had been steady after a percent plan and other steps replaced race-conscious admissions.

But those numbers were only part of the story. In all three states, demographic changes meant that Latinos were a larger part of the potential applicant pool every year. In Texas, for example, the percentage of Hispanics among new high school graduates rose from 29 percent in 1996 to 33 percent in 2002. All other things being equal, that increase should have led to a concomitant rise in Latino admissions. Instead, Hispanic admissions to UT-Austin slid from 15 percent in 1996 to 14 percent in 2002.

Even more damaging to the administration's position were the figures from the top institutions in those university systems. At the University of California at Berkeley, black admissions plummeted from 7.8 percent of the entering freshman class in 1997 to 3.7 percent the next year, after Prop 209 had gone into effect. As of 2002, that number had recovered only to 4.3 percent. A similar drop-off occurred at the state's other premier school, the University of California at Los Angeles.

The problem was especially acute in California, where students admitted under the 4 percent program were guaranteed admission only to the UC system, not to the campus of their choice. But the phenomenon also occurred to a lesser extent in Texas and Florida. Texas A&M hadn't fully rebounded from the decline in black enrollment in the wake of the *Hopwood* ruling. And at the University of

Florida, African American enrollment fell from 11.8 percent in 2000 to 7.2 percent in 2001, after race-based admissions were abolished.

Even if percent plans had been fully effective in those states, their feasibility in Michigan was questionable. Michigan drew from a national applicant pool. More than half the applicants to Michigan's freshman class were from out of state, compared with 14 percent at UT-Austin. Because few Hispanics lived in Michigan, virtually all the university's Latino students came from out of state. A percent plan that focused on Michigan high schools would do little to guarantee Latino enrollment at Michigan.

And how percent plans might help law schools was anything but clear. The Florida, California, and Texas rules applied only at the undergraduate level, guaranteeing a university seat to top-performing high school students in the state. No similar mechanism existed for Michigan Law School, particularly since it drew from a national pool. Would Michigan need to guarantee a spot to the top graduates from every college in the country? If so, the percentage would have to be a low one to ensure the law school wouldn't be swamped by guaranteed applicants. That low percentage, in turn, would mean that few blacks would be admitted because, countrywide, only a handful of African American students graduated at the very top of their college classes.

Beyond workability, percent plans posed deeper problems. They reduced the discretion of admissions officers to assemble their classes and make nuanced judgments about the qualifications of particular applicants. To the extent the goal was to look at each prospective student as an individual, percent plans were an obstacle. And percent plans threatened to dilute the academic quality of the student body, forcing admissions officers to accept students from the lowest-performing high schools in the state, even if their test scores and applications suggested they weren't prepared to do the work.

Finally, percent plans were laden with irony. They may have been race-neutral on their face, but their aim seemed to be race-conscious. And to the extent percent plans succeeded in achieving racial diversity at the university level, they did so only because so many high schools weren't diverse. It was the existence of predominantly minority high schools that guaranteed a significant percentage of black and Latino students would qualify. If those racial concentrations were to lessen, so would the effectiveness of the percent plans.

Chapter Fifteen

Friends of the Court

THE PLANNING MEETING for the military brief had energized Joe Reeder. He and Virginia Seitz put together a short summary describing what they hoped the filing ultimately would say. Reeder then started working the phones, calling military leaders he hoped would sign the brief and faxing them the summary.

All along, Krislov and Cannon had focused on winning support from leaders tied to the academy admissions process—former superintendents of West Point, for example. Reeder agreed with that goal, but he wanted to add an important additional layer of support: endorsements from retired commanders, men who knew about race relations in the military from their own experience in preparing troops and leading them into battle. Reeder knew many of the country's most esteemed former military leaders, and he was convinced that most of them appreciated the value of diversity in the officer corps as much as he did.

Reeder wanted only top officers, people whose qualifications on military matters would be unimpeachable. The team agreed that no one below the rank of four-star general or admiral would be solicited, unless the person carried special qualifications. Reeder was concerned that putting lower-ranking officers on the list might prove counterproductive as he tried to woo the biggest names. "Four-stars like to affiliate with four-stars," he told his colleagues.

Before long, Reeder, with considerable help from Senator Levin, was compiling a respectable list. Lieutenant General Daniel W.

Christman, a former West Point superintendent, enthusiastically lent his support, as did William J. Perry, the highly respected former secretary of defense. Several four-stars joined, including Admirals Dennis Blair and Joseph W. Prueher, both former commanders in chief of the U.S. Pacific Command. The group soon added a former Marine Corps commandant, General Carl E. Mundy Jr., as well as a former Air Force chief of staff, General Ronald R. Fogleman.

Seitz, meanwhile, was seeing the brief itself come together much as she envisioned it. Her research team succeeded where Krislov's office had come up short, uncovering a wealth of detail about affirmative action and racial diversity in the military. Drawing from General Accounting Office studies, congressional hearings, Board of Visitors reports, speeches by academy officials, and a wide range of books, Seitz's associates helped her paint a picture of a military that consciously relied on race-based admissions to improve its ability to defend the country. She sent each draft to Reeder, who got back to her quickly with suggestions for honing the arguments.

By the middle of January, even Krislov was convinced the brief was going to happen—and might be a big hit. A pair of news stories in late January, the first in the *Wall Street Journal* and the second in the *New York Times,* added to the momentum. The articles quoted the current deans of admissions at West Point and the Naval Academy as saying they strove to admit a racially diverse class. The stories put the academies on the record saying they were doing precisely what the Bush administration contended was unconstitutional.

Word of the effort spread, and some former military leaders contacted Reeder on their own accord. By the end of January, the group had well over a dozen signatories, unquestionably enough to make the brief workable.

As the February 19 deadline for the brief approached, the group had so many names that they were becoming a bit of a problem. Not only did Seitz and Reeder now have to circulate each redraft to dozens of people—some of whom differed over the nuances of the arguments—the list of names and qualifications itself created a space crunch. With a thirty-page limit, each new signatory meant Seitz had to cut four or five lines from her argument. Eventually, the lawyers decided they simply couldn't add any more names, arbitrarily capping the list at twenty-nine.

The final list, kept secret until the end to prevent any of its members from being pressured to back out, was a virtual who's who of the American military leadership. There were two former secretaries of defense (Perry and William Cohen), three ex-chairmen of the Joint Chiefs of Staffs (Generals William J. Crowe, Hugh Shelton, and John M. D. Shalikashvili), and five current or former U.S. senators with military expertise (Levin, Cohen, Max Cleland of Georgia, Bob Kerrey of Nebraska, and Jack Reed of Rhode Island). The group included former superintendents from the Army, Navy, and Air Force academies and fourteen four-star generals and admirals, each of whom once exercised authority over hundreds of thousands of men and women. General H. Norman Schwarzkopf, perhaps the best-known American war hero, was on board, his name coming right after that of Reeder, who had decided to serve as both lawyer and client. The alphabetical listing meant the first person named on the brief was a black man, Lieutenant General Julius W. Becton Jr., a former university president as well as a forty-year Army veteran.

Just before the filing deadline, nature threw a last scare at the lawyers. Seitz spent the President's Day weekend with her husband and two children in Connecticut, planning to return to Washington to spend a final day in the office finishing the brief and getting it to the printer. Two feet of snow blanketed the East Coast that weekend, stranding Seitz hundreds of miles away. By the time she arrived in Washington, the brief was due in a matter of hours, and Krislov and Reeder were beginning to panic. Seitz went straight to the subway stop, leaving her husband to shovel out a space for the family car, and worked late into the night to complete the document.[1]

————

THE FINAL BRIEF told the story of a military that learned the hard way about the dangerous and combustible mix created by a racially diverse enlisted corps under the command of overwhelmingly white officers. In 1962, fourteen years after President Harry Truman integrated the military, only 1.6 percent of all commissioned officers were black. During the 1960s and early 1970s, hundreds of race-related incidents occurred in the military, the brief said. Racial violence erupted among the Marines at Camp Lejeune and on three Navy vessels. "In each case, the officer corps was caught off guard, unable to bring the situation under control, due to the absence of trust and communication between the predominantly white officer corps and frustrated African-American enlisted men," Seitz wrote.

By the time of the Vietnam War, "racial tensions reached a point where there was an inability to fight," Seitz said, borrowing a comment made by a lieutenant general to the *Washington Post* in 1990. Black troops had little confidence in the military as an institution, and many white officers had no clue how serious the problem was, she wrote. Eventually, Seitz said, quoting from a book on the subject, the military "recognized that its race problem was so critical that it was on the verge of self-destruction."

That realization led directly to the use of affirmative action, as the military sought to ensure its officer ranks would be more racially balanced, Seitz wrote. Drawing from public records, she showed how the three major service academies all used race-conscious recruiting, preparatory, and admissions policies. According to a 1994 GAO report, West Point maintained "goals for each class for desired percentages of scholars, leaders, athletes, women, blacks, Hispanics and other minorities." Another GAO report said the Naval Academy had targets of 7 percent for blacks and 4 percent for Hispanics. Seitz had fewer details about the Air Force Academy process, but its admissions numbers suggested that it considered the race of applicants, and an academy official removed any doubt by confirming the practice to the *New York Times*.

The services also relied heavily on the preparatory schools they had set up to give minority students, as well as enlisted men and women, an extra year of pre-academy training. With minority enrollment as high as 40 percent, the prep schools were the single largest source of black and Latino students for the academies, Seitz wrote.

Finally, Seitz pointed to the ROTC programs that produced almost half the military's active duty officers. Not only did the services rely on host universities such as Michigan to admit and educate minority ROTC students, but the ROTC scholarship programs themselves were race conscious. Each ROTC program targeted its recruiting at minorities and made a large number of scholarships available at historically black colleges, the brief said.

So what did all this mean for the Michigan cases? With so many clients, some more outspoken than others, Seitz had to choose her words carefully. She wasn't in a position to endorse the specifics of the Michigan policy. But she argued forcefully that the "zero option"—that is, no use of race in a nonremedial setting—would ravage the military. Challenging the Bush administration head on, she said that only race-based admissions could keep the officer corps diverse. "Today, there is no race-neutral alternative that will fulfill the military's, and thus the nation's, compelling national security need for a cohesive military led by a diverse officer corps of the highest quality to serve and protect the country," she wrote.

Seitz suggested that it was a short step from race-based admissions at the military academies to affirmative action at civilian universities. "The crisis that resulted in integration of the officer corps is but a magnified reflection of circumstances in our nation's highly diverse society," she wrote. "In a highly diverse society, the public, including minority citizens, must have confidence in the integrity of public institutions, particularly those educational institutions that provide the training, education and status necessary to achieve prosperity and power in America."

————————

THE HIGH COURT'S DECISION to hear both cases spared the university from ever having to name a single lawyer for the lead role. Mahoney would brief and argue the *Grutter* case, while Payton would handle *Gratz.*

Mahoney's brief for Michigan Law School included some subtle changes in emphasis. Mahoney readily acknowledged that the university paid attention to numbers in its admissions of racial minorities. In a sense, Mahoney was simply acknowledging reality; Judge Friedman had found that the law school sought minority enrollment of 10 to 17 percent every year. But Mahoney also took the view that a quota was something far more definite than President Bush or CIR contended. A quota was a "certain fixed number or proportion" reserved exclusively for particular minority groups. If an institution was instead simply trying to fall within a range, that was a goal, she said. Mahoney added that the high court had repeatedly permitted the use of goals in affirmative action plans. The Harvard plan endorsed by Powell specifically acknowledged "some relationship between numbers and achieving the benefits to be derived from a diverse student body, and between numbers and providing a reasonable environment for those students admitted." Mahoney wrote: "If the Law School did not pay attention to these educational concerns, then its policy would not be narrowly tailored to the interests it seeks to promote."

Mahoney also gave new stress to the unique needs of higher education. "[R]acial diversity," she wrote, "is simply far more *relevant* to the core mission of a university or professional school than to virtually any other government endeavor." Seeking to distinguish the minority contracting set-asides struck down in the *Croson* case, she added: "Although the City of Richmond could install the finest possible plumbing fixtures in its jail using an all-white work force, ... the Law School cannot provide the finest possible legal education with a nearly all-white student body."

Mahoney pressed the university's main theme at the Court: *Bakke* has served America well. Overruling it, she argued, would force either "dramatic resegregation" or an abandonment of high standards. It would slash the number of new minority lawyers and leave a near absence of racial minorities at those law schools that produce the vast majority of the nation's federal judges, prosecutors, and law clerks. "That," she wrote, "is a chilling prospect."

Payton had a tougher assignment with his brief in the undergraduate case. He tried to convince the Court that the point system was more flexible than it seemed at first blush. Payton described the special committee that was set up in 1999 to review "more complex admissions cases." He said admissions counselors had "broad discretion" to decide whether to flag an application for that more in-depth review.

Payton took aim at the percent plans the Bush administration advocated, calling them "a blunt instrument that deprives admissions professionals of the flexibility to achieve the broad diversity that is crucial to the University's mission." Implementation of a percent plan would force a radical change in Michigan's character as a national institution, he said. "The effect of such a sea change on its ability to define itself cannot be overstated: the University would be an entirely different institution."

THE MILITARY FILING was only the beginning of the amicus support for Michigan. The final Fortune 500 brief, arguing that university affirmative action was important for American business, netted sixty-five signatory companies. General Motors filed its own brief in support of Michigan, as did a group of seventeen media companies that targeted minority audiences. The AFL-CIO also lent its support.

In a noteworthy shift, eight Jewish groups backed Michigan, including the prominent American Jewish Committee. Many Jews had long been suspicious of university quotas, a view that stemmed from efforts by top universities in the early twentieth century to limit Jewish enrollment. In *Bakke,* leading Jewish civil rights organizations had united against racial preferences. But in the Michigan cases, the American Jewish Committee and its allies argued that the admissions policies didn't suffer the same infirmities as the one at issue in *Bakke.* "The historic Jewish opposition to quotas does not mandate rejection of carefully tailored goals," the groups said in their brief.

Conspicuously absent from that filing were two other top Jewish civil rights groups. One, the Anti-Defamation League, filed its own brief urging the Court to strike down the Michigan policies, faulting them for making race "a proxy for diversity." But the ADL said the Court should stop short of banning all race-conscious admissions. The second organization, the American Jewish Congress, had intended to submit a similar brief but got bogged down in internal debates, ran out of time, and never filed.

While some briefs were important because of who filed them, others made notable substantive contributions to Michigan's argument. The American Educational Research Association took the lead in making a detailed argument about the social science research into the educational benefits of diversity. Several briefs offered lengthy critiques of percent plans and other "race-neutral" alternatives.

In a brief filed by Walter Dellinger, the Law School Admission Council laid out the consequences if law schools were to rely solely on numerical criteria. In the fall 2002 class, Dellinger wrote, 4,461 law school applicants had both LSAT scores of 165 or above and a GPA of 3.5 or better. Of that group, only 29 were black and just 114 were Hispanic. "The simple, demonstrable statistical fact is that most selective law schools in this country will have almost no students of certain races unless they adopt admissions policies designed to alter that outcome," Dellinger wrote.

Many of the filers were organizations that had been at Krislov's December meeting. Others came from the grassroots that Miranda Massie and Shanta Driver had been cultivating, like the 13,922 law students who filed an eight-page brief supporting affirmative action, along with a 202-page appendix listing all their names. All told, seventy-four entities (or groups of entities) filed amicus briefs supporting Michigan, the most ever on one side of a Supreme Court fight.

—■—

KRISLOV'S MANY SUCCESSES masked one disappointment. The school had hoped Gerald Ford would sign the military brief in his capacity as former commander-in-chief, but he had resisted the university's entreaties. Days before the filing deadline, Krislov asked Jim Cannon if he would make one last appeal to his old boss.

Cannon was skeptical. He thought Ford's presence on the brief would skew its message, making it seem too much like a political document, rather than a military one. Nonetheless, he agreed to place the call.

Seconds into his conversation with Ford, Cannon realized his mission was doomed to failure. The former president thought he had done enough.

"Jim, there's no use arguing," Ford said. "I'm just not going to do it."

The tone of voice reminded Cannon of his days at the White House. He knew when Ford had made up his mind. "I understand, Mr. President," Cannon said.[2]

—■—

TERRY PELL DIDN'T HAVE any inflated illusions about his power to influence the outcome. In his mind, CIR had a very limited role: to make the best legal case possible against race-conscious admissions. Pell was convinced his team had the law on its side, but he also suspected that being right might not be enough. Politics would also play a role, and CIR had very little control over that.

The Bush administration's position was a prime example. CIR's attorneys had made their case to the solicitor general's office but otherwise hadn't directly lobbied the administration, leaving that task to other like-minded groups. What resulted was an administration brief that struck Pell as more political than legal. Pell had been buoyed somewhat by the president's speech and was happy to have the Bush administration on his side. And he certainly agreed that race-neutral methods to seek diversity were preferable to race-conscious ones. But he didn't see the percent plans as quite the panacea the administration held them out to be; to Pell, they were legally murky. Pell thought the Bush administration was trying to have it both ways, decrying the Michigan policies while nonetheless suggesting that racial diversity was a legitimate goal for a state-run university to be pursuing. Pell doubted the brief would have much impact.

Similarly, CIR was helpless to match Michigan's success on the amicus front. CIR's general counsel, Michael Rosman, had done some loose coalition-building, but nothing approaching the extent of the efforts on the other side. CIR's allies included the Asian American Foundation, a civil rights organization whose support proved that Michigan didn't have a monopoly on the backing of racial minorities. "[D]iversity-based admission schemes are almost always used to exclude Asian Americans from educational institutions," the group wrote in a brief. The state of Florida and Governor Jeb Bush filed a brief on CIR's side, as did Ward Connerly. The National Association of Scholars filed to rebut the Gurin report and the rest of Michigan's social science case. Gurin "simply did not assess whether a racially diverse student body affects learning," NAS argued.

In total, seventeen entities or groups of entities filed briefs supporting CIR, and several others argued against affirmative action without formally coming down on Gratz and Grutter's side. Notably, CIR lacked the type of major institutional support Michigan enjoyed from business, the military, and education. In almost any other case, CIR's list would have been more than respectable. In the affirmative action fight, it paled by comparison.

The problem for CIR was that politicking simply wasn't the group's area of expertise. Pell had almost a disdain for the practice, and it certainly wasn't part of his job description. CIR was set up to spearhead important litigation, not to lobby the White House or corporate general counsels. And CIR didn't have the muscle of the University of Michigan and its allies. Unlike Bollinger, Pell wasn't in a position to call a former president or meet with a top officer of one of America's largest corporations. Nor did Pell have the connections to get four-star military leaders on his side.

CIR also lacked the financial wherewithal of its opponent. By the time of the amicus briefs, UM had paid almost $8 million to its outside lawyers, even though Wilmer Cutler Pickering had agreed to deepen its discounts and cut 60 percent from its usual rates. In addition, lawyers, administrators, and spokespeople throughout the university had collectively spent many thousands of hours working on the cases. By contrast, CIR, relying on Kolbo's pro bono work, had incurred less than $4 million in expenses. Although donors had stepped up to meet those costs, Pell was in no position to be extravagant. And even after cleaning up the budget mess left by Greve, Pell had only ten people on staff, just a handful of whom could devote much time to the Michigan cases. CIR also had to deal with more than a dozen active cases, plus fund-raising and administrative tasks.

Pell wasn't above giving Michigan credit. He thought the university had done an admirable job putting together a coalition. Pell wasn't impressed with the substance of those briefs; he saw them more as public-relations efforts than as genuine legal advocacy. But he had to confess that the very presence of so many important names might have an impact on the justices. If the Supreme Court was going to rule for Gratz and Grutter, it would have to buck the establishment.[3]

THE WEEKS LEADING UP to the April 1 argument were a flurry of activity, with a dose of controversy thrown in.

The dispute surrounded the allocation of argument time. At trial and appeals court levels, Payton had made a practice of sharing his time with Massie and Shaw. The move was part of the university's broader strategy to welcome the intervenors into the case without adopting their arguments. When the case reached the Supreme Court, Payton informally told Shaw he would try to find a way to share time. Months earlier, Massie had understood one of Payton's partners to have made similar assurances to her. But with the case now set for argument, and with the solicitor general's office joining CIR in opposition to the policies, the UM team decided the university needed its full allotted argument time, a half-hour in each case.

Massie was furious when she got the word through Shaw. In her view, the intervening students were the ones best positioned to challenge the administration's "race-neutral" alternatives. Part of Massie's argument at trial was that traditional admission criteria were anything but neutral; they were biased toward white applicants. She stated her case to Payton and Mahoney on the phone but made no headway.

Shaw decided to see whether the Court would help. He filed a motion seeking an additional ten minutes for each side, with the pro-affirmative action share going to his clients. Shaw knew his chances of success were slim—the high court rarely deviated from its hour-per-case format—but he figured it was worth a shot. A few days later, Massie filed a similar motion. The university chose not to oppose the extension of time, saying it was satisfied so long as it was allotted thirty minutes per case.

The Court promptly denied the motion. In Detroit, Shaw's local counsel, Godfrey Dillard, exploded in frustration. "They led us to believe they were going to give us time, and at the last minute they pulled the rug out from under us," Dillard told the *Detroit Free Press*. "They are supposed to be representing us, and now the black man is up in the damn gallery again."

Shaw, despite his disappointment, was more charitable. He was confident his friend Payton hadn't been intentionally misleading. Shaw understood that Payton had a client to represent and that the Michigan lawyers needed to do what they thought would give them the best chance to win. They were, after all, on the same side.[4]

————

IN MAUREEN MAHONEY'S MIND, it was impossible to be too prepared for a Supreme Court argument. Having come into the case in the middle, she had a lot of catching up to do. As the argument date approached, Mahoney read the entire record in the case, consisting of thousands of pages, as well as every precedential Supreme Court decision, several of them more than once. She devoted four twelve-hour days to reading the 100-plus amicus briefs. She created pages and pages of outlines, not stopping until she was confident she understood where each legal and factual nuance to the case fit into her argument. She created hundreds of note cards, each containing a potential question the justices might ask and her planned answer.

She took part in three moot courts, where fellow attorneys played the role of justices, asking probing questions and giving her a chance to test and refine her answers.

Payton likewise buried himself in preparation. He had read the precedential Supreme Court decisions many times before, but he read them again now. He read the briefs and argument transcripts from the most crucial prior cases, including *Brown, Bakke,* and *Adarand.* He got briefings from Michigan officials on a myriad of details about the school that technically weren't part of the case but that Payton knew might crop up at argument anyway. In addition to the formal moot courts with Mahoney, he did several smaller sessions with his colleagues at Wilmer Cutler, occasionally focusing on particular issues.

Alone among the four lawyers who were going to argue, Kolbo had never appeared before the Supreme Court. To acclimate himself, Kolbo went with Herr to Washington a month before the argument date to watch two days' worth of proceedings. He listened to CD recordings of previous affirmative action arguments, including the Croson case Payton had argued. Kolbo also took part in three moot courts, two with Ted Olson. Ten days before the argument, Kolbo moved his entire operation from Minneapolis to Washington, finishing his preparation from CIR's suite of offices.[5]

———■———

JENNIFER GRATZ'S FAMILY spent the final forty-eight hours before the argument huddled under a tarp on the south side of the Supreme Court. Tickets for the argument were in such demand that Jennifer couldn't even guarantee seats for her parents, brother, and husband. So on the morning of March 30—just as snow, sleet, and bitter winds moved into Washington—they put their lawn chairs and blankets in the line that had already begun to form for the fifty publicly available seats. Over the next two days, the group, which included an uncle and the girlfriend of Jennifer's brother, took shifts under the tarp to keep their place in line. Their neighbors, they learned, included a professional line-sitter who was being paid $36 an hour to hold a seat for an unnamed University of Michigan official.

Jennifer joined them when she could, but she had other obligations, including a press conference the day before the argument.

Flanked by Grutter, Hamacher, Pell, and Kolbo's partner Larry Purdy, she made her case to almost thirty journalists. "This case isn't about being accepted or not accepted," she said. "It's about being treated fairly. I was not treated fairly."[6]

———

AGNES ALEOBUA'S MOTHER decided at the last minute to join her daughter for the overnight bus ride to Washington. The four BAMN buses—part of a fleet of seventeen that had been chartered at UM for the trip—pulled up outside the Fleming Administration Building to pick up their passengers. The plan was to meet at the state fairgrounds outside Detroit and caravan with a number of other buses, arriving in Washington a few hours before the argument. When Aleobua's group arrived at the fairgrounds, the organizers realized they didn't have enough seats for everyone. While the other students scrambled to find room, Aleobua's bus went ahead. She had a full plate of media interviews lined up for the next morning and was supposed to serve as master of ceremonies for part of the early-morning rally in front of the Supreme Court.

As the bus rumbled along the highway, the group watched *Eyes on the Prize,* a documentary about the civil rights movement. Aleobua managed to get a couple of hours of sleep. By the time the bus pulled into Washington, it was 9 a.m., and Aleobua was late for the rally and her interviews. The area surrounding the court was thick with thousands of students toting signs in support of affirmative action. It took Aleobua a half-hour to push her way through the crowd to the front of the rally, where she gave a speech and conducted a few interviews.

The demonstrators had descended on Washington from across the country, many wearing shirts and jackets that identified their home schools. They carried homemade placards, glistening banners, and boxes of oranges to feed their friends. Their signs ranged from the clever ("ANGRY WHITE GUYS FOR AFFIRMATIVE ACTION") to the crass ("FUCK BUSH") to the thought-provoking ("AMERICA PREACHES MERIT but PRACTICES PRIVILEGE"). The group was heavily black and Hispanic but also included thousands of white and Asian supporters of affirmative action. By BAMN's estimate, fifty-thousand people took part, although independent observers pegged the number much lower.

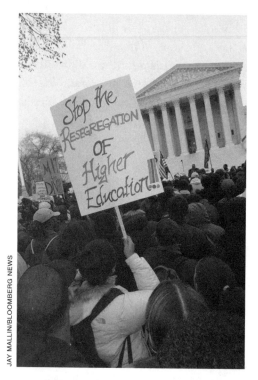

Thousands of student supporters of affirmative action made their way to Washington, D.C., for demonstrations on the day of arguments. A handful of them camped out on the sidewalk outside the Supreme Court to claim seats for the historic session. As they climbed the courthouse steps, the students raised their fists as a sign of solidarity.

The event was the culmination of years of activism for Shanta Driver. Determined that no committed young person should have to stay behind because of insufficient funds, Driver had gone tens of thousands of dollars into personal debt to help pay the organizing, transportation, and setup costs for the event. BAMN raised more money through candy bar sales, door-to-door canvassing, and the Internet. Even so, three weeks before the argument, the group ran out of money, and Driver feared that many students would be unable to attend. Then she appeared on Tom Joyner's syndicated talk show. While on the air, Joyner pledged $2,000 to pay for a bus from South Carolina and urged his listeners to make their own donations. Contributions poured in, including $5,000 from defense attorney Johnnie Cochran to help California students make the trip.

The result on April 1 was a loosely managed chaos, a combination celebration and demonstration. The event began at the court, where in the early morning hours, police told Driver that the stage she planned to erect was too large; she settled for a platform that was so small she couldn't stand on it when Senator Ted Kennedy spoke. Driver found the police restrictions on her sound system equally nettlesome, ensuring that only a handful of the students could hear as civil rights leaders including Al Sharpton, Jesse Jackson, and Martin Luther King III took the microphone.

Near midday, Driver, Aleobua, and Luke Massie tried to start the planned march down Constitution Avenue. They looked back and discovered that just a fraction of the crowd was following. When the rest of the group finally began moving toward the Lincoln Memorial, students danced and sang. As they passed the White House, they parodied a popular rap song, shouting, "Move Bush! Get out the way!"

The crowd gathered at the Lincoln Memorial, which in 1963 served as the backdrop for Martin Luther King's "I Have a Dream" speech. The students heard from more speakers, including Greg Mathis, a one-time Detroit gang member who fulfilled a promise to his dying mother by reforming his ways. He had earned a law degree and now was a judge with his own syndicated television show. The demonstrators raised their right fists and sang the song that had come to be considered the black national anthem, "Lift Ev'ry Voice and Sing." Among the final speakers were some of the middle school students Aleobua had seen at the Detroit fairgrounds. The group had waited eight hours for an additional bus, arriving just in time to catch the end of the rally.

"Our movement," Driver vowed to the crowd, "is just beginning."[7]

—■—

A CAB DROPPED Mahoney off at the court's north side entrance at 8:30 a.m., an hour and a half before the argument was to begin. At the urging of a partner, Mahoney had bought a new navy blue suit and shoes for the occasion. As she approached the building, she saw a long line of lawyers, many of them friends, waiting to pass through the magnetometer so they could claim a seat for the historic event. Mahoney normally would have been happy to chat, but not today. With her head down, she strode purposefully along the brick sidewalk toward the front of the line. Suddenly, her shoe caught in the bricks, and her foot came flying out. Her colleagues burst out in laughter, and Mahoney sheepishly joined in.

Once inside, Mahoney stopped by the court cafeteria for the doughnut that had become part of her pre-argument ritual. (It was an adaptation of a practice she adopted as a girl, when she would eat a candy bar before swim meets to elevate her blood-sugar levels.) She made her way to the clerk's office on the ground floor—the law-yers' lounge that normally served as the gathering point for arguing attorneys was being used for overflow seating—where she met up with Payton and introduced herself to Kolbo. The attorneys made small talk and flipped through their notes until Supreme Court Clerk William Suter broke in. Suter made it a practice to give a fifteen-minute presentation before every argument to remind the attorneys about the particularities of high court procedure and decorum. At 9:25, the lawyers headed upstairs to the courtroom.[8]

Even when empty, the Supreme Court courtroom is an impos-ing sight. At eighty-two by ninety-one feet, the chamber is slightly smaller than a major league baseball infield, all of it ornately adorned with symbols of the law and the majesty of the nation's highest court. Twenty-four columns of Italian marble, fronting deep-red velvet drap-eries, define the room's perimeter. Above the columns, just below the forty-four-foot-high ceiling, are sculpted marble panels depicting his-torical lawgivers—Moses, Hammurabi, Confucius, and Mohammed among them—as well as the Ten Commandments. The nine justices sit behind an elevated mahogany bench, slightly curved so that those on the ends can see one another. Seating for the audience is tight and meticulously arranged, with specified sections for the press, law clerks, guests of the justices, and members of the Supreme Court bar. The room can accommodate up to 350 people.

On the morning of April 1, the gathering crowd lent extra gravity to the courtroom. Senators mingled with lawyers, while former Cabinet secretaries chatted with activists. Jesse Jackson was in the audience, as was U.S. Circuit Judge Harry Edwards, whose 1965 graduation left Michigan Law School without any black students. Shaw and Massie had both obtained seats through the clerk's office, as had Kolbo's mother and sister, and Judges Friedman and Duggan, who came from Detroit with their wives. (Friedman had been disappointed to learn he couldn't get tickets for his law clerks.) Bollinger arrived with a few minutes to spare, stopping to shake hands with Democratic Senators Carl Levin of Michigan and Mary Landrieu of Louisiana. Terry Pell sat near the back alongside his three clients. Just before the argument was to begin, Jennifer Gratz's family took their seats a row behind them, Jennifer's husband leaning over to give her a kiss as he sat down.

A high-pitched beep sounded just as the clock showed 10:00, followed by the sharp, amplified rap of a gavel. The crowd stood, and from behind the red velvet curtain the nine justices appeared, three per opening, each stepping slowly toward a high-backed, black leather chair. Marshal Pamela Talkin called the court to order with the ritual cry, "Oyez! Oyez! Oyez!"[9]

Chapter 16 *Sixteen*

"She's Fabulous"

S UPREME COURT ARGUMENTS are among the most tradition-laden affairs in all of Washington, D.C. From the formal cutaways worn by top court officials and the solicitor general to the quill pens that sit on the counsel table, custom permeates each session. Before taking the bench, each justice shakes hands with the other eight as a symbol of harmony. The justices sit in order of seniority—the chief justice in the middle, the longest serving associate justice on his right, the next most senior justice on the chief's left, and so on down the line. Lawyers, following instructions from the court clerk, invariably begin their presentations with the same words: "Mr. Chief Justice, and may it please the court...."

Rehnquist's commanding presence in the center chair, his seat since 1986, only adds to the air of formality. He uses his booming voice and time-tested script to move the proceedings along with military-like efficiency. Rehnquist's rigidity on maintaining argument time limits is legendary. When the red light illuminates on the counsel lectern, signaling the expiration of time, he expects lawyers to cease immediately. Those who try to make an additional point inevitably find themselves cut off by the chief justice's abrupt, "Thank you." Rehnquist is a stickler for what he considers to be proper attire, even going so far as to bar reporters from dangling press credentials around their necks and female lawyers in the solicitor general's office from wearing brown suits when they argue. (They now can choose between a black suit and a feminine version of the morning suit.)

The arguments themselves, by contrast, can be freewheeling, at times even casual, affairs. Many lawyers say their proximity to the bench—only a few feet separate counsel's lectern from the chief justice's seat—lends an intimate feel to the proceedings. Most of the justices tend to rock back in their chairs, often gazing at the ceiling. Justice Stephen Breyer frequently asks his questions leaning forward with his hand on his cheek. Jokes are commonplace, though the justices tend to prefer their own wisecracks to those of the lawyers.

On the morning of April 1, Rehnquist spent the first few minutes with the ritual swearing in of new members to the Supreme Court bar. Lehman used the occasion to move the admission of Michigan Regent Andrea Fischer Newman; Krislov did the same with Regent Laurence Deitch. (Taking part in the ceremony also ensured that Newman and Deitch would have seats for the argument.) Then the chief justice announced it was time for the *Grutter* case. Kirk Kolbo, clad in a white shirt and shiny blue striped tie, moved to the attorney's lectern.

"Barbara Grutter," Kolbo began, the microphone projecting his South Dakota accent across the courtroom, "applied for admission to the University of Michigan Law School with a personal right guaranteed by the Constitution that she would not have race counted against her. The law school intentionally disregarded that right by discriminating against her on the basis of race, as it does each year in the case of thousands of individuals who apply for admission." The government, he said, has "a solemn obligation to treat all members of our society equally without preferring some individuals over others."

Not two minutes into Kolbo's presentation, O'Connor leaned forward, acting as if she had been itching for months to make a point. She told Kolbo that a university "is faced with a serious problem when it's one that gets thousands of applications for just a few slots." The school must make choices and use a variety of factors to whittle down the applicant pool, she said. "So how do you single this out, and how are we certain that there's an injury to your client that she wouldn't have experienced for other reasons?"

The Constitution, Kolbo responded, makes clear that race is different. It can't be a factor in admissions.

"Well, you have some precedents that you have to come to grips with," O'Connor shot back, "because the Court obviously has upheld the use of race in making selections or choices in certain contexts—for instance, to remedy prior discrimination and other contexts."

"Oh, absolutely, Your Honor."

"Well, but you are speaking in absolutes, and it isn't quite that. I think we have given recognition to the use of race in a variety of settings."

"And we absolutely agree, Justice O'Connor."

Seconds later, Justice Kennedy was upon Kolbo. "Suppose you have a law school with 2 or 3 percent Hispanic and black students. Is that a legitimate concern for the university and for the state officials?" Kennedy asked.

That disparity might justify "broad social and political concerns," Kolbo acknowledged, but not racial preferences in admissions.

"Well, it's a broad social and political concern that there are not adequate members of the profession which is designed to protect our rights and to promote progress," Kennedy said. "I should think that's a very legitimate concern on the part of the state."

The argument couldn't have gotten off to a worse start for the CIR team. O'Connor and Kennedy clearly both were troubled by the idea of an outright ban on the use of race. Neither justice necessarily was embracing the university's position—seasoned Court watchers knew both justices might well have equally sharp questions in store for Michigan's lawyers—but at a minimum they were signaling a reluctance to go as far as CIR wanted.

From her chair next to Kolbo, Mahoney was especially relieved to hear the skepticism from O'Connor, the probable swing vote. Mahoney now was sure she had at least a fighting chance.

Justice Ginsburg asked Kolbo to address the retired military officers' argument.

Kolbo said the academies should look at race-neutral solutions if indeed they had a problem with minority admissions. He added that the academies themselves hadn't actually taken a position in the case.

"Yes, they have," Justice Stevens retorted. According to the briefs, the academies use race in admissions. "Do you challenge that as a matter of fact?"

"We don't challenge what they say, Your Honor. We're just suggesting we don't have a record in this case."

Justice Souter wasn't satisfied. "No, but do you challenge the fact that they are giving the preference?"

"We don't have enough information, Your Honor, to know what the—"

Souter, visibly angry, cut Kolbo off. "Are you serious that you think there is a serious question about that? That we cannot take that green brief as a representation of fact?"

Kolbo was in trouble. He was angering at least one justice on a relatively minor point.

Scalia jumped in to help the lawyer. "It depends on what fact you're talking about, doesn't it? You accept the fact that they're giving preferences, but that doesn't convert to the fact that, if they didn't give preferences, there's no other way to get an officer corps that includes some minority people. Does the brief say that?"

"It does not, Your Honor."

Souter wasn't finished. The issue, he suggested, isn't whether "some" minorities will become officers but whether the affirmative action programs at the academies are necessary to ensure "reasonable number of minorities in the officer corps." Then he pressed Kolbo on another suggestion raised by the Bush administration: that economic disadvantage be used instead of race.

"Do you seriously believe that that would be anything but a surrogate for race?" Souter asked, now less angry but no less incredulous.

"I do, Your Honor, because it's not just minorities that are socio-economically disadvantaged in this country. That happens across racial lines."

Souter clearly disagreed. The objective would still be to increase the percentage of minorities, he said. "If that is the object, then whatever it is, it's not a race-neutral measure."

"Well, I would disagree, Your Honor, because I think if you have a race-neutral means that accomplishes many purposes and one of them is race, that is not necessarily under this Court's precedents unconstitutional."

Kennedy asked whether the military academies could target minorities during their recruiting process. Kolbo said they could.

Breyer broke in. If universities can spend money recruiting blacks, he wondered, why can't they also use race as an admissions factor to ensure that America's future leaders are racially diverse?

The question had come up in one of Kolbo's moot courts, and it was an important one. Kolbo needed to give the justices a clear, principled line that would distinguish race-based admissions from the recruiting efforts that the Court clearly had little interest in questioning.

The difference, Kolbo said, was that race-based admissions constitute discrimination at the "point of competition," making innocent people pay the price.

Why, Breyer wanted to know, are those people any different than those who lose out in the admissions process because they aren't athletes or aren't alumni?

Kolbo again was ready. "There is something special about race in this country. It's why we have a Constitution about it. It's why we have a constitutional amendment."

Justice Ginsburg had a question. If she understood Kolbo correctly, he was saying that the military academies could have minority-only scholarships to attend prep schools. "Why is that permissible?" she asked.

"Because it doesn't prevent someone from applying," Kolbo answered. "The key is to be able to compete on the same footing at the point of competition."

Scalia said he understood that the preparatory schools were open to all races, not just minorities.

Ginsburg said her question focused not on the particular policies in place at the academies, but on the answer Kolbo had given Breyer and the line he was seeking to draw. "I thought you would answer the question, 'Yes, you could have special preparation for minorities only. Yes, you could have recruitment for minorities only.'"

"I believe you can, as part of a broad program, I believe you could," Kolbo replied. "It's very simple, it seems to me, to draw a principled distinction between outreach—casting a wider net—and applying the same standard at the point of competition."

Scalia wanted to make sure Kolbo wasn't leaving a misimpression. "Including at the point of giving the benefit of going to one of these preparatory schools. You wouldn't allow one of these preparatory schools to be for minorities only, would you?"

"No, of course not, Your Honor."

The final questions came from Justice Stevens. Could the governor of Michigan make a commitment to a Native American tribe to admit three members to the University of Michigan every year?

"I don't believe so, Your Honor. Again, it's a distinction drawn on the basis of race."

As Kolbo sat down, his side had reason for concern. Six justices— Souter, Stevens, Ginsburg, Breyer, O'Connor, and Kennedy—had demonstrated at least some skepticism (and in Souter's case outright hostility) toward his arguments. Opposition from the first four was to be expected. But Kolbo needed O'Connor and Kennedy to win the case.

——•——

TED OLSON STEPPED to the lectern. The morning coat trailing behind him was a reminder to the audience that he was unlike any other lawyer who would argue that day—or any day of the term, for that matter. As solicitor general, Olson was part of the Supreme Court's club. The very nature of his office gave him an instant rapport with the justices, beyond even what Mahoney enjoyed as a former clerk.

Olson's skills as an advocate had only enhanced his reputation. Even compared with Supreme Court specialists, the tall, red-haired Olson was a figure of remarkable calm when he addressed the justices. He spoke in soothing tones, even while holding his ground in the face of hostile questions.

Olson's task this day was extraordinarily tricky. He was comfortable enough with the brief to have put his name on it, but it wasn't his preferred approach. The administration was seeking to walk a narrow tightrope, lauding diversity while decrying the step that university administrators said was necessary to achieve that goal.

Three words into Olson's second sentence, Stevens asked the solicitor general to address the military officers' brief.

"The position of the United States," Olson responded, "is that we do not accept the proposition that black soldiers will only fight for black officers, or the reverse." The academies, Olson added, have an obligation to try race-neutral means to accomplish their goals.

Justice Ginsburg jumped in: "But you recognize, General Olson, that here and now, all of the military academies do have race preference programs in admissions?"

Olson acknowledged that all but the Coast Guard Academy did.

Ginsburg asked whether that was illegal.

Olson hedged. "We haven't examined that," he said.

Souter asked Olson what race-neutral mechanisms the military academies might use. Olson pointed to wider recruiting.

"Recruiting with an objective of minority students?" Souter asked.

No, it couldn't be limited to minorities, Olson said.

But, Souter wondered, without a racial objective, how would wider recruiting address the problem cited in the military officers' brief?

Olson said the high court in the past had required government entities to try race-neutral steps first.

Breyer questioned Olson's assertion that the university was stereo-typing students and using race as a surrogate for experience. "That's not what they say," Breyer said. "They say they're not using race as a surrogate for anything because if you have a person who went to Exeter who's very rich and happens to be black and is a conservative Republican, it's great for the class to know that, too. And that's why they want a certain number."

But that person is getting an edge because of race, not because of experience, Olson said. Race "is used as a substitute for any examination of the individual."

O'Connor asked whether Olson agreed with Justice Powell that race could be used as a "plus factor."

Olson noted that Powell spoke only for himself.

"I don't think it commanded a court," O'Connor responded. "I'm just asking if you agreed with that approach."

Olson, of course, had wanted the administration to take the position that race could never be used, but the White House wouldn't go along. "We're reluctant to say never, Justice O'Connor," Olson said. "But this test, every test that Justice Powell applied in that opinion, the law school program here fails."

A moment later, Stevens said he wasn't satisfied with that answer. "Do you agree with Justice Powell's suggestion that race could be used as a plus in something like the Harvard program?"

Olson said the Harvard plan wasn't before the *Bakke* court and wasn't fully examined. "We would not [agree] based on what we see in that opinion."

"Would you agree with his use of the term 'diversity' as being a permissible governmental goal?" Kennedy asked.

Again, Olson, unable to give the direct answer he had urged in private, sidestepped the question. "The only way to answer that, Justice Kennedy, is that the word 'diversity' means so many things to so many different people." What the law school was doing was seeking racial diversity for its own sake, he said. "If it's an end in and of itself, obviously it's constitutionally objectionable."

———•———

REHNQUIST SAVED HIS first question of the day for Mahoney, his former clerk. Suppose the medical school in *Bakke* wanted to enroll sixteen disadvantaged minorities but couldn't reach its goal using race-neutral means, he said. Could it then go back and set aside sixteen seats?

Mahoney seized on the chance to help the Court draw a line that would favor her client. "Well, if the program was designed to have a fixed sixteen seats, no matter what the qualifications of the applicant pool, no matter what the disparities between the minority and majority students would be, then I think it's fair to say that that would be a quota, if that was the nature of the program. But here the record indicates that the law school's program is nothing of the kind."

Scalia leaned forward. "Ms. Mahoney, I find it hard to take seriously the state of Michigan's contention that racial diversity is a compelling state interest, compelling enough to warrant ignoring the Constitution's prohibition of distribution on the basis of race. The reason I say that is that the problem is a problem of Michigan's own creation. That is to say, it has decided to create an elite law school. It is one of the best law schools in the country." If Michigan really cares about racial diversity, Scalia went on, "why doesn't it do as many other state law schools do: lower the standards, not have a flagship elite law school? Solves the problem."

"Your Honor, I don't think there's anything in this Court's cases that suggests that the law school has to make an election between academic excellence and racial diversity."

"If it's important enough to override the Constitution's prohibition of racial discrimination, it seems to me it's important enough to override Michigan's desire to have a super-duper law school."

It was a typical Scalia exchange. The Court's bomb thrower, he loved to debate lawyers with whom he disagreed. Much like Danny

Boggs on the Sixth Circuit, Scalia relished a chance to point out what he saw as the logical fallacies of an argument.

"Your Honor, the question isn't whether it's important enough to override the prohibition on discrimination. It's whether this is discrimination. What Michigan is doing benefits—"

"No, no, no," Kennedy broke in. "The question is whether or not there is a compelling interest that allows race to be used."

Mahoney paused. "That's correct, Your Honor."

"And Justice Scalia's question is designed to put to you the fact that this isn't a compelling interest, because it's a choice that the Michigan Law School has made to be like this."

"There is a compelling interest in having an institution that is both academically excellent and richly diverse," Mahoney responded.

Kennedy moved on to a different issue and in the process made clear that his skepticism wasn't reserved for Kolbo's case. "Suppose there's a reasonable disagreement as to whether or not the so-called critical mass is, in fact, a disguised quota. You would say it is not. Suppose there's a reasonable disagreement on that point. If that's so, you lose, is that not correct?"

Kennedy seemed to be suggesting that the Court might be bound by Judge Friedman's conclusion that the policy operated as a quota. Even the Supreme Court can't overturn the factual findings of a trial judge unless they are clearly wrong.

Mahoney argued that Friedman had no evidence of a quota. The trial judge concluded only that the law school "wants" 10 to 17 percent of its class to consist of blacks, Latinos, and Native American, she said.

Her answer prompted a rare, unintentional breach of etiquette from the normally punctilious Rehnquist. Apparently unable to understand his former clerk, the chief justice sought a clarification, inadvertently addressing her by her first name. "It says 'once' or 'wants,' Maureen?"

"Wants, Your Honor," said Mahoney, so caught up in the argument that she didn't even notice the slip. "That's an aspiration. That is not a fixed minimum. He made no findings that there was a fixed minimum."

A moment later, Scalia pressed Mahoney further on that point. "When you say 'sufficient numbers,' that suggests to me that there is some minimum. Now you don't name it, but there has to be some minimum. But you say there isn't a minimum?"

"It can be related to numbers without being a quota," Mahoney replied.

Souter tried to buttress Mahoney's case. Didn't *Bakke* make clear that there is a "permissible zone between a purely token number and a quota or a set-aside?" he asked.

"Absolutely," Mahoney answered.

Kennedy was skeptical. "It's hard to see that that's true here, when every day the admissions staff looks to see what the numbers are based on race," he said.

"Your Honor, that's not correct. There's a report, which is called the daily, but it is not looked at every day."

"They just have a daily report they look at once a week?" Kennedy asked, drawing laughter from the audience.

Mahoney wasn't flustered. "The reason it's called a daily is that it is a running database that allows for the report to be printed at any time. And the evidence indicated that—"

"To show how well they're doing in getting the so-called critical mass, which is just a synonym for a number," Kennedy interjected.

Scalia tried again on the quota issue, triggering what would prove to be the sharpest exchange of the argument. "Is 2 percent a critical mass, Ms. Mahoney?"

"I don't think so, Your Honor."

"Four percent?"

"No, Your Honor. What—"

"You have to pick some number, don't you?" Scalia thundered.

"Well, actually what the—"

"Eight, is 8 percent?"

"Your Honor, the—"

"Now, does it stop being a quota because it's somewhere between 8 and 12, but it is a quota if it's 10? I don't understand that reasoning. Once you use the term critical mass, you're into quotaland."

"Your Honor, what a quota is under this Court's cases is a fixed number. And there is no fixed number here. The testimony was that it depends on the characteristics of the applicant pool."

"As long as you say between 8 and 12, you're okay? Is that it? If you said 10, it's bad, but between 8 and 12 is okay because it's not a fixed number. That's what you think the Constitution says?"

Mahoney held her ground, convinced her answer was right. "No, Your Honor, if it was a fixed range that said that it will be a minimum of 8 percent, come hell or high water, no matter what the qualifications of these applicants look like, no matter what it is that the majority applicants could contribute to the benefits of diversity, then certainly that would be a quota, but that is not what occurred here."

O'Connor broke in with a gentler question. Every affirmative action program the Court had approved in the past had come with a fixed expiration date, she said. "There is none in this, is there? How do we deal with that aspect?"

Later, Mahoney would say the question, even though she had prepared for it, was the toughest of the argument. She knew there wasn't any fully satisfactory answer. She had nothing concrete to offer O'Connor.

Speaking in more measured tones than she had with Scalia, Mahoney answered that, some day in the future, an improved minority applicant pool might mean that universities don't have to consider race. And perhaps some day the experience of being a minority won't matter so much in American society, she added.

"Have we approved any other affirmative action program with such a vague, distant termination date?" O'Connor asked, making clear that, like Kennedy, she was concerned about what Michigan was doing.

In *Bakke*, Mahoney responded. Plans modeled after the Harvard plan have been in effect for twenty-five years, she said.

Rehnquist asked whether statistics indicated that things were improving. He asked whether more minorities were now gaining admission to Michigan without racial preferences. He broke into a sheepish grin after he inadvertently referred to the program as "quotas."

"They're not quotas, Your Honor," Mahoney shot back, failing to suppress her own smile. "Aspirations!"

Kennedy remained unsatisfied on the quota question. "I don't think the answer that you gave to Justice Scalia was in all respects complete.... Suppose the pool is large enough so that you can find minorities to fill your 15-percent aspiration. Why isn't that a quota, even if they're qualified?"

"The difference between a quota and a goal is the flexibility," Mahoney responded. A quota is when "you have to automatically and blindly promote people in order to meet the goal."

Rehnquist asked how the school determines from year to year exactly what the percentage of minorities would be. "Do they make a conscious decision? Just toss a coin?" Though his tone was polite, his words suggested that Mahoney had made little headway in convincing him.

"It's responsive to the applicant pool," the lawyer responded.

Scalia wasn't finished. "Ms. Mahoney, do you know any quota program that would take somebody to fill the quota, no matter what? All the quota programs I know start off by saying, 'We will only take qualified applicants,' but then setting the level of qualified low enough that they can fill the quota."

Mahoney tried a different approach. In *Bakke,* she said, the school barred white applicants from competing for particular slots. "That doesn't happen at the University of Michigan. When someone applies, whether they're white, it doesn't matter how many minorities have been accepted or rejected. They are considered on their merits just like every other applicant."

"But they aren't just like every other applicant," Scalia responded. "Some applicants are given a preference because of their race."

Ginsburg tried to help. Isn't it the case, she asked, that universities look at a wide range of factors to fill out their classes?

Scalia jumped in, treating Mahoney almost as a prop. "Does the Constitution prohibit distribution against oboe players as opposed to flute players?"

"No, Your Honor," Mahoney replied.

"Does it prohibit discrimination on the basis of alumna status?"

"No, Your Honor, but—"

"But it does prohibit discrimination on basis of race."

"But the question is whether this is prohibited discrimination, and the answer that we would ask this Court to give is that a minority applicant brings something special."

Breyer asked Mahoney for more help in line-drawing. What else, besides a quota, would be going too far?

Mahoney cited three considerations: whether the university is giving flexible consideration to the diversity contributions of each candidate, whether the minorities who are admitted are well-qualified, and whether the burden on the rejected students is excessive. In Michigan's case, she said, of the two thousand five hundred rejected law school applicants every year, only eighty would have gained admission under a race-blind system. "That is a very small and diffuse burden.... It's not one to be minimized, ... but this is extremely limited in scope and relative to the benefits to students of all races and to our nation."

Just as the red light came on, Scalia jumped in. "I don't know any other area where we decide the case by saying, 'Well, there are very few people who are being treated unconstitutionally.' I mean, if this indeed is an unconstitutional treatment of this woman because of her race, surely it doesn't make any difference whether she is one of very few who have been treated unconstitutionally."

Rehnquist cut his former clerk a break. "I think you can regard that as a statement, rather than a question," he said, drawing laughter from the audience.

It was a fitting ending. All told, Scalia's questions and Mahoney's responses to him had occupied a third of her allotted thirty minutes.

A moment after Mahoney took her seat, Ginsburg leaned over to Souter and, in words barely picked up by the Court's recording system, shared her assessment about what she had just heard.

"She's very good," Ginsburg said.

"She's fabulous," Souter answered.

———■———

THE *GRATZ* UNDERGRADUATE case got off to a dry start. For the first six minutes the justices discussed the arcane rules of standing, specifically, whether Patrick Hamacher had a legal right to be before the court. The exchange surprised Kolbo; the topic hadn't arisen at any of his moot courts.

Kolbo eventually moved the conversation to the merits of the case. "The fundamental problem with the diversity rationale is that it depends upon the standardless discretion of educators," he said. "If that is the rule we end up accepting, then universities are free in their discretion to choose which races are discriminated against, which are favored."

Rehnquist wanted to know how Michigan decided whether someone qualifies for a preference. "Is it just a self-reporting type of system on the application?"

That's correct, Kolbo replied.

Breyer, a former professor, said he wasn't bothered by the possibility that universities would have broad discretion. "So is it entirely discretionary when you read a set of exam books," he said. "You know, it's highly subjective.... I'm not sure of the constitutional relevance of that when what you're trying to do is something lawyers don't normally do, which is to select among people, individually considered, which one is better for this particular slot. Businesspeople do that, lawyers don't except when they're hiring." The issue of discretion "seems to me to grow out of the nature of the problem," he said.

Kolbo responded: "What I'm suggesting is the Court itself has made clear that for an interest to be compelling, one of the considerations that the Court must look at is whether there are standards—independent, ascertainable standards ... to determine whether the interest is one that's compelling and one that the Court can oversee."

Stevens tried to pin Kolbo down on the circumstances under which race could be used in nonuniversity contexts. "I think you are arguing that anything except remedies for past discrimination is impermissible.... I think that's your position, is it not?"

"I would not go that far, Justice Stevens. There may be other reasons. I think they would have to be extraordinary and rare, perhaps rising to the level of life or limb. We do know that the Court has recognized past identified discrimination."

Breyer pressed Kolbo on that point. "The other side says, 'Yes, extraordinary. We're 280 million people, we have large racial diversity within the country, the world is even more diverse, and we think from the point of view of business, the armed forces, law, et cetera, that this is an extraordinary need to have diversity among elites throughout the country. That without it, the country will be much worse off....' How can you say, or can you say, that isn't extraordinary?"

"Your Honor, because there are important constitutional rights at stake. And those rights are the right to equal protection. And a mere social benefit—that is, having more minorities in particular occupations or the schools—simply doesn't rise to the level of compelling interest. It doesn't remedy a constitutional value, like—"

Kennedy interrupted. "So if the university president or the dean told you just what Justice Breyer said, and that we have underrepresentation of minorities, you would tell them there's nothing you can do about it?"

Kolbo returned to the core of his case: "I would say, Your Honor, that racial preferences are not the answer.... If minorities are not competing at the same level as other racial groups, then we should take steps to solve that problem. But racial preferences, because they injure the rights of innocent people, because it's a prohibition contained in our Constitution, simply aren't permissible to remedy that problem."

——◼——

OLSON TRIED TO convince the Court that the current system for undergraduate applications to Michigan was functionally identical to the older one Judge Duggan had declared unconstitutional. "The university acknowledges that its pre-1999 admissions program used separate grids, separate qualifications, separate standards, and protected seats.... Yet they stipulated that the only changes that they made from that system affected only the mechanics, not the substance of how race and ethnicity were considered in the admissions process."

"Isn't mecha—I mean, mechanics is another word for tailoring," Souter rejoined. "And they are saying, 'We have tailored it differently.'"

"We submit, Justice Souter, that the changes which they referred to as mechanics were cosmetics, that ultimately the system was intended to, and they acknowledge, to produce the same outcome as the prior system."

Kennedy signaled he agreed. "Yes, the stipulation is that it did not change the substance of how race and ethnicity were considered."

Moments later, three of the Court's affirmative action supporters ganged up on Olson. Souter said the goal of the Michigan plan was to show students that there might not be any correlation between race and point of view.

When Olson tried to dodge the issue, Stevens pressed him. "The argument is that you need to have enough of them to demonstrate that the point of view does not always fit just one person."

In response, Olson called that reasoning "self-contradictory." He added: "They've said, first of all, you have these characteristics because you're black, but we must admit enough of you into the class to prove to the other students that black isn't the reason you—"

Breyer interrupted. In a somewhat tortured question, he suggested that young African Americans may share the common experience of facing discrimination, yet react in different ways to it. Michigan, he said, is arguing that "we want people in this school of all kinds who are black because that will be helpful education."

Olson never did address the point head on. Falling back on the absolutist argument he had used in the University of Texas case, he argued: "What this Court has said is that racial preferences, racial stereotyping, which it is, is stigmatizing, it's divisive, it's damaging to the fabric of society, it's damaging to the goal ultimately to eliminate the problems that racial discrimination and racial differences have created."

Olson summed up by referring back to a point Scalia first made. "The Michigan Law School and the University of Michigan ultimately must make a choice. It may maintain its elitist, as it refers to it, selection process without regard to race, or it may achieve the racial diversity it seeks with race-neutral compromises in its admissions standards. But the one thing that it may not do is compromise its admissions standards or change its admission requirements for one race and not another. That is forbidden by the equal protection clause of the Constitution."

Olson started to return to his chair, but Stevens had one more question. "Is it also forbidden for the United States military academy?"

"It may well be, Justice Stevens," Olson conceded. "We're not defending the specifics of those programs but we have not examined them individually."

———■———

As the last lawyer scheduled to argue, Payton knew in advance he would need to be flexible. He had listened silently for an hour and a half, gauging what seemed to be working with the Court and what didn't. By the time his turn arrived, he felt the university's case was in good shape. All it needed, Payton thought, was the overall theme that tied the various points together.

For several minutes, the justices let Payton make his case almost without interruption. Payton told the Court that Michigan is so racially segregated that almost all high school students graduate without having had any significant experience with other races. "The result often is that these students come to college not knowing about individuals of different races and ethnicities and often not even being aware of the full extent of their lack of knowledge. This gap allows stereotypes to come into existence."

College, Payton went on, presents a tremendous opportunity for students to learn from one another. "Here's how critical mass works in these circumstances," he said. "If there are too few African American students ... there's a risk that those students will feel that they have to represent their group, their race. This comes from isolation, and it's well understood by educators. It results in these token students not feeling completely comfortable expressing their individuality."

The first questions were on the polite side. Rehnquist asked what "critical mass" was and how university officials knew when they had achieved it.

Payton was in his comfort zone. Professors know they have a critical mass when they see their students acting as individuals, he said.

Scalia asked whether Michigan had a minority dorm.

No, Payton said. The question was one of those that Payton had anticipated even though he didn't think it was legally relevant.

Kennedy posed the first real challenge. "I have to say that in looking at your program, it looks to me like this is just a disguised quota. You have a minority student who works very, very hard, very proud of his athletics, he gets the same number of points as a minority person who doesn't have any athletics. That to me looks like an overt quota." Kennedy was making clear that his definition of quota was broader than the one in Mahoney's brief.

It's not a quota, Payton said. Every application gets read in its entirety by a counselor who considers a wide range of factors, he said.

"None of that matters," Scalia said, cutting Payton off. "None of that matters. If you're minimally qualified, and you're one of the minority races that gets the twenty points, you're in. The rest is really irrelevant."

"Actually, the way it works is that every application comes through, and it's read in its entirety. It is evaluated, taking all of these factors into account." The application then gets a point score, and each competes against all the other applications, Payton added.

Rehnquist spotted what he thought was a contradiction. He read from a footnote in the university's brief, where Payton had written that "the volume of applications and the presentation of applicant information make it impractical for [the College of Literature,

Science, and the Arts] to use the same admissions system as the much smaller University of Michigan Law School."

"Now you're saying that every single application for admission to LSA is read individually?" the chief justice asked.

"Yes," Payton said. "Sometimes twice."

Rehnquist then asked how Michigan decides that a group is "underrepresented."

"They are underrepresented in our applicant pool," Payton answered.

"Compared to what?" Rehnquist asked.

Payton said underrepresented groups are those with so few qualified applicants that a critical mass wouldn't exist if race weren't taken into account.

Rehnquist was getting frustrated. "When you say underrepresented, it sounds like something almost mathematical, that you're saying, 'We only have a certain percentage of, and we should have this percentage.' Well, what is this percentage?"

"It's actually not a percentage at all," Payton said, "and it really is driven by the educational benefits that we want from our diverse student body. If we had in our applicant pool sufficient numbers of minority students, African Americans, for example—"

"What is a sufficient number?" Rehnquist demanded.

Payton tried to continue his earlier answer. Rehnquist leaned forward and shook his finger. "I asked you, what is a sufficient number? An answer—would you answer it?"

Payton said: "A sufficient number so that when we made our selections, we were achieving the critical mass of students that we need for the benefits I described. That is not a fixed precise number at all."

Payton had answered the question, but the chief justice gave no indication he was satisfied. Like Kennedy, Rehnquist seemed to view Michigan's concept of a "critical mass" as indistinguishable from a quota.

Scalia returned to Michigan's decision to create an elite institution. "Just lower your qualification standards. You don't have to be the great college you are. You can be a lesser college if that value is important enough to you."

Payton responded that the justice was presenting a "Hobbesian choice."

Breyer broke in, asking whether the point system met Powell's requirement of individualized consideration. Breyer offered a hypothetical situation in which the Michigan point system would seem to undervalue the contributions of a poor, white athlete as compared with a black applicant.

Payton told him that the applications might end up with the admissions review committee, which ultimately could ignore the point system. Breyer suggested that fact might prove critical for him.

"So I want a clear answer to this," Breyer said. "That review committee can look at the applications individually and ignore the points?"

"It does," Payton replied. "The answer is yes."

A voice at the other end of the bench was skeptical. "Mr. Payton," Scalia said. "It's easy to say they can ignore the points. Easy to say. Do you know of any case where a minority applicant, one of the minorities favored in your program, who was minimally qualified, got the twenty-point favor and was rejected?"

"I don't know, Justice Scalia," Payton said. His normally forceful tone had grown momentarily plaintive, suggesting a growing exasperation with Scalia.

"As I understand what the other side is saying, it is automatic. If you are minimally qualified, and you get those twenty points, you are in. That's what they claim."

"That's not correctly describing what happens," Payton answered, assertive again. Most qualified minority applicants do get in, he said, but not by design. The goal, he reiterated, is to reach a critical mass.

Payton's answer glossed over an important piece of evidence: the 1995 memo from Admissions Director Ted Spencer saying that minority admissions guidelines were "set to admit all students who qualify."

"So there are some qualified minorities who get the twenty points and who are rejected?" Scalia asked.

"I believe that is the case."

With only a few minutes remaining, Kennedy leaned forward. "Suppose the Court were to say that the twenty-point system and the law school system looked just too much like a quota and that quotas are impermissible. As of that point, is it our burden to tell you what other systems to use, or is it your burden to come up with some other system—say, more individualized assessment—in order to attain some of the goals you wish to attain?"

Coming nearly two hours into the session, the question was perhaps the most dramatic yet, opening a window into Kennedy's thinking. He seemed to be saying that Michigan's goals were legitimate but that its methods needed to be refined.

"I guess I'm not sure what the more individualized assessment would be here," Payton answered. "Obviously there are things that could be done differently. *We've* done things differently. The two schools do things quite differently. But I think we're both trying to achieve the critical mass. I think there's no dispute at all from anyone that the critical mass is essential to get the educational benefits that we're talking about."

There was one last surprise. Justice Clarence Thomas had sat silently for the entire session, as he did during most arguments. Suddenly, as Payton sought to wind up, Thomas's deep, unmistakable voice resonated through the courtroom.

"Mr. Payton, do you think that your admissions standards overall at least provide some headwind to the efforts that you're talking about?"

Payton, misunderstanding the question, answered "yes." Thomas's follow-up clarified that he was rephrasing Scalia's question about the trade-off between racial diversity and the elite status of a university.

"Now I know you don't want to make the choice, but will you at least acknowledge that there is a tension?" Thomas asked.

No, Payton said. "Some of our other schools, the nonselective schools, actually some can end up with completely un-diverse populations as well."[1]

—■—

OUTWARDLY, AT LEAST, both sides were optimistic. The crowd flowed out of the court into the bright sunshine and onto the sweeping plaza that fronts the building. Gratz and Grutter spoke with confidence to the reporters and television cameras that swarmed around the two women. Pell dissected the arguments made by Mahoney and Payton, finding flaws that he hoped the Court would exploit.

Krislov sought out Mahoney to give her a hug. "I'm so proud of you," he said. Krislov later would speculate that the Court was likely

After the Supreme Court argument, the university team spontaneously broke out into a rendition of Michigan's fight song, "Hail to the Victors." Payton is in the middle of the front row, laughing with Michigan's new president, Mary Sue Coleman. To his right is Michigan Law School dean Jeffrey Lehman, who would soon become president of Cornell University.

to give Michigan between 50 and 80 percent of what it sought. As the Michigan group tried to assemble for a photo on the court steps, some of the students started singing the school's fight song, "Hail to the Victors." The lawyers, administrators, and regents joined in.

One person who wasn't in a cheerful mood was Miranda Massie. The arguments had been excruciating for her. At points, she had felt like screaming, as when Scalia suggested that the university consider lowering its admissions standards. To Massie, Scalia's comments carried an implication of black inferiority. Massie was convinced that she, not the university, had the answer to that charge. She vented in her speech to the demonstrators who were still gathered at the court.

Shaw, too, was frustrated at not having had a chance to make his case. He thought Payton and Mahoney had done fine jobs, but they didn't discuss the all-important history of discrimination. Like Massie, he was offended by Scalia's juxtaposition of quality and diversity.

Michigan and CIR arranged massive lunches for their respective teams at nearby restaurants. Some forty CIR supporters—everyone except Pell and Levey, who returned to the office for the anticipated media deluge—dined at a French bistro six blocks from the court. The group burst into applause when Kolbo walked in, then cheered again when Carl Cohen introduced himself.

Mahoney spent the afternoon and much of the next day responding to dozens of e-mails, many of them from new fans. She was particularly touched by one from a man who said he was a beneficiary of affirmative action and wanted to make sure his sons didn't need it. Friends sent her bouquets of flowers. Later, two people would ask her to autograph copies of her brief.[2]

Chapter Seventeen

"Race Unfortunately
Still Matters"

O N THE FRIDAY AFTER the arguments, the nine justices met in
their private conference room to discuss the Michigan cases as
well as other pending matters. Even by Supreme Court standards,
conferences are top-secret affairs. Only the nine justices are allowed
in the formal, wood-paneled room when a conference is in session.
The most junior justice sits by the door and answers it if someone
knocks with a message or delivery. Not even the law clerks, who often
work intimately with their justices to craft opinions, may attend.

In most cases, the public doesn't learn for years, if at all, what
transpired at conferences. But a few months after the Michigan cases
were decided, Justice John Paul Stevens took an unusual, perhaps
unprecedented, step. Relying on notes he made after the argument,
Stevens told an audience of Chicago lawyers about the comments he
made at conference about the *Grutter* case. Although Stevens didn't
reveal the remarks of his colleagues, his own words nonetheless give
a rare glimpse into some of the Court's internal deliberations.

Stevens was a firm vote in favor of the Michigan Law School policy.
At conference, he urged his colleagues to adhere to stare decisis—the
principle that says the Court should abide by its settled precedents.
Stevens's argument was less a technical interpretation of *Bakke* than
a recognition of how that decision had been received. Universities,
lawmakers, corporations, and military leaders had relied on Powell's
opinion as authoritative, he said.

Stevens was especially impressed by the military brief. He told his colleagues that he found it convincing and that, if diversity was compelling in a military setting, it also should be compelling in a law school setting.

He argued that the *Grutter* case was distinguishable from the quota program struck down in *Bakke*. Unlike the University of California-Davis Medical School, Michigan Law School had the same minimum standards for white and black applicants, Stevens said. Everyone who was accepted met the basic qualification standards. The point was important, Stevens said, because it alleviated concern that minorities accepted under affirmative action would be stigmatized as unqualified. The justice also argued that Michigan's flexible targets were not the same as a quota.

Stevens tried to assure his colleagues that affirmative action wouldn't become a permanent fixture. He pointed to a brief that described how affirmative action for Asians had "worked itself out" and was no longer necessary.

The ultimate question for Stevens was who should decide whether affirmative action was warranted. Should it be, he asked his colleagues, "the nine of us or the accumulated wisdom of the country's leaders?"

———•———

ALMOST THREE MONTHS PASSED with no signal from the Court. On the morning of Monday, June 23, 2003, Ted Shaw was supposed to be in Budapest for a conference about school desegregation. He had reluctantly decided at the last minute to cancel, fearing that the Supreme Court would issue the affirmative action opinions that morning.

As with so much of its work, the Supreme Court is intensely secretive about its plans for releasing opinions. The Court typically gives a few days' notice that decisions were coming on a particular day (at 10:00 a.m., except in extraordinary cases) but won't say which opinions or even how many. Like other Court-watchers, Shaw could do no more than engage in educated speculation. His best guess was the Court would issue the opinions on the final day of its term, either later that week or the following Monday. Still, he didn't want to risk being out of the country if he was wrong.

Shaw caught the 6:30 a.m. shuttle flight, arriving at Reagan National Airport in Arlington, Virginia, at 8:00. He knew he needed to hurry to reach the Court in time to claim a seat. As he hustled through the airport to catch a taxi, he saw a crowd gathered around a large man who had collapsed and was lying on the floor. The man's face was so drained of color that Shaw didn't even realize until later that it belonged to someone he knew well, Maynard Jackson, an affirmative action pioneer and former mayor of Atlanta. Jackson died of heart failure in an ambulance a short time later.

Payton was already in line when Shaw got to the Court. Soon, Mahoney arrived. Like Shaw, she had almost decided not to come. She figured the rulings, like so many other major decisions in the Court's history, wouldn't come out until the final day of the term. By happenstance, Krislov and Michigan president Mary Sue Coleman were also in town. Coleman had given a speech at the National Institutes of Health that morning and was caught in traffic, but Krislov arrived in time to secure a seat in the court.

The turnout was smaller on the other side of the case. Pell made it, along with his CIR colleague Michael Rosman, but Kolbo stayed in Minneapolis, knowing the clerk's office would call him immediately if a decision was issued. Gratz was in San Diego, preparing to leave for work. She usually left before 7:00 local time, but on this morning her husband persuaded her to wait a few more minutes as he monitored CNN.

At the sound of the buzzer and rap of the marshal's gavel, the justices entered and took their seats. Breyer presented the Court's first decision, which ruled in favor of a financial-services company in a consumer-lending dispute. Souter then announced the Court had struck down a California law that would have required insurance companies to disclose information about policies issued in Europe during the Holocaust. As Ginsburg summarized her dissent in that case, Rehnquist and O'Connor chatted quietly, out of range of the microphones.

When Ginsburg finished, Rehnquist leaned forward and announced that Justice O'Connor would announce the next opinion, No. 02-241, *Grutter v. Bollinger.*

A couple of hundred people straightened up in their seats.

—■—

That O'Connor was delivering the opinion was a good sign for the university. Hers was the vote Michigan had to get to prevail. Mahoney, for one, figured that if the Court was going to uphold the law school policy, O'Connor was a likely bet to write the opinion.

"The University of Michigan Law School," O'Connor began, "strives to assemble a highly capable, diverse student body by focusing on academic ability as well as on each applicant's talents, experiences, and potential."

In some other context, O'Connor's words might have seemed a neutral description of the university's argument. But as the opening line of her presentation, her comments were highly suggestive. O'Connor was characterizing the policy much as the university had. Krislov had brought a pad of paper and, his hand shaking, began to write.

O'Connor went on: "The Law School's admissions policy does not define diversity solely in terms of race, but it does reaffirm the Law School's commitment to the inclusion of African American, Latino, and Native American students who might otherwise not be present in meaningful numbers."

That was all Payton needed to hear. O'Connor was acknowledging the value of critical mass.

"We have won," he whispered to Shaw.[1]

———■———

THE VOTE TO UPHOLD the law school policy was five-to-four. Stevens, Ginsburg, Breyer, and Souter joined O'Connor in the majority, reaffirming and expanding on Powell's *Bakke* opinion and endorsing Michigan Law School's approach to diversity.

Kennedy, in dissent, said he would apply Powell's standard—making six votes for that principle—but concluded that the school hadn't met the test. Rehnquist declined to take a position on the diversity rationale, while agreeing with Kennedy that the admissions policy failed the narrow tailoring inquiry. Scalia and Thomas both concluded that universities couldn't use diversity as a basis for race-based admissions.

Moments after O'Connor's announcement, Rehnquist released the *Gratz* opinion, striking down the undergraduate admissions policy, six-to-three. O'Connor and Breyer switched sides, saying the undergraduate admissions policy was too mechanistic and flunked the narrow tailoring test.

Some early news reports characterized the outcome as a split decision. That was true on the surface—each side had won one case—but not as a practical matter. By upholding the law school policy, the high court had given universities a road map, telling them what they could do to achieve a racially diverse class.

———■———

MUCH AS SHE SUGGESTED at argument, O'Connor wasn't interested in making a technical case that Powell's decision was a binding precedent. She and her four colleagues instead embraced diversity, giving it their own, independent endorsement.

O'Connor's first hurdle was strict scrutiny, the principle that race-based distinctions by government must be narrowly tailored to meet a compelling government interest. In *Croson* and again in *Adarand*, O'Connor had joined the Court majority in making strict scrutiny the test for affirmative action, rejecting arguments that a more relaxed standard should apply when the race discrimination is "benign."

In *Grutter*, O'Connor put a new gloss on strict scrutiny, characterizing it as a far more flexible test than many had imagined. "Strict scrutiny must take 'relevant differences' into account," she wrote, quoting from her own opinion in *Adarand*. "Not every decision influenced by race is equally objectionable and strict scrutiny is designed to provide a framework for carefully examining the importance and the sincerity of the reasons advanced by the governmental decision-maker for the use of race in that particular context."

O'Connor's interpretation of strict scrutiny paved the way for a crucial aspect of her decision: the deference that she said courts owed to educators. Student admissions, she wrote, was "an area that lies primarily within the expertise of the university." She added: "We have long recognized that, given the important purpose of public education and the expansive freedoms of speech and thought associated with the university environment, universities occupy a special niche in our constitutional tradition." She said the Court would presume the university was acting in good faith, absent evidence to the contrary.

The benefits of racial diversity "are substantial," O'Connor wrote. She pointed to the expert studies that Payton had introduced at trial, as well as the American Educational Research Association brief and its contention that diversity leads to better learning. O'Connor cited the

Fortune 500 and General Motors briefs for support. "These benefits are not theoretical but real, as major American businesses have made clear that the skills needed in today's increasingly global marketplace can only be developed through exposure to widely diverse people, cultures, ideas, and viewpoints," she said. She quoted at length from the military brief. "At present, 'the military cannot achieve an officer corps that is *both* highly qualified *and* racially diverse unless the service academies and the ROTC used limited race-conscious recruiting and admissions policies.'"

O'Connor gave a nod to the legacy of *Brown v. Board of Education,* citing the connection that case made between education and good citizenship. She invoked the Bush administration's brief, citing it for the proposition that "the diffusion of knowledge and opportunity through public institutions of higher education must be accessible to all individuals regardless of race or ethnicity." She added: "Effective participation by members of all racial and ethnic groups in the civic life of our Nation is essential if the dream of one Nation, indivisible, is to be realized."

Moreover, law schools, particularly highly selective law schools, are the pathway to leadership in America, O'Connor wrote. "In order to cultivate a set of leaders with legitimacy in the eyes of the citizenry, it is necessary that the path to leadership be visibly open to talented and qualified individuals of every race and ethnicity. All members of our heterogeneous society must have confidence in the openness and integrity of the educational institutions that provide this training."

O'Connor said the law school's admissions policies weren't based on stereotypes and in fact were aimed at tearing them down. At the same time, she suggested that race often played an important role in a person's viewpoint. "Just as growing up in a particular region or having particular professional experiences is likely to affect an individual's views, so too is one's own, unique experience of being a racial minority in a society, like our own, in which race unfortunately still matters."

O'CONNOR BEGAN her discussion of narrow tailoring by adopting a definition of "quota" similar to the one Mahoney had urged. "Properly understood, a 'quota' is a program in which a certain fixed number or proportion of opportunities are 'reserved exclusively for certain minority groups,'" she wrote, quoting from *Croson.* "'[S]ome attention to numbers,' without more, does not transform a flexible admissions system into a rigid quota," she wrote, quoting Powell's *Bakke* opinion. She said the actual enrollment figures—ranging from 13.5 percent to 20.1 percent black, Hispanic, and Native American—were "inconsistent with a quota."

The key for O'Connor was the flexibility of the law school's admissions policy. "[A] university's admissions program must remain flexible enough to ensure that each applicant is evaluated as an individual and not in a way that makes race or ethnicity the defining feature of his or her application." Michigan Law School "engages in a highly individualized, holistic review of each applicant's file, giving serious consideration to all the ways an applicant might contribute to a diverse educational environment," she said. Unlike the Michigan undergraduate admissions office, "the Law School awards no mechanical, predetermined diversity 'bonuses' based on race or ethnicity." She noted that all admitted students were deemed qualified for admission. And she said Michigan Law School "seriously weighs many other diversity factors besides race that can make a real and dispositive difference for nonminority applicants as well."

O'Connor wasn't impressed by the race-neutral alternatives the Bush administration and other litigants had suggested. Using a lottery system or reducing the emphasis on undergraduate grades and LSAT scores "would require a dramatic sacrifice of diversity, the academic quality of all admitted students, or both." As for percent plans, O'Connor chided the Bush administration for failing to "explain how such plans could work for graduate and professional schools." And she said they suffered from a fundamental flaw: "[E]ven assuming such plans are race-neutral, they may preclude the university from conducting the individualized assessments necessary to assemble a student body that is not just racially diverse, but diverse along all the qualities valued by the university."

Finally, O'Connor addressed the aspect of the case that had troubled her during argument: the time frame of race-conscious admissions programs. All government uses of race must have "a logical end point," she said. Universities should conduct periodic reviews to assess whether preferences are still necessary and, over time, should draw on "the most promising aspects" of the alternative programs in Florida, California, and Washington. "We take the Law School at its word that it would 'like nothing better than to find a race-neutral admissions formula' and will terminate its race-conscious admissions program as soon as practicable."

She concluded:

> It has been 25 years since Justice Powell first approved the use of race to further an interest in student body diversity in the context of public higher education. Since that time, the number of minority applicants with high grades and test scores has indeed increased.... We expect that 25 years from now, the use of racial preferences will no longer be necessary to further the interest approved today.

———■———

REHNQUIST'S OPINION for the Court in *Gratz*, the undergraduate case, started with the presumption that O'Connor's *Grutter* opinion was the law. Although Rehnquist himself never took a position on the issue of diversity, his opinion assumed diversity was a compelling interest. The question now was narrow tailoring.

The fundamental problem for Rehnquist was the automatic nature of the twenty-point preference. Powell's opinion had "emphasized the importance of considering each particular applicant as an individual, assessing all of the qualities that individual possesses, and in turn, evaluating that individual's ability to contribute to the unique setting of higher education," the chief justice wrote. "Powell did not contemplate that any single characteristic automatically ensured a specific and identifiable contribution to a university's diversity.... Instead, under the approach Justice Powell described, each characteristic of a particular applicant was to be considered in assessing the applicant's entire application."

Rehnquist pointed to a section in the Harvard plan that Powell had praised. In seeking to foster diversity, that policy said that "the crucial criteria are often individual qualities or experience not dependent upon race but sometimes associated with it." Harvard's plan also posited an example in which a white applicant "with extraordinary artistic talent" might earn a seat in the class over two black applicants.

At Michigan, even if a white student had artistic talent that "rivaled that of Monet or Picasso," that student could earn only five extra points, compared with the twenty allotted to every minority who submitted an application, Rehnquist said. "Clearly, the LSA's system does not offer applicants the individualized selection process described in Harvard's example."

Rehnquist wasn't swayed by Payton's description of the "flagging" process that allowed a special committee to ignore the point system and look at selected applications holistically. "[I]t is undisputed that such consideration is the exception and not the rule in the operation of the LSA's admissions program," Rehnquist wrote.

—■—

O'CONNOR JOINED Rehnquist's opinion and wrote separately in an effort to harmonize the two rulings. Joined by Breyer, she said that the automatic nature of the undergraduate selection index "ensures that the diversity contributions of applicants cannot be individually assessed." She went on: "This policy stands in sharp contrast to the law school's admissions plan, which enables admissions officers to make nuanced judgments with respect to the contributions each applicant is likely to make to the diversity of the incoming class."

—■—

REHNQUIST'S DISSENT in *Grutter* was a remarkable opinion, centering around his own statistical analysis of the law school's admissions and making a series of arguments that Kolbo and CIR themselves hadn't raised. Scalia, Thomas, and Kennedy all signed the opinion.

Rehnquist broke down the law school's minority application and admissions numbers, separating blacks, Latinos, and Native Americans from one another. From 1995 through 2000, the number of blacks admitted ranged from 91 to 108, Hispanics from 47 to 56, and Native Americans from 13 to 19. In Rehnquist's view, the numbers proved that "critical mass" was a farce. "If the Law School is admitting between 91 and 108 African-Americans in order to achieve 'critical mass,' thereby preventing African-American students from feeling 'isolated or like spokespersons for their race,' one would think that a number of the same order of magnitude would be necessary to accomplish the same purpose for Hispanics and Native Americans,"

Rehnquist wrote. Even if every admitted Native American was to enroll, "how can this possibly constitute a 'critical mass' of Native Americans in a class of over 350 students?" In a footnote, Rehnquist added that at one point Native American enrollment at Michigan Law School dropped to three students.

Rehnquist had put his finger on a weakness in the university's case, even though he somewhat mischaracterized Michigan's position. As described by the university, "critical mass" worked collectively. Blacks, Latinos, and Native Americans didn't each have their own, separate critical mass, as Rehnquist suggested; clearly, that would have been all but impossible given the tiny numbers of Native Americans who applied. The law school instead sought a single critical mass of all underrepresented minorities. The problem was that the concept of critical mass, at least as Michigan had defined it, didn't lend itself to the inclusion of multiple minority groups under the same umbrella. If the goal was to prevent a handful of Native American students from being isolated or feeling as though they needed to be representatives of their race, the presence of large numbers of black students would seem to be of little help.

Rehnquist said the differing numbers were the product of uneven admissions standards for the three groups. Borderline black candidates, the chief justice said, had a much better chance of admission than Latinos with similar credentials. As one example, Rehnquist pointed to 2000, when, of twelve Hispanic applicants with a 159 or 160 LSAT score and a 3.0 or higher GPA, only two were admitted. By contrast, all twelve of the black applicants with similar qualifications got offers. The university and its lawyers "have *never* offered any race-specific arguments explaining why significantly more individuals from one underrepresented minority group are needed in order to achieve 'critical mass' or further student body diversity," Rehnquist wrote. "They certainly have not explained why Hispanics, who they have said are among 'the groups most isolated by racial barriers in our country,' should have their admission capped out in this manner." The notion that the law school was seeking a critical mass, Rehnquist added, "is simply a sham."

Rehnquist then compiled three charts, one for each of the racial groups that benefited from affirmative action. For every year from 1995 to 2000, the charts compared the percentage a race represented in the law school's applicant pool with the percentage it comprised of the group that was admitted. The correlation was striking. In 1995, 9.7 percent of the applicants were black, compared with 9.4 percent of the admittees. For Latinos that year, the comparable numbers were 5.1 and 5.0. For Native Americans, they were 1.1 and 1.2. Even in the year with by far the most variation, 1997, the disparities in the percentages were small: 9.3 versus 8.3 for blacks, 4.8 versus 3.9 percent for Hispanics, and 1.1 versus 1.6 for Native Americans.

That outcome, Rehnquist concluded, "must result from careful race based planning by the Law School." The correlation "suggests a formula for admission based on the aspirational assumption that all applicants are equally qualified academically, and therefore that the proportion of each group admitted should be the same as the proportion of that group in the applicant pool." The school operated a "carefully managed program designed to ensure proportionate representation of applicants from minority groups," he said. And even the majority had conceded that racial balancing would be illegal.

—■—

THOMAS BEGAN his *Grutter* dissent by quoting Frederick Douglass, who in 1865 told a group of abolitionists that the best thing they could do for blacks was to leave them alone. "Like Douglass, I believe blacks can achieve in every avenue of American life without the meddling of university administrators," Thomas wrote.

More so than any other member of the Court, Thomas evinced a deep-seated antipathy for government-sponsored racial distinctions. "Every time the government places citizens on racial registers and makes race relevant to the provision of burdens or benefits, it demeans us all," he wrote. He accused Michigan of admitting "overmatched" minority students who "take the bait, only to find that they cannot succeed in the cauldron of competition." He said racial preferences engender resentment among whites and, quoting from one of his earlier opinions, "stamp minorities with a badge of inferiority and may cause them to develop dependencies or to adopt an attitude that they are 'entitled' to preferences."

Thomas, the Yale graduate, was equally contemptuous of the upper-crust status afforded to some universities. The justice used the words "elite" or "elitist" no fewer than twenty-one times in his opinion. Taking up the contentions Scalia had advanced at argument, Thomas said that Michigan "maintains an exclusionary admissions system that it knows produces racially disproportionate results." Thomas went on: "Racial discrimination is not a permissible solution to the self-inflicted wounds of this elitist admissions policy."

Michigan, Thomas said, "has no compelling interest in having a law school at all, much less an *elite* one." He listed five states with no accredited state-run law school, much less one of the caliber of Michigan's. He noted that less than 16 percent of Michigan Law School graduates remain in the state. "The Law School's decision to be an elite institution does little to advance the welfare of the people of Michigan or any cognizable interest of the State of Michigan."

Thomas questioned the assertion that racial diversity was of value in a college environment. He said the *Grutter* majority ignored "the growing evidence that racial (and other sorts) of heterogeneity actually impairs learning among black students." He said the logic of the majority's deference to the university's judgment would mean that a historically black college would have the right to reject white applicants if it concluded that students would learn better in a segregated environment. And he pointed to a precedent in which the Supreme Court refused to defer to the judgment of a state-run university—the Court's 1996 decision requiring the all-male Virginia Military Institute to admit women.

Thomas tried to twist O'Connor's language to his advantage, characterizing her reference to the future as a twenty-five-year "time limit" on racial preferences. The majority had issued a "holding that racial discrimination will be unconstitutional in 25 years," according to Thomas.

"It has been nearly 140 years since Frederick Douglass asked the intellectual ancestors of the Law School to '[d]o nothing with us!' and the Nation adopted the Fourteenth Amendment," Thomas concluded. "Now we must wait another 25 years to see this principle of equality vindicated."

———•———

Scalia concurred in the bulk of Thomas's opinion and added a few words of his own. Scalia predicted the majority decision would mean a litany of future lawsuits. Some suits would question whether a particular admissions program treated each applicant as an individual, others whether a policy operated separate admissions tracks, he said. Still other suits might contend that a university had "so zealously pursued its 'critical mass' as to make it an unconstitutional *de facto* quota system, rather than merely 'a permissible goal,'" he said. Opponents also might argue that, whatever educational value racial diversity has at Michigan, no such benefits exist at various other institutions, he said. Still other suits might "challenge the bona fides of the institution's expressed commitment to the educational benefits of diversity" or argue that preferences "have gone below or above the mystical *Grutter*-approved critical mass." Finally, Scalia said, particular minority groups might sue, claiming they were short-changed much as Rehnquist described in his dissent. "I do not look forward to any of these cases," Scalia wrote.

———

KENNEDY SAID Powell's *Bakke* opinion "states the correct rule for resolving this case." But, he said, the majority didn't apply the type of strict scrutiny that Powell had required. The problem, Kennedy said, lay in the broad deference O'Connor afforded university administrators. "The Court confuses deference to a university's definition of its educational objective with deference to the implementation of this goal," he wrote. "In the context of university admissions the objective of racial diversity can be accepted based on empirical data known to us, but deference is not to be given with respect to the methods by which it is pursued."

As he had foreshadowed at argument, Kennedy said the pursuit of a critical mass was "a delusion used by the Law School to mask its attempt to make race an automatic factor in most instances and to achieve numerical goals indistinguishable from quotas." For support, Kennedy looked to the enrollment numbers of minority students at the law school from 1987 to 1998. Although the percentage of minorities varied considerably over that period—ranging from 12.3 percent in 1987 to 20.1 percent in 1994—Kennedy said the school may have simply adjusted its targets over time. In any event, "[t]he narrow fluctuation band raises an inference that the Law School subverted individual determination," he wrote. For additional support, he pointed to the daily reports the admissions office used to track the racial composition and other characteristics of the incoming class. Race, Kennedy said, may be "one modest factor among many others," but it may not become "a predominant factor."

Kennedy said he feared that the right to use quotas, or their equivalent, would leave schools with "few incentives to make the existing minority admissions schemes transparent and protective of individual review." That, Kennedy said, would "perpetuate the hostilities that proper consideration of race is designed to avoid."

—•—

OF THE THREE JUSTICES who dissented in *Gratz,* only Ginsburg and Souter considered the substance of the university's undergraduate selection index. Stevens, ever the maverick, dissented on the grounds that neither Gratz nor Hamacher had standing to seek a change in Michigan's admissions policies. "There is a total absence of evidence that either petitioner would receive any benefit from the prospective relief sought by their lawyer," Stevens wrote.

Souter joined Stevens's opinion, while also concluding the policy was constitutional. Souter said the undergraduate policy avoided the pitfalls that had doomed the UC-Davis Medical School policy in *Bakke.* In particular, Michigan eschewed separate admission systems for majorities and minorities, instead putting all applicants into a single pool, he said.

As for the automatic nature of the twenty-point award, Souter said he wasn't troubled. If race is a legitimate consideration, it necessarily will increase the chances of admission for some applicants, he said. "Since college admission is not left entirely to inarticulate intuition, it is hard to see what is inappropriate in assigning some stated value to a relevant characteristic, whether it be reasoning ability, writing style, running speed, or minority race," Souter wrote. "Justice Powell's plus factors necessarily are assigned some values. The college simply does by a numbered scale what the law school accomplishes in its 'holistic review.'"

Souter saved his harshest words for the position advocated by the White House. The percent plans, Souter said, amounted to "deliberate obfuscation." They are "just as race conscious as the point scheme (and fairly so), but they get their racially diverse results without saying directly what they are doing or why they are doing it," he wrote.

"In contrast, Michigan states its purpose directly and, if this were a doubtful case for me, I would be tempted to give Michigan an extra point of its own for its frankness. Equal protection cannot become an exercise in which the winners are the ones who hide the ball."

—•—

GINSBURG, JOINED BY Souter and Breyer, attacked the notion that affirmative action plans should be held to the same strict scrutiny standard as government policies designed to exclude minorities. That would be fitting "were our Nation free of the vestiges of rank discrimination long reinforced by law," she wrote. "But we are not far distant from an overtly discriminatory past, and the effects of centuries of law-sanctioned inequality remain painfully evident in our communities and schools." Racial disparities abound, she said, pointing to unemployment, poverty, health-care access, education quality, and job discrimination.

"[G]overnment decision-makers may properly distinguish between policies of exclusion and inclusion," Ginsburg said. "Actions designed to burden groups long denied full citizenship stature are not sensibly ranked with measures taken to hasten the day when entrenched discrimination and its after effects have been extirpated."

Ginsburg seconded Souter's argument that Michigan was being penalized for the candor of its point system. Writing now only for herself and Souter, she predicted that colleges "will seek to maintain their minority enrollment ... whether or not they can do so in full candor through adoption of affirmative action plans of the kind here at issue." Universities "may resort to camouflage," she said. "If honesty is the best policy, surely Michigan's accurately described, fully disclosed College affirmative action program is preferable to achieving similar numbers through winks, nods, and disguises."

That last contention drew a response from Rehnquist, who added a footnote to his majority opinion. "These observations are remarkable for two reasons," the chief justice said. "First, they suggest that universities—to whose academic judgment we are told in *Grutter v. Bollinger* ... we should defer—will pursue their affirmative-action programs whether or not they violate the United States Constitution. Second, they recommend that these violations should be dealt with, not by requiring the universities to obey the Constitution, but by changing the Constitution so that it conforms to the conduct of the universities."

Ginsburg responded: "Contrary to the Court's contention, I do not suggest 'changing the Constitution so that it conforms to the conduct of the universities.' ... In my view, the Constitution, properly interpreted, permits government officials to respond openly to the continuing importance of race."[2]

Hail to the Victors

Dᵁᴿᴵᴺᴳ ᴛʜᴇ ꜰɪᴿꜱᴛ twenty-five years after *Bakke*, university affirmative action rested on a set of slim reeds. The predominant legal justification came from a single justice, Lewis Powell. The model he had offered, the Harvard plan, hadn't been tested in the courts. Some of the language in his opinion suggested that race could be only a minor factor, a small "plus" that would propel a minority candidate over a majority applicant with similar credentials. And the Supreme Court itself had gradually clamped down on racial preferences in other post-*Bakke* contexts, hinting that the same fate eventually would greet university affirmative action.

Instead, the *Grutter* decision bolstered the legal foundation for affirmative action, leaving race-based admissions more secure than they had ever been. Six justices adopted Powell's reasoning, five of them expanding and in many ways strengthening it. The majority approved a program that was properly before them, creating a model for other universities to emulate. The Court approved "critical mass" as a constitutional goal.

One of the weaknesses of Powell's explanation was that it focused almost exclusively on the benefits of diversity to the university and, by extension, to the nonminority students in the class. Powell said little about the value to the direct beneficiaries of affirmative action themselves. Given the long, tragic history of discrimination against American racial minorities, his reasoning was, to say the least, ironic:

it focused mainly on the benefits of diversity to white people.

O'Connor's explanation, by contrast, emphasized the stake that blacks and Hispanics had in affirmative action. She explained how an education and degree from a top university served as a doorway to future prosperity. She cited *Brown* for the notion that education was the "foundation of good citizenship."

O'Connor also described how society at large, not just people on college campuses, would benefit from the successes of minority groups. By welcoming members of all races, she said, universities cultivated "a set of leaders with legitimacy in the eyes of the citizenry." Society needed "[e]ffective participation by members of all racial and ethnic groups" in civic affairs, she added. O'Connor specifically noted the importance of having minorities in the ranks of the officer corps in the military.

In effect, O'Connor was invoking one of the justifications Powell explicitly rejected: the goal of producing more minority college graduates and professionals. Granted, O'Connor disclaimed any endorsement of "racial balancing," calling that concept "patently unconstitutional." But the rest of her opinion made clear that universities could consider both their own racial composition and that of key sectors of society. And they could act to rectify the imbalances they saw. Indeed, Rehnquist's dissent in *Grutter* makes a strong case that critical mass couldn't fully explain the racial aspects of the law school's admissions decisions, even if he may have overstated the mathematical precision of the process. None of the affirmative action supporters on the Court effectively rebutted the suggestion that the school seemed to have at least a rough racial breakdown in mind for each entering class.

To be sure, the majority opinions had their share of logical shortcomings, particularly when taken together. Neither O'Connor nor Rehnquist answered the argument made by Souter and Ginsburg that the undergraduate point system simply made explicit what was implicit at the law school; at both schools, race was a factor that mattered and that sometimes could make the difference between admission and rejection. In addition, O'Connor raised more questions than she answered by trying to marry the incompatible principles of strict scrutiny and deference, leaving a conceptual mess for future Supreme Courts to clean up.

O'Connor did little to address the concern she first raised at argument: the lack of a clear expiration point. Despite Thomas's insistence that O'Connor had imposed a twenty-five-year sunset provision on racial preferences—something she lacked authority to do even if that was her intention—her language made it more of an aspiration. She fell back on the deference she had afforded university administrators, trusting that they would seek and find alternatives that would make race-based admissions unnecessary. She expressed the hope that minority grades and test scores would improve significantly, but could give no real assurance that they would.

Michigan and its supporters, of course, would have preferred to see the Court uphold the undergraduate admissions policy along with the law school system. As CIR would point out repeatedly over the coming weeks, the nation's highest court found that Michigan's largest academic unit violated the Constitution. The university might have to pay damages to wrongly rejected applicants, and it would have to rewrite its admissions policy.

But O'Connor and the rest of the Court also gave Michigan and every other selective university in America the key to fashioning a constitutional affirmative action policy: treat every applicant as an individual. Point systems were out; holistic review was in. Universities that followed that prescription would go a long way toward shielding themselves from future lawsuits.

All told, it was a stunning victory for affirmative action, one few could have envisioned when CIR filed its first complaint against Michigan in October 1997. The cases that aimed to topple racial preferences, in the end, saved them.

For advocates of affirmative action, heroes abounded. Shaw helped craft a law school admissions policy that stood a fighting chance at the Supreme Court. Bollinger made the decision to mount a full-scale defense, then used his stature to marshal outside support. Payton skillfully put together the core legal case from the ground up. Krislov relentlessly pursued Bollinger's vision of corporate and military backing, then coordinated what became a sprawling team of supporters. Mahoney wowed the high court with her advocacy skills. A slew of other figures also played important roles: Nancy Cantor, Jane Sherburne, Randy Mehrberg, Jim Cannon, Harry Pearce, Joe Reeder, Virginia Seitz, Mary Sue Coleman, as well as dozens of other people, only some of whose names appear in this book. And Miranda Massie and Shanta Driver, questionable though their tactics were in places, succeeded in starting a movement to highlight the real-world impact of affirmative action on minority students.

For the CIR lawyers, the decisions represented the failure of what had been a calculated gamble. When they sued, they thought, not unreasonably, that they had the law and the Supreme Court on their side. By the time the cases reached the high court, CIR was outnumbered. Too many powerful institutions had told the Court that race-based admissions were crucially important to the nation's well-being. Even the Bush administration refused to rule them out altogether, instead peddling an awkward compromise that gained little traction at the Court. Pell and his predecessors McDonald and Greve did succeed in raising the national consciousness about racial preferences and in forcing the high court to provide some clarity to a muddled area of the law. Yet the ultimate prize they sought not only eluded them but, in light of the *Grutter* ruling, grew more distant. Race-based admissions would be around for at least another generation.

———•———

IN NEW YORK, Bollinger found himself surrounded by champagne and flowers. In Washington, Mahoney signed autographs again, this time on stapled copies of the *Grutter* decision. In Ann Arbor, Aleobua and hundreds of her fellow students chanted and cheered in celebration amid a handful of dissenters.

Outside the Supreme Court, Pell tried to cast a favorable light on the rulings. "We've moved the ball forward," he told a reporter. "We are seeing the beginning of the end for racial preferences." The Supreme Court, he pointed out, had found Michigan to have engaged in unconstitutional race discrimination in its undergraduate admissions policy. In the days that followed, Pell would grow aghast at the giddy reactions from university officials in Michigan and around the country.

The Bush administration put its own spin on the decisions. Even though O'Connor had upheld an admissions program decried by the president as a "quota" and even though she had rejected the government's contention that percent plans were an adequate alternative, the White House claimed victory. "I applaud the Supreme Court for recognizing the value of diversity on our Nation's campuses," Bush said in a statement. "Today's decisions seek a careful balance of equal treatment under the law."

Greve was under no illusions that the rulings were any sort of partial victory. They were, he thought, a complete loss. "The Court has held that quotas are okay—so long as universities lie about them," he wrote.

Payton hit the speaking circuit over the next few weeks. He was hailed as a hero at the annual convention of the liberal American Constitution Society. (His cheering audience included Judge Boyce Martin, who was happy to show his broad support for affirmative action despite his misgivings about Michigan's undergraduate admissions policy.) In his remarks, Payton pointed to one of his favorite themes from the decisions: the optimism they offered for the future of American race relations.

"We have had major problems relating to race," Payton said. "They're confounding to us. But in this area, higher education, we've learned that having a diverse student body makes us a better country. This is something we can and must do.... These are optimistic decisions on race. And that ought to prompt all of us to turn to the underlying problems that still afflict our country."[1]

Epilogue

IN ANTICIPATION OF the Michigan decisions, the pro–affirmative action Civil Rights Project at Harvard had scheduled a meeting to take place in mid-July 2003, a few weeks after the end of the Supreme Court's term. The intent was to provide a forum for university presidents and other officials to discuss how to maintain racial diversity under whatever new restrictions the Court might impose.

Although some eighty university presidents were invited, only half a dozen showed up, and many schools didn't even send a representative. The low turnout was a testament to the sense of relief felt by many university administrators in the wake of the *Grutter* and *Gratz* rulings. Their worst fears hadn't been realized. They could continue to use race in admissions to diversify their campuses.

The nonchalance among college officials masked significant changes that occurred at many institutions in the months following the decisions. Some universities amended their admissions systems to make the use of race less explicit, continuing a trend that had begun even before the Court ruled. Ohio State and the University of Massachusetts at Amherst both scrapped point-based systems that bore similarities to the Michigan policy struck down in *Gratz*. Each school substituted a more flexible process that included an increased focus on essay questions. Each also hired additional readers to cull through the thousands of applications that began arriving in the fall of 2003.

Michigan's undergraduate admissions office made similar alterations, abandoning the point system that was at issue in *Gratz* in favor of a holistic evaluation. The new application posed additional questions to prospective freshmen, seeking such information as family educational history, household income, and "significant intercultural experiences." Another question specifically offered students

309

an opportunity to describe how they would add to campus diversity. Under the new system, two readers looked at each application, considering race as one of many factors, and forwarded a recommendation to an assistant director of admissions. The assistant director then either made a final decision or submitted the application to a committee for a judgment.

The new Michigan policy came at a steep cost. In the first year alone, the university spent close to $2 million putting the system in place. Most of that money went toward salaries for fifty-one additional permanent and temporary staffers, including the new admissions counselors and readers who were needed to give each application individual attention.

To the extent Michigan's goal was to maintain racial diversity, the policy was a partial success. Minority admissions dropped slightly for the fall 2004 entering class. As of May 16, black, Latino, and Native American students accounted for 11.1 percent of the admittees for the fall of 2004, down from 13.0 percent in 2003 on the same date. Perhaps more striking was the sharp decrease in applications, down 25.4 percent for blacks, 20.7 percent for all underrepresented minorities, and 18.0 percent overall. Michigan officials speculated that some high school students might have been turned off by the lengthier application.

While some universities became less rigid in their use of race, the University of Texas at Austin moved in the opposite direction. Freed from the restrictions of the Fifth Circuit's *Hopwood* decision, UT-Austin President Larry R. Faulkner announced plans to resume race-conscious admissions. Faulkner also called on state lawmakers to scale back the "top ten percent" law, which he said tied the hands of admissions officers by accounting for more than two-thirds of the school's entering class. In contrast, his counterpart at Texas A&M, President Robert M. Gates, said his institution would continue to use only race-neutral admissions criteria.

More sweeping changes were made in non-admissions contexts. With few exceptions, universities concluded that the Court's requirement of individualized consideration meant colleges could no longer maintain minority-only scholarships, summer programs, and orientations. From early 2003 to early 2004, almost seventy colleges opened previously restricted programs to people of all races, according to the *Chronicle of Higher Education*. Harvard began welcoming white and Asian participants into a one-week summer preparatory program at its business school. Indiana University made changes to a program that had awarded scholarships to 150 black, Latino, and Native American freshmen, opening it to white and Asian students who could make the case that they would contribute to campus diversity. Saint Louis University replaced a scholarship program for African Americans with one for students who would promote Martin Luther King Jr.'s "dream of a diverse but unified America." Princeton University discontinued a summer program that had been designed exclusively for minority college students interested in graduate study in public service.

Conservative organizations kept the pressure on universities to reduce their reliance on race. Groups that initially had been furious about the Supreme Court rulings found that the decisions nonetheless contained nuggets that could be exploited. The Center for Equal Opportunity, which had stayed in the background while CIR pressed the Michigan suits, cruised the Internet looking for evidence of race-exclusive policies that might run afoul of the Court's reasoning. CEO, as the group was known, then wrote to colleges that were operating questionable programs, demanding changes or at least clarifications. CEO also filed complaints with the U.S. Department of Education's Office of Civil Rights against Rice University in Houston and Texas Tech University, saying *Grutter* required those schools to continue using the race-neutral admissions criteria they had been employing since the *Hopwood* decision. Another anti-preference group, the National Association of Scholars, took the lead in filing Freedom of Information Act requests covering admissions policies at Michigan and in nineteen other states.

At CIR, Terry Pell and his team were as interested in the subject as ever. Pell harbored suspicions about the changes Michigan was making—he wondered whether the university was simply repackaging its admissions system to disguise the importance of race. CIR also had additional work to do in the courtroom, pressing ahead with damage claims against Michigan on behalf of Jennifer Gratz, Patrick Hamacher, and other rejected undergraduate applicants. The group also continued to litigate its preference case against the University of Washington. And CIR joined the National Association of Scholars and Center for Equal Opportunity in filing the FOIA requests.

But for the time being, Pell and his colleagues were content to let other groups take the lead on university racial preferences. After spending six years and some $4 million on the Michigan lawsuits, they found that other matters now were demanding attention. The group was suing the U.S. Department of Housing and Urban Development over its employment goals and preferences for women and minorities. CIR also was representing a California Polytechnic State University student who had been disciplined after posting a flyer about an upcoming lecture by an author who believed blacks were too dependent on government programs. CIR's style had always been to move deliberately, selecting its lawsuits carefully for maximum impact. The group wanted to let matters settle a bit before launching any major new initiative on college admissions.

Had CIR achieved its goal of color-blind admissions, the social and political consequences might have been enormous. Although no firm numbers exist, various statistical estimates suggest that, at the undergraduate level alone, between 300 and 400 institutions—recipients of more than a million applications every year—have relied on racial preferences over the years. For good or bad, virtually every student who attended a top American university would have felt the impact of a fundamentally different admissions system. And tens of thousands of students each year likely would have wound up at a different school and with a different career track. The effect would have rippled across society for decades to come.

Indeed, a year after the Supreme Court rulings, the most striking legacy of the Michigan affirmative action cases was what the Court chose *not* to do. The justices didn't force universities to ignore the race of applicants. Nor did the rulings precipitate sharp cuts in minority enrollment at top universities. Those outcomes had seemed plausible, perhaps even likely, in the fall of 1997 when CIR filed its two lawsuits. In many ways, the rulings were akin to the Court's 1992 decision in *Planned Parenthood v. Casey;* in that case, anti-abortion activists had hoped the Court would overturn the landmark *Roe v. Wade* decision, only to see the justices reaffirm its central tenets. Likewise, the justices easily could have used *Grutter* and *Gratz* to unleash the social revolution sought by conservatives. As with abortion—and with Sandra Day O'Connor again in the lead—the Court opted instead to make changes at the margins.

FOR SOME OF the people on the winning side, the lawsuits seemed to serve as a springboard for career advancement. A week after the Supreme Court decision, Jeff Lehman followed Lee Bollinger to the Ivy League, taking over as president of Cornell University. Marvin Krislov's name would surface later in connection with other presidential searches. The board of the NAACP Legal Defense and Educational Fund in January 2004 selected Ted Shaw to take over as president and director-counsel, replacing Elaine Jones, who was stepping down.

Ted Olson spent another year as solicitor general before deciding to return to private practice. In a June 24, 2004, resignation letter to the president, Olson said his work "has been exciting, inspiring and, at times, breathtaking."

Others involved in the cases found their lives complicated as a result. The Republican chairman of the House Judiciary Committee, Representative James Sensenbrenner of Wisconsin, launched an investigation into Judge Boyce Martin's handling of the affirmative action cases. Then a private watchdog organization, Judicial Watch, filed a complaint against Martin with the Sixth Circuit, accusing him of misconduct in the Byrd and Michigan cases. Under the court's operating rules, the complaint was referred to Danny Boggs, whose seniority made him the acting chief judge when Martin was unable to handle a matter. Boggs recused himself, sending the matter to the next-most senior active judge, Alice Batchelder. As the one member of the court who had joined Boggs's scathing "procedural appendix," Batchelder might have disqualified herself as well. Instead, she wrote that, although no punishment was warranted, Martin had bent the court's rules. Martin appealed to a larger panel of his colleagues, who agreed that punishment was unnecessary, while declining to take a position on the allegations of wrongdoing.

Shaw's departing boss, Elaine Jones, also came under fire. According to a Senate Judiciary Committee memo leaked to the press, Jones had spoken to an aide to Senator Ted Kennedy in April 2002—a month before the Sixth Circuit's decision in the *Grutter* case—and asked that the committee not approve a new judge for that court until it had decided the Michigan appeals. The memo portrayed

Jones as being concerned that a new judge would have the right to vote on the affirmative action cases. After the leak, four conservative groups filed an ethics complaint against Jones with the Virginia State Bar, accusing her of improperly trying to influence the outcome of the cases. In April 2004 the bar rejected the complaint. The irony of the whole episode was that, if indeed Jones feared the impact of a new judge on the Michigan cases, those concerns were misplaced. Even if a nominee had been confirmed by the Senate and sworn into office before the Sixth Circuit's ruling, the new judge couldn't have taken part; under the court's rules only judges who were active at the time of argument were eligible to participate.

For many of the central participants, the *Gratz* and *Grutter* cases marked not the end of the fight over college racial preferences, but the beginning of a new stage. Michigan would remain a battleground. In July 2003 Jennifer Gratz and Barbara Grutter joined Ward Connerly on the steps of the University of Michigan's Hatcher Graduate Library to announce a new effort to put the question of preferences to the state's voters. The initiative was designed to sidestep the Supreme Court ruling by making preferences illegal as a matter of Michigan law. Midway through the presentation, they were interrupted by shouting and chanting protestors, including Agnes Aleobua. Before long, police had placed Aleobua under arrest. Charges against her were eventually dropped.

In January 2004, Gratz announced that she was moving back to Michigan to accept a paid position with the Michigan Civil Rights Initiative, which was waging an uphill fight to collect the 317,757 petition signatures needed to put the anti-preference proposition on the November ballot. Carl Cohen, who set the legal fight in motion eight years earlier with a Freedom of Information Act request, was the first to sign his name.

Acknowledgments

W HEN I APPROACHED Bloomberg News editor-in-chief Matt Winkler about this project, my hope was that he would grant me a leave of absence so I could make a pitch to an outside publisher. Matt was so enthusiastic that he instead encouraged Bloomberg L.P.'s publishing unit, Bloomberg Press, to acquire the book. Before I knew it, writing the book had become my new job at Bloomberg. I'm grateful to Matt for both his confidence in the idea and his willingness to let me pursue it. It is a rare and enriching opportunity for a beat reporter to take such a long step back, to spend a year studying an important issue, and to write 100,000 words in his own voice.

By writing the book in-house, I was able to take advantage of the many resources of Bloomberg, none more valuable than the colleagues who sit near me in the newsroom. Jim Rubin was a constant source of support and wisdom, as he has been since becoming my news editor in 1998. James Rowley was a terrific sounding board, providing the insight on public policy issues I've come to expect from him. Laurie Asseo not only gave great advice but also graciously assumed responsibility for Bloomberg's day-to-day Supreme Court coverage. Both Jims also gave priceless feedback on an early version of the manuscript; thanks to them and to others who read drafts and excerpts: Richard Stohr, Carolyn Stohr, Anne Tumlinson, and Greg Baumann.

Working through Bloomberg Press gave me a chance to meet and work with a fabulous book editor, Jared Kieling, whose wealth of ideas and reassuring presence helped me overcome many an obstacle. I'm grateful as well for the valuable contributions of the rest of the Bloomberg publishing team, including Bill Inman, Tracy Tait, Barbara Diez Goldenberg, JoAnne Kanaval, Mary Macher, John

Crutcher, Andrew Feldman, Lisa Goetz, Priscilla Treadwell, Charles Glasser, and Karen Verde. I also benefited from the fine research services of the Bloomberg library, especially Karen Heitz.

Finally, I offer a necessarily inadequate thanks to the five people who matter most in my life: my parents, Dick and Carolyn, who always insisted that I should follow my own star; my two children, Grace and James, who are far too young to realize how inspirational they are; and my wife, Anne, who every day for more than ten years has made me a better person.

Notes

THE STORY OF the Michigan affirmative action cases was in some respects a highly public one. I was fortunate to be able to witness some of the most important episodes first-hand, including the arguments before the Supreme Court and Sixth Circuit. I also relied heavily on the many volumes of court documents generated by the litigation. (The record of the lower court proceedings alone, as sent to the Supreme Court, filled some forty boxes.) I'm grateful to the litigants, particularly the University of Michigan, for making many of those documents available online.

To learn those parts of the story not on the public record, I interviewed more than sixty people, some of them repeatedly and extensively. I am especially grateful to Carl Cohen, Terry Pell, Kirk Kolbo, Larry Purdy, David Herr, Marvin Krislov, Lee Bollinger, John Payton, Maureen Mahoney, Ted Shaw, Miranda Massie, and Agnes Aleobua, each of whom fielded questions for hours. In addition, Julie Peterson and Tony Collings at Michigan and Curt Levey at CIR were valuable public-affairs sources.

Two judges, Bernard Friedman and Boyce Martin, spoke to me at length after the Supreme Court ruling. In my view, the public benefits when judges step out from their robes, tell their personal stories, and explain how they reach decisions in important and difficult cases. Three other judges also spoke with me briefly: Patrick Duggan, to discuss his personal background; Danny Boggs, to clarify a handful of matters; and John Feikens, to explain his perspective on the "companion case" issue at the district court. Judges Anna Diggs Taylor and Julian Abele Cook Jr. did not respond to requests for interviews.

I regret that no one involved in the White House decision-making process would consent to an on-the-record interview, despite repeated requests through a variety of channels. My account is based on background interviews I conducted with people who took part in the administration's deliberations. I also relied on a background briefing given to reporters by a senior official on the day of the president's announcement.

The lawsuits against Michigan generated a great deal of news coverage from the beginning. The *Detroit Free Press*, the *Detroit News*, the *Ann Arbor News*, the *Michigan Daily*, and the *University Record* all provided invaluable reading. Two beat reporters I've never met, Maryanne George of the *Free Press* and Jodi Cohen of the *Detroit News*, merit special mention because of the thoroughness of

317

their work and the extent to which I relied on their stories. I've drawn from news accounts in places, particularly in the early part of the book, attributing the information where necessary.

What follows are more detailed descriptions of sources.

PROLOGUE

1. The section on Jennifer Gratz came from interviews with her, a transcript of her deposition, and other court documents.

2. William G. Bowen and Derek Bok, *The Shape of the River: Long-Term Consequences of Considering Race in College and University Admissions* (Princeton, NJ: Princeton University Press, 1998).

3. *University of California Regents v. Bakke,* 438 U.S. 265 (1978).

4. *Hopwood v. State of Texas,* 78 F.3d 932 (5th Cir. 1996).

CHAPTER 1
A TALE OF TWO PROFESSORS

1. The sections on Cohen came from interviews and correspondence with him and documents he provided.

2. The sections on Bollinger came from interviews with him, contemporaneous news stories, an interview with Samuel Issacharoff, and the transcript of Bollinger's deposition in the *Hopwood* case.

3. On the history of race relations at the university, I interviewed Michigan President James Duderstadt and former Michigan Law School Dean Terrance Sandalow. I also relied on contemporaneous news stories and the following two books: Howard Peckham, *The Making of the University of Michigan,* 1817–1992 (Ann Arbor: University of Michigan Press, 1996); and Robben W. Fleming, *Tempests Into Rainbows: Managing Turbulence* (Ann Arbor: University of Michigan Press, 1996).

CHAPTER 2
GETTING LAWYERED UP

1. My sources for the sections on the Center for Individual Rights included interviews with Michael Greve, Michael McDonald, Terry Pell, and Michael Carvin. CIR's website, www.cir-usa.org, provided additional information, as did CIR newsletters provided by Greve. The Pioneer Fund donations are documented in that organization's tax returns, IRS form 990-PF, for the years in question. Greve was the primary source for the accompanying narrative on the Pioneer Fund. Other information on donations can be found through www.mediatransparency.org and an article by Terry Carter, "On a Roll(back)," *ABA Journal* (February 1998). The case on funding of religious student organizations is *Rosenberger v. Rector and Visitors of the University of Virginia,* 515 U.S. 819 (1995).

2. Sources for the section on Bollinger's preparation for the lawsuit included interviews with Bollinger and Nancy Cantor and contemporaneous news articles. Elsa Kircher Cole confirmed that Bollinger sought her resignation.

3. The account of the discussions between Greve and the Michigan legislators came from interviews with Greve and Deborah Whyman. David Jaye, who was teaching in Korea at the time I wrote the book, did not respond to requests for interviews sent to two e-mail addresses supplied by his attorney.

4. The section on Kolbo's hiring is based on interviews with Kolbo and McDonald.

5. 458 U.S. 886.

6. Sources for the section on John Payton's hiring included Bollinger and Payton. The Croson citation is: *Richmond v. J. A. Croson Co.,* 488 U.S. 469 (1989).

CHAPTER 3

GRATZ, GRUTTER, AND HAMACHER

1. The section on Gratz came from interviews with her and from her deposition transcript.

2. The section on finding plaintiffs came primarily from interviews with Whyman, McDonald, Kolbo, and Gratz.

3. For the BAMN section, I relied on interviews with Shanta Driver and contemporaneous news articles. The Brown case can be found at *Brown v. Board of Education of Topeka,* 347 U.S. 483 (1954).

4. On the Jaye event, I relied on: Jeffrey Kosseff and Katie Plona, "Four Arrested at Hearing on Affirmative Action," *Michigan Daily,* September 30, 1997.

CHAPTER 4

EQUAL PROTECTION

1. The case is *Gratz, et al. v. Bollinger et al.,* 97 Civ 75231 (U.S. District Court for the Eastern District of Michigan, October 14, 1997).

2. Four disputes captioned together as *Civil Rights Cases,* 100 U.S. 3 (1883).

3. *Plessy v. Ferguson,* 163 U.S. 537 (1896).

4. *Korematsu v. United States,* 323 U.S. 214 (1944).

5. *Brown v. Board of Education of Topeka,* 349 U.S. 294 (1955) ("*Brown II*").

6. *Loving v. Virginia,* 388 U.S. 1 (1967).

7. *Green v. County School Board of New Kent County, Virginia,* 391 U.S. 430 (1968).

8. *DeFunis v. Odegaard,* 416 U.S. 312 (1974).

9. *United Steelworkers v. Weber,* 443 U.S. 193 (1979).

10. *Fullilove v. Klutznick,* 448 U.S. 448 (1980).

11. *Metro Broadcasting v. Federal Communications Commission,* 497 U.S. 547 (1990).

12. *Adarand Constructors Inc. v. Pena,* 515 U.S. 200 (1995).

13. Sources on reaction to the lawsuit included interviews with Pell, Gratz, Driver, and Bollinger and contemporaneous news stories.

CHAPTER 5
ARGUMENTS MICHIGAN WOULDN'T MAKE

1. For the sections on Patrick Duggan and Bernard Friedman, I relied on interviews with the two judges and on news articles. The law school case is *Grutter v. Bollinger et al.,* 97 Civ 75928 (U.S. District Court for the Eastern District of Michigan, December 3, 1997).

2. The description of Payton putting the case together came largely from interviews with Payton and Cantor.

3. The discussions of Shaw, Massie, and their respective involvement in the cases came from a series of interviews with each of them.

4. The section on Connerly's visit to Ann Arbor came from him and contemporaneous news stories.

CHAPTER 6
A CLASH IN CHAMBERS

1. The sections on the companion case issue are based largely on an interview with Friedman, documents he provided, and public court records. I also spoke briefly with Judge Feikens.

2. The Connerly section is based on an interview with him.

3. The account on Krislov's hiring is based on interviews with Krislov and Bollinger.

4. The discovery section is based on public documents and interviews with Kirk Kolbo, Larry Purdy, and David Herr.

5. The sections on the Gratz and Bollinger depositions were based primarily on transcripts.

CHAPTER 7
ACCEPTED ON THE SPOT

1. The section on Agnes Aleobua is based on a series of interviews with her.

2. Linda F. Wightman, "The Threat to Diversity in Legal Education: An Empirical Analysis of the Consequences of Abandoning Race as a Factor in Law School Admissions Decisions," *New York University Law Review* (April 1997).

CHAPTER 8
BOLLINGER'S NEW FRONT

1. News reports provided the basis of my description of the proceeding before the Sixth Circuit. Shaw described his reaction in an interview. Herr, Kolbo, and Luke Massie all confirmed the encounter in the elevator.

2. Bollinger was the primary source on his early efforts to woo outside support, including his call to Gerald Ford. Lehman described his encounter with Clinton.

3. Shaw and Massie provided their reactions to the Sixth Circuit intervention decision.

4. The section on the change in leadership at CIR was based in part on interviews with Greve, McDonald, Pell, and CIR Director Jeremy Rabkin. I received additional information from people who did not wish to be identified.

5. For the section on activities during the delay, I relied on interviews with Shaw, Kolbo, and Massie.

6. My description of Aleobua's deposition is based on a transcript.

7. Krislov, Bollinger, and Pearce all shared their recollections of the meeting at General Motors.

8. Jim Hackett, Jon Botsford, Randy Mehrberg, and David DeBruin were sources for the section on corporate support.

9. Bollinger and Jim Cannon both described their lunch meeting.

CHAPTER 9
DUGGAN'S DISTINCTION

1. The accounts of the hearings before Judges Duggan and Friedman come from court transcripts. Descriptions of goals and reactions come from the particular lawyers.

2. The section on Gratz's move is based on an interview with her.

3. *Smith v. Univ. of Washington*, 233 F.3d 1188 (9th Cir. 2000).

4. *Bush v. Gore*, 531 U.S. 98 (2000).

5. *Gratz v. Bollinger*, 122 F.Supp.2d 811 (E.D. Mich. 2000).

CHAPTER 10
PREFERENCES ON TRIAL

1. Most of the description of the trial comes from court transcripts. The attorneys added additional insight through interviews.

2. The descriptions of Friedman's thinking came from an interview with him.

3. *Grutter v. Bollinger*, 137 F.Supp.2d 821 (E.D. Mich. 2001).

4. The account of the freeze in law school admissions came from an interview with Christina B. Whitman, former associate dean for academic affairs.

CHAPTER 11
A COURT DIVIDED

1. The account of CIR's deliberations on its en banc petition came from interviews with Kolbo and other attorneys.

2. Massie was the source for the discussion of her finances.

3. In August 2001, a Macomb County, Michigan, judge ruled that Jaye violated his probation on a drunken-driving conviction by assaulting his fiancée, Sonia Kloss, while in Florida. The judge determined there was not enough evidence to prove Jaye had assaulted Kloss in a separate incident in Bay County, Michigan. Local prosecutors declined to press assault charges in either case. Jaye did not face criminal charges with respect to his laptop computer.

4. Interviews with Bollinger and Krislov were the basis for the section on their efforts to win military backing.

5. Much of my account on Bollinger's departure was based on interviews with people who were familiar with the process and did not wish to be identified. Bollinger declined to comment on the specifics of his discussions with Michigan and other universities. Krislov was the source for his reaction to Bollinger's departure.

6. Court documents were the primary source for the discussion of the Byrd case. Martin's explanation came from an interview with him.

7. Kolbo, Payton, and Pell were the sources for their reactions to the hearing postponement.

8. *Johnson v. Bd. of Regents of Univ. of Georgia*, 263 F.3d 1234 (11th Cir. 2001).

9. Kolbo, Herr, and Payton described their preparations for the argument. The account of the student rally in Cincinnati came from personal observations and an interview with Aleobua.

CHAPTER 12
MARTIN v. BOGGS

1. The account of the hearing at the Sixth Circuit and its aftermath came from my notes and observations, a court transcript, and interviews with the attorneys.

2. My account of the university's decision to retain Mahoney is based on a series of interviews of people with a variety of perspectives on the discussions. The group included five people with direct knowledge of the internal university deliberations. Each of those people asked not to be identified with respect to at least some of the information provided. Coleman, Shaw, and Ogletree described their meeting with Bollinger. Mahoney is the source for her biographical information.

3. For the section on behind-the-scenes maneuvering, Boggs and Moore laid out their versions in their opinions. Martin's account came from an interview and documents he provided. Boggs also gave a short interview in which he described why he did not vote on the en banc petition. The citation for the Sixth Circuit decision is *Grutter v. Bollinger*, 388 F.3d 732 (6th Cir. 2002).

4. The attorneys described their reactions to the decision. I also relied on contemporaneous news accounts.

5. Coleman provided some of the information for the biographical section on her.

CHAPTER 13
LOOKING TO THE HIGH COURT

1. Martin described in an interview his decision not to issue a decision in the undergraduate case.

2. 418 U.S. 483 (1974).

3. Kolbo, Pell, and Levey were sources for CIR's deliberations on its cert-before-judgment petition. Kolbo and Payton both described their phone conversation on the subject.

4. The description of Mahoney's thoughts on Michigan's opposition to the cert position came from an interview with her.

5. Shaw is the source for the section on his thoughts on the respective merits of the two cases.

6. The military sections came from interviews with Cannon, Dellinger, Krislov, and Reeder.

7. The section on John Paul Stevens was based on a speech he gave to the Chicago Bar Association on September 18, 2003.

8. The account of the scene in the press room came from personal observations.

CHAPTER 14
THE MOST POWERFUL WOMAN IN AMERICA

1. Some of the background on Sandra Day O'Connor came from her memoir, Sandra Day O'Connor and H. Alan Day, *Lazy B: Growing Up on a Cattle Ranch in the American Southwest* (New York: Random House, 2002).

2. For the section on the amicus meetings, I relied primarily on interviews with Krislov, Cannon, Seitz, and Reeder.

3. Ward Connerly is the source for his encounter with Ted Olson.

4. The sections on the deliberations of the Bush administration came from interviews with people who took part in the process and asked not to be identified.

CHAPTER 15
FRIENDS OF THE COURT

1. The primary sources for the sections on the military briefs were interviews with Krislov, Seitz, Reeder, and Dan Christman.

2. Cannon described his phone call to Gerald Ford.

3. Pell is the source for the section on his thoughts on the cases.

4. The section on argument time at the Supreme Court was based on Court documents and interviews with Shaw and Massie.

5. Mahoney, Payton, and Kolbo all discussed their preparation in interviews.

6. Gratz and her relatives described their wait for tickets.

7. Aleobua and Driver were sources for the section on the demonstration.

8. Mahoney described her activities on the morning of the argument.

9. The description of the scene in the courtroom is based on personal observations.

CHAPTER 16
"SHE'S FABULOUS"

1. The description of the hearing comes from my notes, transcripts, and audio recordings, which are available on the www.oyez.org website. The praise for Mahoney by Souter and Ginsburg is audible at the beginning of the *Gratz* argument, after Rehnquist announces the case and before Kolbo begins his presentation.

2. My description of the reactions to the argument came from first-hand observations and interviews with the participants.

CHAPTER 17
"RACE UNFORTUNATELY STILL MATTERS"

1. Justice O'Connor provided a copy of her statement from the bench. Payton described his comment to Shaw.

2. *Grutter v. Bollinger,* 539 U.S. 306 (2003). *Gratz v. Bollinger,* 539 U.S. 244.

CHAPTER 18
HAIL TO THE VICTORS

1. Shaw, Payton, Mahoney, Krislov, Bollinger, Kolbo, and Pell all provided accounts of their activities on June 23 and their reactions to the decisions.

Index

About Bloomberg

Bloomberg L.P., founded in 1981, is a global information services, news, and media company. Headquartered in New York, the company has sales and news operations worldwide.

Bloomberg, serving customers on six continents, holds a unique position within the financial services industry by providing an unparalleled range of features in a single package known as the BLOOMBERG PROFESSIONAL® service. By addressing the demand for investment performance and efficiency through an exceptional combination of information, analytic, electronic trading, and Straight Through Processing tools, Bloomberg has built a worldwide customer base of corporations, issuers, financial intermediaries, and institutional investors.

BLOOMBERG NEWS®, founded in 1990, provides stories and columns on business, general news, politics, and sports to leading newspapers and magazines throughout the world. BLOOMBERG TELEVISION®, a 24-hour business and financial news network, is produced and distributed globally in seven different languages. BLOOMBERG RADIO℠ is an international radio network anchored by flagship station BLOOMBERG® 1130 (WBBR-AM) in New York.

In addition to the BLOOMBERG PRESS® line of books, Bloomberg publishes *BLOOMBERG MARKETS®* and *BLOOMBERG WEALTH MANAGER®*. To learn more about Bloomberg, call a sales representative at:

London:	+44-20-7330-7500
New York:	+1-212-318-2000
Tokyo:	+81-3-3201-8900

FOR IN-DEPTH MARKET INFORMATION and news, visit the Bloomberg website at **www.bloomberg.com**, which draws from the news and power of the BLOOMBERG PROFESSIONAL® service and Bloomberg's host of media products to provide high-quality news and information in multiple languages on stocks, bonds, currencies, and commodities.

About the Author

Greg Stohr has been the Bloomberg News Supreme Court reporter since 1998. In 2001 he won a New York Press Club award for best spot news coverage for a Bloomberg story on the Supreme Court's *Bush v. Gore* decision. He is a former law clerk to U.S. District Judge Frank A. Kaufman and graduated with honors from Harvard Law School in 1995. He served as Congressional and campaign press secretary for U.S. Representative Tom Campbell from 1989 to 1992. A native of St. Louis, he now lives in Washington, D.C., with his wife and two children.

THE SUPREME COURT OPINIONS can be read at
www.bloomberg.com/blackandwhitecase